STUDY TEXT
Professional Banker Certificate

In this 2016/17 edition

- A **user-friendly format** for easy navigation
- **Updated** on recent developments
- A **chapter review** at the end of each chapter
- A full **index**

Chartered Banker
Leading financial professionalism

Published April 2016

ISBN 978 1 5097 0418 7

British Library Cataloguing-in-Publication Data
A catalogue record for this book
is available from the British Library

Published by

BPP Learning Media Ltd
BPP House, Aldine Place
London W12 8AA

www.bpp.com/learningmedia

Printed in the United Kingdom by

Ricoh UK Limited
Unit 2
Wells Place
Merstham
RH1 3LG

Your learning materials, published by BPP Learning
Media Ltd, are printed on paper obtained from traceable
sustainable sources.

The contents of this book are intended as a guide and
not professional advice. Although every effort has been
made to ensure that the contents of this book are
correct at the time of going to press, BPP Learning
Media makes no warranty that the information in this
book is accurate or complete and accepts no liability for
any loss or damage suffered by any person acting or
refraining from acting as a result of the material in this
book.

BPP
LEARNING MEDIA

CONTENTS

INTRODUCTION

Aim

The aim of the *Professional Banker Certificate* module is to provide you with an overview of the banking profession and enable you to:

- Develop the values, attitudes and behaviours set out in the Chartered Banker Code of Professional Conduct

- Demonstrate a general knowledge of banking practice

- Relate your banking knowledge to a range of practical banking applications

- Use a range of banking skills to serve customers, and address routine issues at work

- Apply your banking knowledge and understanding, and practise your skills to enhance customer service, improve work performance, and develop your professional banking practice

Learning Outcomes

On completion of the module, you should be able to:

1   Explain the purpose and functions of a bank and describe the business and economic environment in which banks operate

2   Describe key regulatory, cultural and legal requirements that apply to banking and explain how these requirements influence the way a bank operates

3   Describe a range of banking products and services and assess their suitability for different customer needs

4   Explain the key principles of credit and lending and how these can be used to make professional and ethical lending decisions

5   Describe the role of risk management in banking

6   Explain the importance of high standards of conduct in banking and the practicalities of applying those standards

On successful completion of the module, you will be awarded the *Professional Banker Certificate* and be eligible for membership of the Chartered Banker Institute. Attainment of the *Professional Banker Certificate* also supports achievement of the CB:PSB Foundation Standard for Professional Bankers, published by the Chartered Banker Professional Standards Board (CB:PSB).

The Chartered Banker Professional Standards Board (CB:PSB)

The Chartered Banker Professional Standards Board (CB:PSB) was launched in October 2011. It aims to enhance and sustain a strong culture of ethical and professional development across the UK banking industry by developing a series of professional standards at Foundation, Intermediate and Advanced levels. The CB:PSB intends to help build, over time, greater public confidence and trust in individuals, institutions and the banking industry overall, and to enhance pride in the banking profession. To find out more about the standards and the work of the CB:PSB, visit www.cbpsb.org.

Preparing to Study: Personal Learning Goals

Before you start to study Professional Banker, you may find it useful to think about what you personally want to get out of it, and why. The following activity has been designed to help you clarify your own goals for the programme and think about how best you can achieve these.

Activity: Personal Learning Goals

Although there are formal learning outcomes for the module, you will also have your own goals in terms of what you specifically want to achieve from studying this module. Clearly, passing the exam will be a key goal. What else, though, is an important outcome for you in either the short or the long term? For example, you may want to use what you learn to help you achieve the CB:PSB Foundation Standard for Professional Bankers, improve your performance in your current role at work, or enhance your future career prospects; or perhaps having a professional qualification and being a member of a professional body is important to you. Whatever you personally want to get from your studies, the following questions will help you clarify what these are and why they are important to you.

Although this activity is for you personally, you might want to discuss your thoughts with your line manager so that you can agree goals that will help you apply what you learn at work.

Apart from passing the exam, what specifically do you want to achieve by studying *Professional Banker*?

Apart from passing the exam, how will you know that you've got what you wanted from your studies? What will you see, hear and feel that lets you know you have it?

For what purpose do you want this? What will achieving what you want from studying *Professional Banker* do for you or allow you to do?

Are you doing this only for you? Who else will benefit? In what ways?

What will you gain if you achieve what you want from your studies? What will you lose?

What key skills, qualities and strengths do you have that will help you complete *Professional Banker* and pass your exam?

On a scale of 1 to 10, where 1 is the lowest and 10 is the highest, where are you now in relation to what you want to achieve from your studies?

1   2   3   4   5   6   7   8   9   10

What would need to happen to get you from where you are now to the next number on the scale? For example, what further resources or support do you need and from whom?

On a scale of 1 to 10, where 1 is the lowest and 10 is the highest, how motivated do you feel to make this happen?

1   2   3   4   5   6   7   8   9   10

If less than 8, what would need to happen in order for this to be a 10? (For example, if you're not feeling particularly motivated at the moment, think again about what could be good about this and what's in it for you.)

What are you going to do now, and during the next six months, to make sure you achieve what you want from studying Professional Banker?

Now that you have a clearer idea about what you want to get out of your studies and why, you are well on your way to making it happen.

chapter 1

THE BUSINESS OF BANKING AND THE ECONOMIC ENVIRONMENT

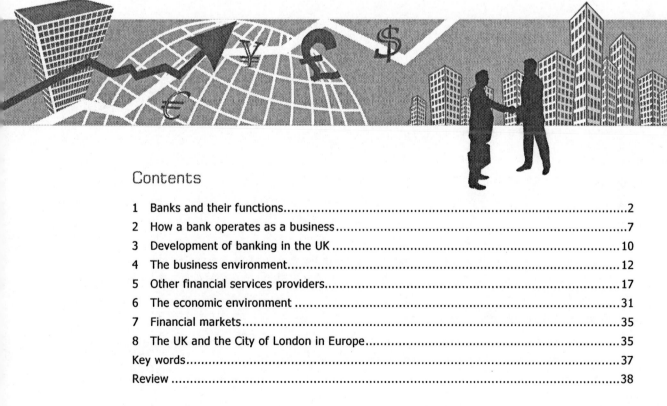

Contents

Learning objectives

On completion of this chapter, you should be able to:

- Describe types of banking activity
- Explain the evolution, purpose and functions of the banking sector as a financial intermediary
- Explain how a bank operates as a business and its requirement for both liquidity and profitability
- Describe how the political, economic and business environment influences bank operations

Introduction

This first chapter of the Study Text introduces you to the business of banking.

We will consider what a bank is, what it does, and how it makes money. We will also look at the development of UK banking and the different types of banks and other financial services organisations that operate in the current business environment.

We will conclude by considering key elements of the economic environment in which banks operate, including the role of financial markets and the UK as an international finance centre.

1 Banks and their functions

1.1 What is a bank?

The word 'bank' comes from the Italian word *banco* meaning a bench or a table at which Italian money lenders used to conduct business in the Middle Ages (approximately 1200-1500 AD). This Italian connection continues, as the oldest bank still in business today is Monte dei Paschi di Siena, founded in 1472.

QUICK QUESTION

When you hear or see the word 'bank', what immediately comes to mind?

Write your answer here before reading on.

You may have thought about the word 'bank' in terms of being a building, a company, a business, or an employer; or perhaps you thought of it in terms of storing something for safekeeping, or something completely different.

Here is one dictionary definition of a bank:

> *'A bank is a financial establishment that uses money deposited by customers for investment, pays it out when required, makes loans at interest, and exchanges currency.'*

Source: The Oxford English Dictionary

The definition provided by the British Bankers' Association is as follows:

> *'A bank is an organisation which accepts deposits, makes loans, pays cheques, and performs related services.'*

http://www.bba.org.uk/customer/glossary-entry/Bank

The **universal bank** model involves providing 'related' financial services of various kinds, including advisory services, in addition to deposit and lending services.

QUICK QUESTION

If banks did not exist, what would be the impact on you, others, and society?

Write your answer here before reading on.

Thinking about the answer to this question as you study *Professional Banker* will help you understand the purpose of the bank, what banks do, and the role they play in society.

1.2 Types of banking

Banking is the business conducted, or the services offered, by a bank. Banking in some form began as far back as the 18th century BC in ancient Mesopotamia. It subsequently developed and expanded in ancient Greece, Rome and medieval Italy.

Traditional divisions within banking have become blurred in recent decades. Retail banks have joined other types of institution in raising funds in wholesale markets, and have moved away from purely 'direct' lending to advising commercial clients on various financial matters.

A bank's business may include different types of banking activities, such as those within the spheres of:

- Commercial banking
- Investment banking, and
- Bancassurance

Each of these is described further in what follows.

These activities have evolved due to the merging of different types of banks and other financial services organisations over the years.

1.3 Commercial banking

Commercial banking is essentially about taking deposits and making loans. When a commercial bank takes deposits, it is effectively borrowing that money from the depositor because it is based on a condition that the money can be returned to the depositor on demand, that is immediately, or on expiry of a notice period.

Commercial banking includes:

- Retail banking
- Business banking, and
- Wholesale banking

Retail banking is about taking deposits (ie, borrowing) from and lending to **individuals**, through a range of delivery channels, typically including a branch network. **Business banking** involves similar activities where the customers are small or medium-sized business enterprises.

Wholesale banking is about borrowing from and lending to large corporate clients, other financial institutions, public agencies, and governments. It involves dealing in large sums of money, which can be raised in London's money markets.

1.4 Investment banking

Investment banking is about:

- Providing advice to corporate customers who want to raise finance

- Managing corporate mergers and acquisitions

- Buying and selling shares and bonds on behalf of both corporate and private customers (typically high net worth customers), as well as for the bank

- Managing customers' investments and share portfolios

1.5 The purposes of a bank

The central activities of a commercial bank involve taking deposits from and lending to individuals and companies. The bank collects money from people or companies who have surplus funds they want to deposit for safekeeping, and lends money to those who want or are short of funds.

- Customers who deposit money are the bank's **creditors**, because the bank is effectively borrowing their money.

- Customers to whom the bank lends money are the bank's **debtors**, because these customers owe them the money they have borrowed.

The bank thus acts as a go-between for those who have extra money and those who want to borrow. As customers deposit money in the bank for safekeeping, the bank has a duty to look after it on their customers' behalf.

Banks also provide mechanisms that enable customers to make payments into and out of their accounts and offer a range of other products and services to meet their customers' financial needs.

1.6 The purpose of a bank for deposit customers (the bank's creditors)

Customers deposit money in a current account to hold their cash in a form that is liquid (easily available) and to transact payments. Customers deposit money in a savings account to earn interest, that is, make a small profit at low risk.

Customers therefore want banks to:

- Reduce, or bear, the risks of their payments
- Look after their money and financial investments

The bank therefore has a duty to:

- Reduce risks for their deposit customers
- Administer customers' accounts reliably, securely and confidentially

The bank does this by:

- Facilitating and coordinating payments
- Providing safe custody for deposits under conditions that preserve their liquidity (availability)
- Creating opportunities for the investment of capital (the money available for investment), invested without risk whilst ensuring modest rates of return

1.7 The purpose of a bank for credit customers (the bank's debtors)

Customers who borrow from the bank want their bank to offer them money at an affordable price. The purpose of the bank is to make finance available. In doing so, the bank has a duty to lend responsibly. This means remaining objective, while having the courage to take some level of risk that comes with the decision to lend.

1.8 Intermediating between borrowers and savers

By providing loans to borrowers and collecting deposits from savers, the bank functions as a financial intermediary between borrowers and savers, as shown in the following diagram.

The bank as financial intermediary

SAVERS **BANK**  **BORROWERS**

Financial intermediation is the process of pooling funds from different sources and using these to provide loans and make investments. The people and companies who supply these funds and make deposits into the bank (for example, savers), receive interest for allowing their money to be used for loans or investments. Borrowers pay interest for the privilege of borrowing other people's money.

Therefore, by channelling funds from savers to borrowers, the bank creates a mechanism for making best use of the funds it has collected and pooled from different sources. It is this that leads to more efficient utilisation of funds within the economy as a whole.

QUICK QUESTION

In what way is there a conflict between the bank's duties to its savers and borrowers?

Write your answer here before reading on.

The bank's respective duties to its savers and borrowers conflict because, on the one hand, the bank must be risk-averse and cautious with savers' money; on the other hand, it must embrace a level of risk in order to lend money.

The bank therefore needs to reconcile these duties and to intermediate between deposit customers' expectations that risk will be avoided and borrowers' expectations that there will be some risk.

1.9 Bancassurance

The development of insurance and life assurance provision by banks is known as **bancassurance** (or *all finanz*). The Association of British Insurers (ABI) defines bancassurers as 'insurance companies that are subsidiaries of banks and building societies and whose primary market is the customer base of the bank or building society'.

The UK financial services industry developed through the creation of many specialisms, with groups of financial institutions tending to stick to quite rigidly defined products and services. Therefore, as recently as the 1980s, it was quite usual for a typical household to operate a current account with a bank, a savings account with the Post Office and/or a building society, a mortgage with a building society, a life assurance policy with a life company and general insurance through a general insurance company. It was rare for banks to offer mortgages, or for building societies to offer any loans other than mortgages. Insurance companies were not interested in banking, and although it was possible to purchase insurance in the branch of a bank, the product itself would be sold on behalf of the insurance company by the banker for commission.

By contrast, the financial services industry in continental Europe tended to adopt a more integrated approach through which most of the services described above would be purchased from, and created by, a single financial services group. This bancassurance approach developed originally in **Germany** and **Switzerland** and gradually extended to many other European states. The bancassurance model is well established in Europe.

CASE STUDY

In Germany there is no strong tradition of owner-occupation and until recently it was relatively rare for a couple to aspire to buying a property until they were perhaps in their mid-thirties. Indeed, Germany had, and continues to maintain, a strong private rented housing sector, so young people naturally chose to rent rather than buy, and could do so at an affordable price. However, at household formation stage (on marriage, or leaving the parental home), young people would enter into long-term relationships with financial institutions in order to provide for current banking needs and to build up long term savings and investments that would enable them to purchase homes later.

This was not only desirable but necessary, as German banks traditionally created mortgages with much lower loan-to-value ratios than in the UK. Mortgage terms were traditionally for terms of 10 to 15 years, and customers rarely traded up – if a bigger house was required, they would build an extension or commission an attic conversion.

The merits of the one-stop shop facilitated by the bancassurance model was not lost on the UK financial services industry, but a major impediment to its development was the fragmented nature of the industry.

Each set of financial institutions had their own products and services, their own legislation and their own regulators. The deregulation of the 1980s changed that. For the first time, banks could freely enter into the insurance market, building societies could offer current accounts and insurance companies could offer mortgages and banking products. As a result, the demarcation lines between types of financial institution eroded.

It is now possible to buy a wide range of financial products and services from a single provider. All of the major banks have subsidiary companies to which they can refer business. If it is not cost-effective to do so, they enter into agency arrangements with other organisations. The availability of comprehensive product ranges under one roof lends itself to the creation of long-term banking relationships, and advances of information technology help providers to anticipate or predict customer needs quite accurately and offer suitable products to customers to meet these needs.

QUICK QUESTION

Which type of banking activity do you contribute to in your role at work – commercial banking, investment banking, or bancassurance?

In what way do you contribute to the provision of this service?

Write your answer here before reading on.

2 How a bank operates as a business

2.1 Overview

Commercial banks are operated as companies to generate profit for shareholders. They make money by dealing in money. The major functions of a commercial bank are to:

- Accept deposits
- Grant loans
- Act as an agent for payments
- Provide a range of other services

Banks make money in three main ways:

1   Lending some of the money deposited by savers to borrowers and charging these borrowers interest on the sums loaned (i.e. the bank makes money by lending at rates higher than the cost of the money they lend)

2   Charging fees for products and services

3   Investing the money deposited by savers

While some bank customers are looking for a safe place to keep their money, others want to borrow money to buy or invest in something, or expand a business, for example. If customers kept their surplus money under their mattress instead of depositing it in the bank, the bank would have little or no money to lend. The more the banks lend, the more interest and profits they have the potential to make.

Pause for thought ...

Imagine you are a merchant in ancient times. You make your living selling exotic oils and spices. You want to tap into new markets and dream of setting sail for foreign shores in a ship laden with precious cargo. You are confident that when you reach your destination, you will be paid well for your cargo. There's only one problem – you need money to get a ship and crew together. You've heard that there is a particularly wealthy group of people in the town who have loads of money sitting idle so you seek them out and tell them about your exciting new business venture. They agree to give you the money to fund your voyage in exchange for a share of the profits when you return. Yet, in your view, they want too large a share of the profits because, if your calculations are correct, not only would they be getting all of their money back, they would also be getting a hefty sum on top of that. When you object, they say that your voyage is perilous and, should something happen to you and the ship, they risk losing all the money they'd be giving you. They're not going to give you the money for nothing – there's a price to pay. Looking at this from the lender's perspective, there is no guarantee that they'll get their money back, so why take the risk? They take the risk because lending the money provides an opportunity to make even more money – and the bigger the risk, the higher the price.

Adapted from: Banking Basics, Federal Reserve Bank of Boston (2011)

What do you do?

QUICK QUESTION

What do you understand by 'liquidity'?

Write your answer here before reading on.

2.2 Liquidity and profitability

In a bank's **balance sheet**, the money a bank lends to its customers and other banks appears as assets because this money is a source of income and profits. The money deposited by customers appears as liabilities because this money is repayable to customers, either immediately on demand or on expiry of a notice period.

In accounting terms, liquidity is a measure of the ability of a debtor to pay their debts as they fall due. This suggests that the bank, which has effectively 'borrowed' the money its customers have deposited, must keep enough cash available to repay this money to customers who want to withdraw it. Yet, as a

BPP
LEARNING MEDIA

business, the bank needs to make a profit and if it were to keep enough cash available to meet all likely withdrawals, it would not be able to invest it to make a profit.

Retail banks are therefore pulled in opposite directions – on the one hand towards liquidity (holding enough cash on hand to meet the immediate demands of customers) and, on the other, towards profitability. As operators of the payments system, the retail or 'clearing banks' (so-called because of their role in clearing cheques and payments), cannot allow their liquidity to fall too low, even though liquid assets offer a poor return.

2.3 Assets held by banks

Look at your own bank's **balance sheet** in the annual report and accounts. What does it include?

The main types of asset we would expect to see a bank holding are as follows.

Notes and coin: this is the physical cash that is held in tills, branch safes, cash machines and in centralised cash-handling areas of the bank. It is up to each bank to decide how much cash to keep to meet customers' withdrawal demands.

Balances with the Bank of England: there is a statutory requirement for banks to hold non-operational, non-interest bearing deposits with the Bank of England. The amount of these deposits is a percentage of 'eligible liabilities' – these are sterling deposit liabilities of less than two years until maturity, net foreign currency liabilities and some inter-bank liabilities. Banks also hold non-interest bearing operational balances with the Bank of England to meet both cash needs and make inter-bank settlements.

Loans and advances to banks: these are short term loans made by one bank to another.

Bills: these are promises to pay money on a stated date – often three months (13 weeks) after the date of issue, although maturities could alternatively be one month (4 weeks), or six months (26 weeks). Once one of these bills is purchased by a bank, it becomes a short-term loan from the purchasing bank to its customer. These bills are negotiable, which means that they can be bought and sold in the market. The bills may be Treasury bills, or other bills. Treasury bills, as the name implies, are issued by the UK Treasury as short-term loans to the Government. Banks will often buy these bills on the secondary market when they are near to their maturity date. Other bills include local authority bills and trade bills.

Investments: these can consist of Government stock (gilts) and shares in other companies, as well as shareholdings in subsidiary companies of the bank, such as a finance house.

Advances: it would be expected that this would be the biggest asset of a bank – it represents the loans made by the bank to its customers.

Premises and equipment: these are the properties owned by the bank to conduct its operations – branches, processing centres, contact centres and regional/head offices. Equipment would include, for example, computers and vehicles.

Cash and operational balances at the Bank of England pay no interest. In fact, when we take account of the cost of protecting cash from theft, it can be said to have a negative yield. Having said that, 70% of deposits are virtually payable on demand (at least in theory) and so the banks must keep enough cash or its equivalent (for example, balances at the Bank of England) to meet all likely withdrawals. This does not mean that banks keep 70% of their deposits in cash. If they did, they would earn very little profit indeed.

From experience, banks know that only a small proportion of deposits will actually be withdrawn at any given time. Provided the banks maintain sufficient cash to meet these likely withdrawals and a margin of liquid assets which can be converted into cash rapidly to meet any unexpected demands, they can lend the remainder of their funds for longer periods.

As with any company, profit is important to a bank as profit provides for future growth and a return for shareholders. A bank considered to be earning inadequate profits could find itself subject to a takeover bid by a competitor. A management team unable to earn sufficient profit could well be replaced. This pursuit of profit conflicts with the need for liquidity since the most profitable assets (loans) tend to be the least liquid. The asset structure of a bank is a compromise between the desire for profit and the need for liquidity. Success depends on striking the right balance between the two.

Liquidity thus represents the ability of a bank to convert its assets into cash quickly and without loss. Government securities can be speedily converted into cash via the stock exchange, but the price of these securities fluctuates and so losses might be incurred if some of these need to be sold at the wrong time.

Advances are slow to realise, because it is not normal practice to call them in as this might force the borrower into liquidation or bankruptcy. The usual way of contracting advances is to slow down the granting of new advances while allowing repayment of existing advances to continue, thereby reducing the total amount of advances outstanding. Advances are thus slow to convert into cash for the purpose of repayment.

2.4 The bank's role in society

In conducting its business, a bank also has an important role to play in society as a whole, in the following ways.

The bank:

- Acts as a financial intermediary between savers and borrowers which results in efficient use of pooled resources

- Facilitates the creation of money by expanding the supply of money through deposit and loan transactions

- Creates financial products and services that benefit its customers

- Develops mechanisms for transferring money

- Contributes to the development of the banking industry

We consider the social responsibilities of a bank in more detail in Chapter 6.

3 Development of banking in the UK

3.1 Banking in England

In the early 19th century, English private banks were restricted to six partners. This was due to an Act in 1708 which gave the Bank of England a monopoly in joint stock banking (a bank with a large number of shareholders) in England. Most banks were small, local and unregulated. In 1825 over 60 private banks failed in England, the outcome of which was the Country Bankers Act 1826. This Act represented a milestone in the development of English banking. It broke the Bank of England's monopoly and permitted the creation of joint stock banks outside a 65-mile radius of London with the right to issue notes. New banks could raise more capital than the old ones to open branches and thus lend to a variety of industries, thereby spreading their risks.

In 1833, a Bank Charter Act authorised joint stock banks to open branches within the 65-mile radius provided they did not issue notes. In 1834 the London and Westminster Bank was established; ultimately through mergers it became the National Westminster Bank plc, which in turn became part of the RBS Group. The number of joint stock banks increased during the next few decades while the number of private banks diminished through mergers and takeovers. Barclays Bank grew out of a series of mergers by private banks from 1896 onwards.

The period 1890 – 1918 witnessed the increased concentration of banking in England whereby a few banks dominated deposit taking and lending business. This trend was encouraged by the public's greater confidence in large banks, a view also held by the authorities.

Bank mergers were seen as strengthening the financial system. In 1918 a Treasury Committee was set up to examine bank mergers as fears began to be expressed about the size and influence of large banks.

A proposed legal ban on mergers was dropped, but the banks did agree to consult the authorities before proceeding with any further amalgamations. For the next 50 years the pattern of banking in England remained stable. Five banks dominated the banking scene – Barclays, Lloyds, Midland, National Provincial and Westminster, plus six smaller joint stock banks.

A strong argument for bank mergers in the 1960s was that English clearing banks faced increased competition from both home and abroad, from finance houses, building societies and foreign banks. In 1968 Barclays merged with Martins Bank while the National Provincial, District and Westminster Banks became the National Westminster Bank.

These mergers resulted in three major benefits:

- Strengthening of bank balance sheets and thereby greater lending capacity
- Cost savings via branch mergers and reduced staff requirements
- More funds available for investment in new technology available at that time

3.2 Banking in Scotland

The Bank of Scotland was established in 1695 to meet the needs of commerce and began by issuing notes and making loans. In 1727, the Royal Bank of Scotland was established; thus, Scotland gained two joint stock banks to England's one. Both were legal corporations with limited liability for their shareholders. Fierce competition ensued over the issue and presentation of notes until both realised the mutually destructive nature of such competition.

As time passed, more banks were set up in Scotland to meet the needs of expanding industry and commerce. The prohibition of having more than six partners did not exist in Scotland and so, by the 19th century, most major Scottish towns and cities had joint stock banks issuing their own notes. For example, Clydesdale Bank was set up in Glasgow in 1838. Similar to the situation in England, a process of amalgamations took place which reduced the number of Scottish banks to eight by 1907. The 1950s and 1960s witnessed further mergers until there was only the Bank of Scotland, Royal Bank of Scotland and Clydesdale Bank.

The following innovations originated from the Scottish banking system.

Overdrafts – the overdraft developed from the cash credit introduced by the Royal Bank of Scotland in 1728. Under this system, the bank agreed to honour claims against a person's account up to an agreed amount. The sum was debited against the customer's account and interest was charged on the outstanding balance.

Branch banking – Scotland developed a network of branches which added to the stability of the banking system and allowed banks to tap a wider source of funds and spread risks associated with lending over a wider geographical area.

Joint stock banking – this form of banking meant that shareholders in a bank were protected from personal liability for the bank's debts should it fail. Limited liability encouraged a greater number of people to become investors in banks, thus providing them with a larger capital base.

The clearing house – in 1771, the Scottish banks introduced a note exchange in Edinburgh which meant that each bank's notes were more acceptable to the public. This example of interbank cooperation encouraged the concept of a clearing house for cheques.

The Chartered Banker Institute – established in 1875, the Institute was the world's first professional body for practising bankers. It dedicated itself, as it does today, to the training and educating of bankers and other financial services practitioners both in the UK and globally.

Note issue – a distinctive feature of Scottish banking is the right of Scottish banks to issue their own notes. The *Bank Charter Act 1844*, which gave the Bank of England an eventual monopoly of the note issue in England and Wales, did not apply to Scotland. Thus the Scottish joint stock banks retained the right to issue their own notes.

Under the Bank Notes (Scotland) Act 1845, each bank was granted an authorised circulation based on its average circulation for 1844; thereafter any notes issued above this figure were backed by gold.

Today, that privilege appears very small for the three Scottish banks which issue their own notes, as only £3m out of over £2,000m in circulation does not need to be covered at the Bank of England. Scottish clearing banks must meet the cost of printing and security for their own notes. However, the banks appreciate the prestige, advertising and appeal to Scottish patriotism of issuing their own notes. There are also sound financial benefits from maintaining the separate Scottish note issue. These stem from the fact that Scottish notes do not need to be covered until in circulation with the public; this reduces the cost of till money. If the Scottish note issue were abolished, Scottish banks would have the expense of holding all their till money in the form of Bank of England notes for which a fee is payable.

4 The business environment

4.1 Introduction

The UK clearing banks share numerous characteristics. They are all large financial institutions, offering a wide range of services within their respective banking groups. Their deposits have a fixed monetary value and so, unlike investments in stocks and shares, they cannot lose their capital value.

What if a bank cannot pay back its depositors? There is always the potential for this to happen, as the banks are commercial organisations that utilise their deposits to create loans and other assets. If enough depositors asked for the immediate withdrawal of all their funds, all at once, the banks would not be able to meet these demands. In practice, banks can usually predict the level of withdrawals over time and can also call upon funds from other institutions should the need arise. Unusual conditions can however arise, for example if people fear a banking crisis and no longer consider that their money is safe with the bank. This is called a 'run on the bank'. Governments and central banks should generally try to avoid a situation in which there is an unfounded loss of confidence in banks but, if a run on the banks does occur, in these extreme circumstances banks may have to stop allowing withdrawals and close their doors. As we shall see in the Case Study that is described a little later, in September 2007, thousands of customers of the UK bank Northern Rock queued for hours at branches of the bank in the hope of withdrawing funds. The run on deposits slowed after the Government issued an emergency pledge to Northern Rock customers to assure them that their money was safe.

4.2 Regulation of deposit takers

The Banking Acts 1979 and 1987 established a formal system for the supervision and control of **deposit taking institutions (DTIs)** in Britain. The Bank of England became responsible for granting recognition to banks. A bank deposit protection fund which was also established under the 1979 Act has been replaced by the Financial Services Compensation Scheme. In 1998, responsibility for the authorisation and supervision of banks was transferred from the Bank of England to the Financial Services Authority (FSA).

In April 2013, the FSA was superseded by two separate regulatory authorities, the Financial Conduct Authority (FCA) and the Prudential Regulation Authority (PRA). The FCA's primary role is to regulate conduct in the financial services industry: its aim is to protect consumers and promote competition between financial services providers. The PRA is the prudential regulator, responsible for ensuring the safe and financially sound operations of over 1,000 DTIs, as well as insurers, investment banks and some other institutions.

4.3 Late 2000s credit crisis

The safety of deposits with banks was once rarely questioned, but the credit crisis that started in 2007 caused severe difficulties, both in terms of pressure on their capital resources and customer confidence. Given the importance of public confidence in the banking sector, the Government stepped in during 2008

BPP
LEARNING MEDIA

to ensure that the banks had access to capital. At the same time, the Government reinforced the protection provided to personal customers by increasing the deposit guarantee threshold to £50,000 (from £31,700). At the end of 2010, this limit was increased to the sterling equivalent of 100,000 euros, and now stands at £75,000.

CASE STUDY

Northern Rock

In July 2007, Northern Rock announced a set of upbeat results and stated that the outlook for their business was 'very positive'. However, within a month of this announcement, the Governor of the Bank of England was made aware by the FSA (now the FCA) and the Treasury that the developing global credit squeeze was having an effect on Northern Rock. Soon after, the Governor announced that the Bank of England would be willing to provide funds to any bank that encountered short-term difficulties as a result of temporary market conditions. On the following day, the BBC announced that Northern Rock had received funding from the Bank of England in the Bank's role as lender of last resort.

On the next day, Northern Rock announced that the 'extreme conditions' on the financial markets had forced it to turn to the Bank of England for assistance and a statement was issued by Northern Rock, the Bank of England and the Treasury to the effect that Northern Rock was solvent. However, this cut little ice with many customers who formed queues outside the bank looking to withdraw their deposits.

Over the next few days, the queues continued and the bank's share price continued to plunge, causing the Chancellor of the Exchequer to guarantee all of the bank's deposits – even those in excess of the legal compensation limit. This move seemed to appease depositors.

One week later, the bank cancelled its proposed dividend and stated that it had commenced talks with parties interested in buying all or part of the business.

In the weeks and months that followed, Northern Rock was rarely out of the news as others sought to buy the bank, before it was eventually nationalised. The FSA was heavily criticised for its part in the process. For most people, the abiding memory of the Northern Rock story was television pictures of customers queuing to get their savings out of the bank. Then, on 1 January 2012, Northern Rock was acquired by Virgin Money.

4.4 The retail market

The public regards the products offered by banks as close substitutes for each other. This public perception has recently come even closer to reality, as the old differences between clearing banks and building societies have now largely disappeared. All now provide a range of payment facilities including money transmission, cash dispensers, direct banking and credit cards as well as lending facilities which, although they are not identical, do overlap, particularly in personal lending and mortgages. This operating environment has resulted in intense competition between deposit-taking institutions (DTIs).

The UK clearing banks are mostly involved in retail banking, although they also have some wholesale activities. Retail banking implies a large number of customers generating volume business on standard terms and conditions. The interest rates payable on the different varieties of deposits are normally advertised and thus are widely known. Lending rates are widely publicised and rates to borrowers are based on these.

Competition among clearing banks and between them and other DTIs takes the following forms:

- Range of services available online and over the telephone line
- Extent and location of branch networks
- Interest rates charged on loans and paid on deposits
- Fees charged for arranging loans
- Range and quality of additional services provided

- Perceived stability and trustworthiness of the organisation

Although clearing banks vary in size, to some extent they all enjoy economies of scale, the particular advantages being that:

- The branch network makes the clearing banks accessible to a wide range of customers

- A comprehensive direct banking service can be offered

- Risk is spread over a range of sectors of the economy and parts of the country (a bank is much more vulnerable when it is involved with only a few customers)

- A larger bank can afford to employ experts and have specialist departments and services, or they can afford to outsource some operations

- Larger banks require proportionally lower levels of liquid assets as risk of unexpected withdrawals is spread more widely

- Larger banks can maximise use of modern technology

A clearing bank's cash inflow consists of customers' deposits and loan repayments (including interest) while cash outflow is customers' withdrawals and new loans. The amount of loan repayments will be fixed at any given time, depending on the amount of lending in previous periods, but the inflow of deposits and the amount of lending and withdrawal of deposits will depend on prevailing interest rates and other conditions attached to deposits and loans.

Rates and terms can be varied, consequently varying the level of inflows and outflows. As clearing banks are very similar in the range of services offered, altering interest rates would appear to be the main variable, but they do not choose to actively compete through interest rates, although they are free to do so.

They do not operate an interest rate cartel, although the tendency to simultaneously adjust interest rates might suggest otherwise. This apparent coordination of rate adjustments, the banks would claim, derives from them all operating in the same money markets and thus being subject to precisely the same market forces.

Interest rates on loans and deposits are adjusted to give each bank a desired level of liquidity – a balance between inflows and outflows. They will not normally be keen to alter these rates relative to each other, unless the existing balance appears to have been permanently upset – an abundance or shortage of liquidity within a bank.

The distinction between retail and wholesale banking has become blurred in recent years. Most of the UK clearing banks are now banking groups which provide through subsidiaries a wide range of services, for example, deposit taking, share issues, leasing. The key distinction of clearing banks from other DTIs is that they play a major role in money transmission services and hold a high proportion of demand deposits in the economy.

Banks are not the only financial institutions to accept deposits from the public. Some **finance houses** are authorised by the FCA to accept deposits. Others, such as **building societies**, **credit unions** and **National Savings & Investments (NS&I)**, are covered by separate Acts of Parliament which authorise their acceptance of deposits from the public. A feature of most of these institutions is that they accept deposits for small sums of money from large numbers of personal customers.

A final group of financial institutions comprises those which do not accept deposits from the public but instead provide facilities for long-term saving and investment, comprising:

- Investment trusts, unit trusts and Open Ended Investment Companies (OEICs)
- Insurance companies, and
- Pension funds

4.5 Recent developments

The period since 2007 has been turbulent for the UK banking sector. It was characterised by a tightening of credit conditions brought about largely by international factors, notably the credit crisis in the USA.

During the crisis of the late 2000s, several banking institutions had to seek government support and some were taken wholly or partially into public ownership. There was also significant rationalisation in the UK financial services sector.

A credit crunch is defined as 'a severe shortage of money or credit'. In August 2007, bad news from French bank BNP Paribas triggered a sharp rise in the cost of credit, causing the financial world to realise just how serious the situation was. Lehman Brothers was the first major bank to collapse in the credit crisis.

The crisis had a major impact on all organisations that relied to any extent on the wholesale markets, and as many UK-based financial institutions were heavily reliant on wholesale funds from the USA, deteriorating conditions in the US economy quickly had a major impact in the UK.

Until 2007, the housing market in the USA had enjoyed a period of sustained growth, fuelled by low interest rates and readily available funds, including buoyant inflows from Asian economies and oil-producing countries.

Much of the growth was based on the belief that mortgage assets were generally safe. Many US lenders leveraged their growth by issuing mortgage-based securities, which raised funding based on the perceived quality of existing mortgage assets. In addition to the burgeoning mortgage market, demand for other types of loans, such as credit cards and car finance, was extremely strong. Most economists agree that the UK credit market peaked in late 2006.

The US economy inevitably overheated. Default rates started to increase and lenders became increasingly nervous. The costs of funding started to increase. As recession loomed, the banks in the USA became reluctant to make wholesale funds available. Alarmingly, the five largest investment banks in the USA, major players in the wholesale and derivatives markets, all ran into difficulties. Lehman Brothers collapsed in September 2008. Goldman Sachs and Morgan Stanley became commercial banks. Bear Stearns and Merrill Lynch were bought out. Also in 2008, the Federal National Housing Association (Fannie Mae) and the Federal Loan Mortgage Corporation (Freddie Mac) were placed into conservatorship of the Federal Housing Finance Agency.

All of these developments put pressure on many of the larger banks in the UK, who had to make their lending products competitive but could not secure funding at the right price. The crisis in the UK was triggered by fundamental problems affecting many major players in the market.

Other financial institutions quickly found that they needed government support. In autumn 2008, several large banks were supported by public funds when the Government decided to take shares in these banks in return for capital injections. Further funds were provided by the Government in Spring 2009. These measures – which amounted to part-nationalisation – were intended to be temporary, in that the capital will be repaid to the Government when markets eventually recover.

As previously mentioned, the Government also sought to increase confidence in the banking and finance sector by reinforcing the compensation available to customers of failed organisations, increasing the level of protection for individual (personal) investors.

CASE STUDY

Icelandic banks

The international dimensions of the crisis were brought home by the collapse of the Icelandic banking system, and in particular the failure of Landsbanki. This bank had been offering attractive interest rates for deposits through its subsidiary, Icesave, which provided easy access, online retail banking services to retail customers in the UK and the Netherlands. In October 2008, Icesave stopped processing withdrawals. Initially the Government of Iceland announced that it would only protect domestic depositors, causing diplomatic tensions between the UK and Iceland. Eventually, in October 2009, the Icelandic government announced that it would be making compensation available for non-resident and personal customer account holders.

Some banks took the more conventional route of seeking merger partners and were effectively taken over. Some of the former building societies that had become public limited companies during the 1980s and 1990s had some of their business taken over by other financial organisations.

Ironically, in a sector in which size had become important, some of the smaller institutions with less dependence on wholesale markets were less seriously affected by the crisis. Some observers have commented that none of the former building societies that relinquished their mutual status to become public limited companies survive as independent institutions. By contrast, few of the building societies were seriously affected by the crisis, though there has inevitably been some rationalisation.

The crisis has led to an inevitable restructuring of the financial sector, with several mergers and acquisitions as well as the total demise of some companies. The government has forecast that recovery will be gradual and prolonged, which suggests that there will be further significant developments to come.

The events of 2008 and 2009 focused attention on the ways in which banking organisations conduct themselves, with perhaps an overdue re-evaluation of corporate governance, values and ethics. It was inevitable that regulation of the financial sector would be reformed. Banking institutions will therefore be faced with new compliance challenges, and will also have to consider the extent to which their corporate social responsibility policies go further than simply obeying the law. In building their business models for the future, the larger institutions may have to undergo a period of consolidation and perhaps even fundamental restructuring of the ways in which they do business in order to compete with new challenges, including entirely new players that enter their markets.

A significant outcome of the crisis is the reinforcement of the long-held view of some economists that some institutions are **'too big to fail'**. The financial sector in the UK did much to generate wealth in the quarter century that followed the Second World War, giving successive governments the confidence to deregulate and permit banking institutions to compete with each other, largely without external interference. This led to more innovation and greater choice for consumers, but perhaps also complacency that if and when things were to go wrong, the industry would be able to deal with any problems as they arose. The fact that many financial institutions came to rely on government (and therefore taxpayer) support is a timely reminder that banking has always been, and will remain, a risk business.

As the Government now has substantial holdings in some of the major banks, public scrutiny of banks has probably never been greater.

4.6 Independent Commission on Banking (Vickers Report)

In June 2010, the Chancellor of the Exchequer announced the creation of an Independent Commission on Banking (ICB), chaired by Sir John Vickers. The ICB was asked to consider structural and related non-structural reforms to the UK banking sector to promote banking stability and competition.

With regard to stability, the ICB stated in an interim report that making the banking system safer required a combined approach that:

- Makes banks better able to absorb losses
- Makes it easier and less costly to sort out banks that get into trouble
- Curbs incentives for excessive risk taking.

The two ways to make banks safer were:

- Firstly, by increasing their ability to bear losses, by requiring them to hold a great deal more capital
- Secondly, to alter their structure.

The final Vickers Report (2011) made recommendations on the future of UK banking, in the wake of the late 2000s financial crisis. Stopping short of advocating a full-scale **separation** of **'High Street' banking** from the banks' high-risk 'casino'-style **investment banking** activities, the Report recommended that the main UK banks be required to **'ring-fence'** their retail banking operations within separate entities from their investment banking arms. ('Retail' banking for this purpose can include straightforward banking services provided to corporate customers.)

The Financial Services (Banking Reform) Act 2013 (the 'Banking Reform Act') implements the Report's recommendations. The ring-fencing of retail and investment banking, which will be implemented along with stricter capital requirements for the banks, is intended to avoid financial losses in investment banking from de-stabilising a retail bank and thus possibly requiring a rescue at taxpayers' expense. The banks have until 2019 to complete the ring-fencing process.

The ICB also stated that UK retail banking needs to be more competitive and that the **ability of customers to switch banks** could be greatly facilitated.

5 Other financial services providers

5.1 Introduction

In addition to the clearing banks, other types of banks and financial services organisations include the following:

- Building societies
- Credit unions
- National Savings & Investments (NS&I)
- Investment banks
- Insurance companies
- Pension providers
- Investment trust companies
- Unit trusts and OEICs
- The central bank

5.2 Building societies

A **building society** is a financial institution that offers savings accounts and mortgages as its main business. In recent years a number of building societies have diversified and now offer a wide range of personal financial services.

A building society is a mutual institution. This means that most people who have a savings account, or mortgage, are members and have certain rights to vote and receive information, as well as to attend and speak at meetings. Each member has one vote, regardless of how much money they have invested or borrowed or how many accounts they may have. Each building society has a board of directors who run the society and who are responsible for setting its strategy.

Building societies are different from banks, in that banks are companies that are usually listed on the stock market and therefore owned by, and run for, their shareholders. Societies, which are not companies, are not driven by external shareholder pressure to maximise profits to pay away as dividends. This can sometimes result in building societies offering products at competitive prices. The other major difference between building societies and banks is that there is a limit on the proportion of their funds that building societies can raise from the wholesale money markets.

Building societies originated in the late 18th century among working people who wished to build their own homes. The oldest society for which records survive was Keltey's Building Society founded in Birmingham in 1775. Others were to follow and by 1800 there were 23 building societies.

It was in the Midlands and the north of England, in the rapidly expanding towns of the Industrial Revolution, that the new movement took root and prospered. The names of the towns or regions where the societies began are still to be seen in the titles of today's societies such as the Skipton or the Yorkshire.

Compared with today's financial giants, the early societies were simple. A group of working men would pool their financial resources to purchase some land and build houses for themselves and their families. Each member paid a regular subscription to the society. As each house was completed, lots would be drawn to decide the member to whom it should be allocated. When every member was housed, any loans repaid and all other expenses met, the society would be dissolved. For this reason the early societies were known as **'terminating' societies**.

Modern building societies are 'permanent' societies which means they were not to be dissolved once their founding members are housed, but have a continuing existence. The first permanent society was established in 1845. This development opened up membership to those who wished to save rather than to build or buy a house. The Building Societies Act 1874 made building societies corporate bodies with full legal powers similar to limited companies and it provided the legal basis for their activities over the next 100 years.

The inter-war period. The 20th century saw the growth of the building society movement, particularly in the inter-war period. Even the economic depression of the 1930s failed to halt this expansion; indeed, the building societies were able to benefit from the prevailing low interest rates. This depression was predominantly a regional problem hitting the traditional heavy industries of the north of England, south Wales and central Scotland.

The new consumer goods industries were concentrated in the south and Midlands of England. For those in work, real incomes grew as did the volume of savings and the demand for home mortgages. This period of substantial growth ended with the outbreak of war in 1939.

The post-war period. When the Second World War ended in 1945, the immediate problems were reconstruction and repairing wartime damage. Government housing policy concentrated on building public sector houses to let, which offered little scope for the building societies. In the 1950s, the emphasis switched back to the private sector and there was a rapid increase in the number of houses built for owner-occupiers. This began a new period of growth for the building societies.

The last 25 years. The number of building societies has reduced since the start of the 20th century.

QUICK QUESTION

Why do you think this happened?

Write your answer here before reading on.

Underlying the decline are the following factors:

- The closure of some of the very small permanent societies
- The process of amalgamation by mergers has reduced the number of societies.

While this has occurred over a number of years, you will be aware that some of the smaller societies merged with some larger ones as a consequence of the banking crisis in 2008; for example, the Derbyshire Building Society and the Cheshire Building Society both merged with the Nationwide at the end of 2008.

Under the Building Societies Act 1986, a building society has the right to convert from mutual to company status. The Abbey National converted in July 1989, and other major societies – Halifax, Woolwich, Alliance & Leicester – converted in 1997. Once company status is achieved, the building society is reclassified as a bank (or mortgage bank). Obviously this trend has reduced further the number of building societies and their share of personal sector financial assets and mortgages.

BPP
LEARNING MEDIA

Building Societies Acts 1986 and 1997

The Building Societies Act 1986 provided an entirely new legal framework for the building society movement and replaced all earlier building society legalisation. It removed many of the restrictions which had limited their activities and gave them a much broader remit to enable them to extend their range of financial services. The Act was part of the wider move towards deregulation/liberalisation which affected all financial institutions in Britain in the 1980s. The Act has since been amended and revised by the Building Societies Act 1997 and the Financial Services and Markets Act 2000, but the main provisions of the 1986 Act relating to the constitution, governance and principal purpose of building societies remain in place.

The principal (but no longer the sole) purpose of building societies remains that of raising funds from personal savers to lend out for house purchase to owner-occupiers. To this was added a range of new services such as money transmission, house purchase, non-mortgage lending and other financial services such as share dealing.

The development of building societies in Scotland was quite different to that south of the border. Although some building societies existed in Scotland in the early 19th century, they have always done proportionately less business in Scotland than in the rest of the UK. Unlike banks, none of the large building societies was founded in Scotland. The lack of a major Scottish-based building society can be explained by a number of interrelated factors:

- The dominance of other savings institutions – commercial and savings banks – may have inhibited the development of an indigenous building society movement

- The relative poverty of the working class and lower middle class in the past made house purchase more difficult in Scotland

- The former availability of social housing (council houses) with subsidised rents that bore no relation to the actual interest cost associated with their construction

- The Scottish tradition, up until the 1980s, of renting rather than purchasing a home – in the early 1990s, about only 55% of Scottish homes were owner-occupied as opposed to almost 70% in England

- A previous inadequate stock of suitable housing in Scotland for purchase or acceptance as security for advances by building societies.

In the 1980s and 1990s there was increased home ownership in Scotland, encouraged in part by the sale of council houses, the near cessation of new council house building and higher council house rents. Mortgage business generated by this trend was won mainly by building societies and mortgage banks in England. At the same time, the main building societies, such as Nationwide and the Yorkshire, had branches and agencies in Scotland, the savings deposits of which have partly financed their mortgage operations in Scotland.

CASE STUDY

Dunfermline Building Society

The largest Scottish-based society is the Dunfermline Building Society. It was established in 1869, incorporated in 1887, and is now part of Nationwide. The Society's profitable core business was bought by Nationwide in 2009 when the Dunfermline came close to insolvency due to its exposure to the commercial property market.

Shares and deposits. Personal savings accounts with building societies are share accounts. Holders of share accounts are members of the Society with a right to attend and to vote at general meetings, typically subject to them having a minimum of £100 balance in their account.

Since 1986, those with mortgages have the same membership rights and are referred to as 'borrowing members'. Minimum balances are specified for both types of customer in order to enjoy voting rights.

Unlike members of limited companies, each member of a building society has one vote, irrespective of the sum deposited or owed.

Under the provisions of the 1986 Act as amended, building societies must raise at least 50% of their capital from retail sources, and at least 75% of their commercial assets must be represented by loans secured on land for residential use. Building societies are permitted to accept corporate deposits and engage in lending other than mortgages, subject to the statutory limits. However, deposits from corporate customers must be designated as 'deposit accounts' and not as shares, so the investor has no constitutional rights.

The lower level of dependence on wholesale funding was one reason why the majority of building societies escaped some of the more serious effects of the credit crisis. However, some societies did come under pressure and this led to further rationalisation, such as the takeovers of the Cheshire, Derbyshire and Dunfermline building societies by Nationwide.

5.3 Credit unions

Credit unions are mutual savings and loan societies providing a basic low-cost banking service. Members finance their personal borrowing from their own combined resources.

In many ways credit unions are like the early building societies with the provision that members must share some common bond, such as attending the same church, living in the same locality, or working for the same employer. One possibility is for a firm to support a credit union for its employees and deduct savings automatically from their salary.

Credit union services are common in North America. About 25% of Americans bank with credit unions which offer a wide range of banking and financial services. In the UK, the movement was established first in Northern Ireland, and Irish and West Indian people who were already familiar with the benefits of credit unions brought them to mainland Britain.

Each credit union is a self-governing club owned by the members themselves and run on cooperative principles. Administration is through a board of directors, a credit committee and a supervisory committee elected by and from the members. Many credit unions rely to some extent on voluntary support. Members must be regular savers and can apply for small loans at moderate rates of interest to meet such expenses as holidays, weddings or even, in the winter, high fuel bills. Borrowers must continue to save while repaying their loans. Loan requests are treated in confidence and dealt with by the credit committee.

Part of the strength of credit unions is their size. Managers and members should be known to each other and loans can be granted on the basis of personal knowledge of the borrower. This is important for low income families with no financial assets to offer as security. It is also important for those groups whose needs and culture are outside the experience of the established financial institutions.

Unlike building societies, the demutualisation of credit unions into bank plcs is not possible under current legislation. The operations of credit unions in the UK are governed by the Credit Unions Act 1979.

5.4 National Savings & Investments (NS&I)

The idea of a national savings bank operating through the post office was proposed as long ago as 1807, but it was not until 1861 that the Post Office Savings Bank (POSB) was established. The POSB had a number of advantages over retail and trustee savings banks in that:

- It could provide national coverage through an established network of post offices

- Deposits and interest of 2.5% per annum at the POSB were guaranteed by the state so there was no risk of default

- All deposits were placed in an account at the Bank of England and subsequently invested in government securities

These perceived advantages encouraged the closure of small local savings banks in the south of England as customers transferred their accounts to the POSB, which continued to expand in the first half of the 20th century, reaching a peak of almost £2 billion in deposits in 1946.

Various improvements were made to the service such as the payment of small sums on demand, payment by crossed warrant through a bank, a method of making periodic payments and the sale of savings stamps, although the basic service remained essentially unchanged. POSB accepted deposits at 2.5% and reinvested the funds in government securities.

The subsequent decline in the POSB's popularity in the 1950s and 1960s may be explained by:

- **Reluctance to provide competitive services**. At a time when other savings institutions were broadening their range of services, the POSB continued to offer its one basic account; the management showed no enthusiasm for introducing a payments system such as a giro, nor was the management prepared to offer an investment account.

- An **uncompetitive interest rate**. In the 1930s and 1940s, the 2.5% offered by the POSB was competitive; with rising/fluctuating interest rates from the mid-1950s onwards, the POSB steadily lost ground to its more aggressive competitors who offered higher interest rates.

Reform and revival

In the 1960s a number of developments took place:

- The POSB headquarters was moved from London to Glasgow in 1966

- Also in 1966, investment accounts were introduced offering higher interest rates to long term savers

- In 1969 POSB changed its name to the National Savings Bank (NSB) although it continued to operate through post offices.

The investment account reversed the overall decline of funds held in the NSB. All the funds raised by the NSB were made available to the UK Treasury. Around 2000, NSB was absorbed into the National Savings & Investments (NS&I), a department of the UK Treasury.

NS&I is an **Executive Agency** of the **Chancellor of the Exchequer**. HM Treasury uses the money invested in NS&I to manage the national debt cost-effectively, contributing to the Government's financing needs. NS&I is responsible for providing cost-effective financing to the Government by issuing and selling retail savings and investment products to the public.

The powers governing the way in which NS&I products are structured and managed are derived from specific NS&I legislation and all strategic decisions affecting our products require Ministerial consent. NS&I is expected by HM Treasury to comply with Financial Conduct Authority (FCA) requirements where applicable and appropriate, but this is on a voluntary basis, since NS&I does not formally come within the FCA's regulatory remit.

NS&I raises funds for the Government by offering a broad range of savings products to the general public, including fixed interest savings certificates, index-linked savings certificates, capital bonds, its own Individual Savings Account (ISA) product, and retirement bonds.

About 4,000 NSB staff were transferred to Siemens Business Services as part of a ten-year public private partnership agreement which gave NS&I access to new technology and expertise.

In 2004 the ordinary account facilities were terminated and customers were asked to transfer their business to a more flexible savings account. At this time, 13 million people had ordinary accounts but many of these accounts were dormant. The interest rate was only 0.25% per annum and more than 4 million accounts had less than £10 as a balance.

It was this situation that encouraged NS&I to introduce a new, easy access savings account while continuing to provide an investment account, along with the NS&I Direct Saver account which offers access to funds either online or over the telephone.

5.5 Investment banks

Investment banks have their roots in what used to be known as merchant banks.

Some merchant banks (formerly known as accepting houses) can trace their origin to the overseas trading houses of the 19th century. Banking in many cases developed as a sideline to the main activity of merchant houses which was dealing in commodities. With their knowledge of commodity trading and banking, the merchant houses developed a market for bills of exchange in London.

As Britain grew as an international power during the 18th and 19th centuries, it was necessary for those engaged in international trade to find ways of financing their transactions. The most popular method of doing this was the bill of exchange.

A **bill of exchange** is a document drawn up by a bank on behalf of an exporter. It sets out the amount to be paid on or before a future date by the customer. The bill of exchange is sent to the importer's country and is then accepted by a bank, confirming it as good for payment. The bill can then be endorsed (or indorsed) to facilitate further payments to a third party, or even a series of third parties. Although this function is much less important today, the role of the merchant banks as accepting houses was enormously significant in Victorian times.

Modern investment banks typically have the following functions:

- **Accepting deposits**. As wholesale banks, investment banks deal in large deposits mainly from the corporate sector (industrial and commercial companies) rather than the personal sector. Investment banks' wholesale activities now predominate. Although much of this business is with other banks through the London inter-bank market and with banks abroad, lending to corporate customers in both sterling and foreign currencies remains significant.

  Investment banks do not operate a chain of retail branches or provide the general public with money transmission accounts. While this saves the expense of a branch network and the cost of administering numerous small accounts, it means that the bulk of an investment bank's liabilities are market interest rate bearing deposits.

  Some investment banks provide deposit and money transmission services for high net worth personal and corporate customers. Such services are often provided through subsidiaries set up as private banks.

- **Finance**. Apart from accepting trade bills and thereby providing a source of finance to firms, investment banks often provide their own clients with acceptance credits which enable a customer to issue bills drawn on an investment bank up to an agreed amount. These bills are then discounted to raise finance. The bank pays the bills on maturity and debits the client's account with the bills' face value. Clients pay investment banks for the use of such facilities.

  Investment banks also provide term loans in sterling and foreign currency to companies and institutions. Like finance houses, they also provide leasing and factoring facilities to their clients, but on a larger scale.

- **New share issues**. As issuing houses, investment banks advise companies on the most economical way to raise capital for expansion; this might often take the form of a new share issue to the public. If an issue of shares is considered appropriate, most investment banks will be able to provide the necessary expertise, such as the issue of a share prospectus, and compliance with Stock Exchange requirements, to help their corporate client raise the necessary finance.

  There are several ways that new shares may be issued. The most usual is an **offer for sale** where the issuing house buys the shares from the company trying to raise finance and offers them for sale to the general public at a higher price. Advising on the price at which to issue the shares is another responsibility of the issuing house which will also arrange underwriting to ensure that all the shares are sold. For a commission, an underwriter undertakes to buy any of the shares not taken up by the public.

- **Financial advice**. An area of investment banking activity that sometimes receives considerable publicity is their work in mergers, acquisitions and takeovers. Investment banks advise companies on the tactics and strategy to employ in carrying out a merger or for resisting an unwanted takeover bid.

- **Investment management**. Investment banks provide investment management expertise to a large number of pension funds, investment trusts and funds (unit trusts and OEICs). Some investment banks operate their own unit trusts.

- **Other activities**. Investment banks deal in foreign currencies, gold bullion and other commodities, either on their own account or for clients. Their range of activities is not uniform, dealing only with certain industries or sectors.

QUICK QUESTION

What is the purpose of insurance?

Write your answer here before reading on.

5.6 Insurance companies

5.6.1 Overview

Insurance is about the transference of risk from one party (the **customer**, that is the '**insured**') to another party (the **insurer**, typically an **insurance company**) who pools together the risks taken on from different parties – usually in return for the payment of a fee or premium.

Forms of transference of risk were practised by Chinese and Babylonian traders as early as the second and third millennia BC. If Chinese merchants were travelling across dangerous waters, they would carry their goods in a number of vessels so that, in the event of the loss of a ship, not all of their goods would be lost – in other words, they were spreading the risk. The Babylonians developed a system whereby if a merchant received a loan to fund a shipment, and if he paid the lender an additional sum, then, should the shipment be stolen, the lender would write off the advance – rather like financial protection products in use today.

The concept of life assurance was introduced by the Greeks and Romans when they organised 'benevolent societies' where the societies cared for dependants and paid the funeral expenses of deceased members.

At the end of the 17th century in Britain, London's growing importance as a trade centre increased the demand for maritime insurance. In the late 1680s, Edward Lloyd opened a coffee house which was frequented by ship owners, merchants and ships' captains and, as a result, became a reliable venue for shipping news. Later, people who were interested in insuring cargoes and ships would gather there and thus Lloyds of London was born. After the Great Fire of London, Nicholas Barbon started to insure buildings against fire and, in 1680, established 'The Fire Office' to insure houses.

The business of insurance companies falls into two main categories:

- The spread of risks between persons and organisations – general insurance
- The spread of risk over time – life assurance.

5.6.2 General insurance

General insurance provides cover against certain agreed risks such as fire, theft or accident which may occur during a specified period of time. The types of general insurance you will be most familiar with are motor insurance, holiday insurance and property (house and contents) insurance.

The common feature of these different classes of insurance is that the probability of the risks involved actually happening can be calculated reasonably accurately. These calculations are based on past experience, therefore, for any given group seeking insurance cover against a particular risk, an insurance company can estimate with a high degree of certainty the total value of claims likely to arise. What the company cannot do is predict which of the insured will be the ones to suffer the loss covered and so be the ones to claim. If such risks could be identified, they would be uninsurable.

The service an insurance company offers is to spread a risk of loss over all those who wish to insure against it. The insurance company charges each of its clients a fee or premium based on the degree of risk contributed by that particular client. The fees are paid into a common pool which is used to meet subsequent claims. The aim of an insurance company is to produce sufficient income from its premiums and its return on assets to meet all expected claims, to cover administrative costs, to make a profit and to add to its reserves.

QUICK QUESTION

What is the difference between insurance and assurance?

Write your answer here before reading on.

5.6.3 Life assurance

The difference between insurance and assurance is:

- Insurance offers cover against an event such as theft or an accident which may or may not happen.

- Assurance provides payment of a benefit on an occurrence, such as death or survival to a particular date, which will take place but the time of which is uncertain.

It would be possible to offer life cover for a limited period of say a year, in the same way that general insurance is offered. A problem with this approach is that, as a person grows older, the mortality risk increases and so the premiums would need to increase each year to match this. For older people, the costs of insurance could be prohibitive.

The solution to this problem is the use of **mortality tables**, which indicate the life expectancy of groups by age, sex and possibly other criteria, and so provide the basis for life assurance schemes, the main features of which may be that:

- Premiums are fixed for the duration of a policy – in the early years a policyholder pays a higher premium than is necessary, but the rate remains the same in later, high-risk years.

- Premiums are paid into a professionally managed life fund; income generated is for the benefit of the policyholders; claims are met out of this life fund.

Most assurance companies (or life offices) have a variety of policies available. The main types are as follows.

BPP
LEARNING MEDIA

- **Term assurance.** The assurance company pays a benefit only if the assured person dies within a specified time. There is no payment if the assured survives beyond that date. In view of the limited benefits and the fact that most policies do not result in claims, this is the cheapest form of life assurance.

- **Whole of life assurance.** The company promises to pay a sum of money when the assured person dies, which is a useful way of providing further protection for dependants. It remains in force for the whole of the assured person's life. Premiums may be fixed for an agreed period of time or may be payable throughout the life of the assured. This is more expensive than term assurance since all the policies eventually end in claims.

- **Endowment assurance.** The assurance company pays the benefits of the policy at an agreed date when the policy matures or earlier, on the death of the assured. Benefits may be a lump sum or an annual sum to be paid for a specified number of years or even for life.

  Endowment assurance and whole of life assurance are available with profits or without profits. With profits policies are more expensive, but the benefits are increased to give the policyholder a share of the profits earned by the fund.

- **Annuities.** Annuities are concerned with survival benefits rather than death benefits. On survival to a certain age, the benefits are paid to the policyholder him/herself either in the form of a lump sum or, more usually, a guaranteed income for life. Pension plans offer a form of annuity and life offices are heavily involved in this type of business.

5.6.4 Investment policy

Investment is an important part of insurance business and insurance companies hold a variety of assets including company securities, public sector securities, property and various mortgages and loans. Investment decisions and the range of assets held are greatly influenced by the liabilities incurred.

Insurance companies can reduce their risks by matching assets with liabilities and by holding a broad spread of investments. Life assurance and pension business is concerned with long-term liabilities and so life funds contain mostly long term assets.

5.6.5 Investment-based life policies

An endowment life assurance policy is a financial asset of the customer and represents a claim to future payment. It is not conditional in the sense that payment will be made by the maturity date at the latest. This is not the case with an insurance policy since payment is conditional on the insured event occurring and will not be made if that event does not take place. The longer an endowment policy runs, the more it increases in value which can be calculated.

Such a policy is mainly a long-term savings contract and is designed to run to its maturity date. Early withdrawal is possible, and there are the following several ways this can be done.

- **Convert the policy into a paid-up policy** – the policy continues in force until the original maturity date, but the sum assured is reduced and no further premiums are paid.

- **Surrender the policy for cash** – the policy is discontinued and the holder receives its surrender value based on the current value of the policy's share of the life fund, less all expenses such as commission and administration involved in setting up the policy. Surrendering a policy is a breach of the original contract and is not always allowed. As the early repayment of the policy might interfere with a life office's investment strategy and cause some disorientation of risk, the surrender value will be less than the accumulated premiums in most cases, in the early years considerably less.

- **Sell the policy** – the policyholder sells the policy to another party who will continue to pay the premiums and obtain the benefit at the end of the life of the policy. Although this may be a more lucrative way for the policyholder to raise cash, there will be qualifying criteria to meet, such as the length of time the policy has run for and a minimum level of current surrender value.

- **Use the policy as security for a loan** – most life offices would consider one of its own life policies as excellent security for a loan and would be willing to lend up to 90% of its surrender value. Most offices charge a commercial interest rate linked to banks' base rates. Banks are also willing to grant loans on the security of life assurance policies.

5.7 Pension funds

Pension funds have experienced a tremendous growth in the last forty years. Payments from these funds are used by the beneficiaries to supplement their state pension. In many respects, pension fund management is very similar to the life assurance business discussed earlier in this chapter since both are concerned with building up a substantial fund of assets to meet long term liabilities.

A fund's income consists of contributions from employers and employees as well as earnings from investments. Expenditure, apart from administration, consists mainly of payments to pensioners.

An important principle of a work-based ('occupational') pension fund is the separation of the fund's liabilities from those of the employer. A pension fund is established with a legal identity separate from the employer particularly so that, should the employer run into financial difficulties, the creditors would have no claim on the assets of the pension fund and pensions would be protected.

There are two types of funded pension scheme.

- **Insured schemes** – pension contributions are paid to a life assurance company which guarantees the future pensions. The life assurance fund is responsible for investing the funds and carries the actuarial risk. This is perhaps most attractive to small firms which do not wish to establish their own funds.

- **Self-administered schemes** – the pension fund itself carries the actuarial risk and is responsible for the level of pensions paid. Sometimes the management of a pension fund will be contracted out to professional investment managers such as life assurance offices or investment banks. In other cases, the trustees of a large pension fund may prefer to employ their own staff and manage investments themselves.

Registered pension schemes receive some tax concessions, thus it is not surprising that there are limits on the benefits which may be received. Although personal pension plans (which are **defined contribution** schemes) operate by different rules, the maximum pension which can be received in a final salary (or **defined benefit**) scheme is two thirds of final salary which is reduced if a lump sum is paid. The lump sum itself may be no more than one and a half times final salary. There are also limits on the amounts of **contribution** which may be paid into a pension scheme, generally based on the individual's income, subject to an overall limit.

5.8 Investment trusts

Although called 'investment trusts', these are public limited companies ('plcs') whose business is investment. As a plc, the company must comply with the same rules as other plcs: for example, it will have a Memorandum, and Articles of Association; it will also publish annual financial statements, which will be reported upon by an external auditor.

An investment trust raises funds by offering its own shares to investors. With the money raised, the trust will trade on the market with the aim of making a profit which can then be passed back to the investment trust's own shareholders by the payment of a dividend. The price of the investment trust's shares on the market is determined by the supply and demand for its shares on the market, just like any other company.

Investment trusts are called 'closed-ended funds' as the number of shares issued by the investment trust is fixed and can only be increased if the trust arranges a fresh issue of its own shares.

5.9 Unit trusts and OEICs

A **unit trust** is a trust in the strict legal sense and the idea behind it is that it pools the resources of many people and from this open-ended pool, the manager place the funds in a wide range of investments. Depending on the level of their contribution, investors will be given a registered certificate which shows that they have purchased a stated number of units in the trust.

Unit trust schemes operate under a **deed of trust**. The deed appoints a trustee, such as a bank, to oversee the operation of the scheme. The fund investments are controlled by a fund manager who is responsible for the investment and for valuing the assets in the portfolio and calculating the prices of the units.

There are no limits to the number of units that can be created, therefore unit trusts are often described as 'open-ended funds'. An **Open-Ended Investment Company (OEIC)** is similarly an open-ended scheme for collective investment, and unit trusts and OEICs are often together known as **'funds'**.

QUICK QUESTION

What is a central bank?

Write your answer here before reading on.

5.10 The UK's central bank

5.10.1 The UK's central bank

A central bank is responsible for overseeing the monetary system for a nation, or a group of nations. Central banks have various responsibilities, ranging from overseeing monetary policy to implementing specific goals such as currency stability, low inflation, and full employment. Central banks also generally issue currency, function as the banker of the Government, regulate the credit system, oversee commercial banks, manage exchange reserves, and act as a lender of last resort.

The central bank of the UK is the Bank of England which was established by Royal Charter in 1694 and was promoted by a Scot, William Paterson, who believed that a large joint stock bank with its greater capital would have a considerable advantage over the existing banks, which were actually goldsmiths who also provided banking services. The original intention was to operate as an ordinary commercial bank on a larger scale; only gradually did the Bank assume the functions now associated with central banking.

Under its Charter, the Bank of England was authorised to:

- Accept deposits and make loans
- Discount bills
- Issue notes.

In return for its Charter, the Bank made a loan to the Government of £1.2 million at 8% which was added to Britain's National Debt. The loan took the form of notes issued by the Bank. The Bank thus issued notes and made a profit by making loans in the form of bank notes which it persuaded the public to accept and to hold. In this respect the Bank of England was similar to the other banks of the time. For its part the Bank tried to get a monopoly of the right to issue notes. At various times, the Bank's Charter needed to be renewed which provided opportunities for the Government to increase its borrowing and for the Bank to strengthen its position.

Although the Bank of England was founded as a commercial bank, it differs from other banks in a number of ways.

- **A joint stock company.** The Bank of England was established as a joint stock company and its capital was raised by public subscription which gave the Bank an advantage over the existing private banks which were restricted to six partners and so limited in potential size. An Act in 1708 made the Bank the only joint stock bank allowed to issue notes in England. The Bank did not operate in Scotland and by 1746 Scotland had three joint stock banking companies issuing notes – Bank of Scotland, Royal Bank of Scotland, British Linen Company.

- **Limited liability.** The Bank of England was given the privilege of limited liability which limited the shareholders' liability for the Bank's debts in the event of failure to the amount they had paid for their shares. This reduced the risk of investing in the Bank and so made its shares more attractive.

- **The government's banker.** By granting a loan to the Government, the Bank of England established a special relationship which developed over the years as the Bank undertook new responsibilities such as the circulation of Exchequer bills and the issue of government securities. In 1751, the Bank undertook the administration of the National Debt. Despite the competition that the Bank posed, private bankers in London found it convenient to keep an account with it for their surplus funds, thus the Bank took a step nearer to becoming a central bank by acting not only as the Government's banker but also as the bankers' bank.

5.10.2 Bank Charter Act 1844

The principal aim of the 1844 Act was to control the money supply by regulating the issue of banknotes. This was achieved by placing a limit on the Bank of England's ability to issue notes unbacked by gold and by the gradual phasing out of private bank note issues in England and Wales.

To ensure the proper operation of the note issue, the Bank was reorganised into two departments:

- An Issue Department solely concerned with the note issue
- A Banking Department to carry out the Bank's normal commercial activities.

The Bank was required to redeem its notes for gold at a fixed price (£3.87 per ounce of gold), thus linking the pound sterling to gold.

5.10.3 The Bank and financial crises

During the 19th century, the Bank assumed another function of central banking by acting as the lender of last resort which involved the Bank in providing support to the banking/financial system when major financial panics occurred. In many instances this support resulted in the Bank discounting bills or extending loans against bills offered by banks in need of liquidity. This function of the Bank of England was seen in more recent times during the banking crisis of the late 2000s.

5.10.4 Nationalisation

In 1946, the Bank of England was nationalised and thus passed into public ownership. The Bank's shareholders were compensated with government stock. Public ownership was the culmination of years of close cooperation between the Bank and government.

The Bank often appeared to be as much the Government's agent as an independent bank. With the Government playing a much greater role in the management of the economy after 1945 it seemed inappropriate that the Bank should remain in private ownership.

5.10.5 The Court of Directors

Responsibility for governance of the Bank lies with the Court of Directors which consists of the Governor, two Deputy Governors (both appointed for a term of five years) and sixteen non-executive members (three-year term) appointed for their expertise and drawn widely from industry, commerce and finance. The non-executive members' main role is to review the performance of the Bank as a whole, including the work of the Monetary Policy Committee (MPC) (which sets the base interest rate).

The Bank is managed on a day-to-day basis by the Governor and the two Deputy Governors – one deputy works with the Governor on monetary stability and the other on financial stability. The Governor keeps a close liaison with the City – financial institutions and markets – and represents the Bank at international financial and monetary meetings.

5.10.6 The Bank of England's mission

The Bank has had **monetary stability** and **financial stability** as two core purposes. However, the Bank takes the view that these are not ends in themselves, but necessary pre-conditions for delivering the public good. For that reason, the Bank's previous commitment to two core purposes has been recast into one all-embracing mission which emphasises the contribution that delivering the Bank's statutory responsibilities makes to the end goal.

The Bank has re-stated its single **mission** as being: 'to promote the good of the people of the United Kingdom by maintaining monetary and financial stability'. This is just as it was in the Bank's original Charter of 1694 ('Now know ye, That we being desirous to promote the public good and benefitt of our people...').

The Bank's **monetary policy** objective is to deliver price stability and, subject to that, to support the Government's economic objectives including those for growth and employment. Monetary stability means stable prices and confidence in the currency. Stable prices are defined by the Government's inflation target, which the Bank seeks to meet through the decisions delegated to the Bank's **Monetary Policy Committee (MPC),** explaining those decisions transparently and implementing them effectively in the money markets.

The remit of the MPC, including the definition of the inflation target, is re-confirmed each year by the Chancellor.

Financial stability requires an efficient flow of funds in the economy and confidence in financial institutions.

This is pursued through:

- The Bank's financial operations, including as lender of last resort
- Decisions of the Financial Policy Committee (FPC)
- Prudential regulation of financial institutions by the PRA
- The Bank's role as resolution authority, and
- Bank oversight and regulation of key payment, clearing and settlement infrastructure.

The **FPC** takes action against systemic risks to protect and enhance the resilience of the UK financial system. This Committee of the Bank has a secondary objective to support the economic policy of the Government.

We have already outlined the role of the **Prudential Regulation Authority (PRA),** which is a **subsidiary** of the **Bank of England**. The PRA is responsible for the supervision of around 1,700 banks, building societies, credit unions, insurers and major investment firms. The PRA has a general objective to promote the safety and soundness of these firms and – specifically for insurers – contributes to the protection of policyholders.

The Bank's accountability is ensured by the fact that the decision-making process is fully transparent and by the Government's overall accountability to Parliament for economic policy. The Bank makes reports and gives evidence to the House of Commons through the Treasury Select Committee.

QUICK QUESTION

What are the main functions of the Bank of England?

Write your answer here before reading on.

5.10.7 Functions of the Bank of England

As the UK's central bank, the Bank undertakes a number of important domestic and external functions on behalf of the Government and other financial institutions, are as follows.

- **Government's banker**. The Bank of England keeps the Government's bank accounts. The main government account is the Exchequer Account into which nearly all government receipts are paid and out of which nearly all payments originate. The Bank also keeps the accounts of government departments.

  Revenue flows very unevenly into the Exchequer and on occasions is inadequate to meet current government expenditure. The Treasury has then to make arrangements to bridge the gap between the inflow of revenue and the outflow of expenditure by advances from the Bank or by the issue of Treasury bills.

  The Bank provides temporary finance at market interest rates to the Government by 'ways and means advances' which are often not very large and are provided as an overnight facility. The Bank also advises the Government on economic, financial and monetary matters.

- **Bankers' bank**. The main clearing banks find it convenient to keep part of their cash reserves in operational accounts at the Bank of England. These banks constantly need to make and receive payment from one another due to the operation of the clearing system and these payments are made through the banks' accounts with the Bank of England. The banks need to keep these balances large enough to cover their needs and are expected not to overdraw.

- **Issue of notes**. The Bank is the sole bank of note issue for England and Wales. Scottish and Northern Ireland banks issue their own notes under strict regulation and, once in circulation, must be covered by Bank of England notes.

  There is now no gold backing of notes issued which means that the UK note issue is a fiduciary one, as the note issue is based purely on faith that notes will be acceptable to UK residents in settlement of debts at all times. Notes cannot be exchanged at the Bank of England for gold coins or bullion. As is to be expected with inflation, the note issue has increased over the years.

- **Implementation of monetary policy**. Since 1997, the Bank has implemented interest rate policy which takes account of the current/prospective inflation rate, the level of monetary demand and money supply growth in the economy. Apart from influencing base interest rate changes, the Bank can alter the cash deposit ratio on banks in order to effect changes on credit supply (loans) and/or terms made available by banks to their customers. Ultimately all deposit takers are affected by such action.

- **Lender of last resort.** The Bank occasionally acts as a lender of last resort to individual banks or the banking system which generally involves the provision of liquidity, sometimes at a penal interest rate, secured by first class bills and securities. By undertaking this role, the Bank endeavours to stabilise the banking and financial system and thereby prevent financial panics and depositor runs on banks.

- **International relationships.** The Bank cooperates with the principal central banks of the world, such as US Federal Reserve Banks, European Central Bank and others, and takes part in the work of the International Monetary Fund, Bank for International Settlements and the World Bank.

  It also provides services (gold and foreign exchange business) for the central banks of some Commonwealth countries. The Bank can arrange loans from overseas when necessary in order to add to the UK's foreign currency reserves, thereby increasing confidence in sterling on the world's foreign exchange markets.

- **Manages the Exchange Equalisation Account (EEA).** The EEA was established in 1932 to stabilise the pound's exchange rate in relation to other currencies and consists of the UK's gold and foreign currency reserves (US dollars, euros, Japanese yen) which technically belong to the Treasury. The EEA is managed on behalf of the Treasury by the Bank.

  If there is a temporary fall in the pound's exchange rate, the Bank can buy pounds using its foreign currency reserves on the foreign exchange market to bid up the pound. When the pound is too high, the Bank can sell pounds for foreign currencies and so force down sterling's exchange value. This process is known as official intervention in the foreign exchange market.

- **Private banking.** The Bank has some old-established private banking customers, as well as staff members and pensioners as customers. The general public cannot open accounts at the Bank.

5.10.8 The Bank of England Act 1998

The main provisions of this Act are as follows.

- The monetary policy objectives of the Bank as set out in statutory form are to maintain price stability and support the Government's economic policy.

- A Monetary Policy Committee was established which has responsibility for formulating monetary policy within the Bank.

- A new accountability framework for the Bank based on its statutory duties. The need for greater transparency in the Bank's operations was also identified.

- The Bank's function in relation to the supervision of UK banks was transferred to the FSA.

These were quite sweeping changes and marked a fundamental shift in the Bank's operational and supervisory roles from the position it occupied prior to this Act. Apart from the Bank's statutory responsibility for monetary policy, the most significant step was the transfer to the FSA of responsibility for bank supervision.

6 The economic environment

6.1 Introduction

Traditionally, governments will focus on the well-being of the people that they govern, the idea being that if the electorate is happy with its lot, it will re-elect the existing government. An important indicator of how people are faring is the state of the economy, as a strong economy indicates that the households and firms within the economy are enjoying a good standard of living and, to maintain this, the Government will do all in its power to stimulate economic growth.

6.2 The role of government

Macroeconomics is the study of how a national economy works and the interaction between economic growth in output and national income, employment and the general level of prices. A macro-economy consists of all the different markets for goods and services, labour, finance, foreign exchange and other traded items. Changes in the behaviour of producers and consumers in individual markets will therefore have an effect on the macro-economy and the rate of economic growth, inflation, employment and trade.

Most national governments share similar macroeconomic objectives:

- Low and stable price inflation
- A high and stable level of employment
- Economic growth and prosperity
- Favourable balance of international payments

Governments use policy instruments, including taxes and regulations, to help achieve their objectives through the impact they have on the actions of producers and consumers.

Government has a key role in the regulation of the financial services industry, with the key regulatory bodies being the Prudential Regulation Authority, the Financial Conduct Authority, the Bank of England, and HM Treasury.

6.3 Fiscal policy and monetary policy

There are two types of policy that the Government uses to control the economic environment.

- **Fiscal policy**. This covers the Government's spending activities, for example through capital projects, welfare payments, and defence spending. To do this, the Government must collect money in, through levying tax and borrowing funds. The annual budget outlines this policy. If the Government spends more than it collects, this is a **budget deficit**; if the Government spends less than it collects, this is a **budget surplus**. Another factor to consider is that if the Government collects tax from firms and households, this reduces the purchasing power of these firms and households.

- **Monetary policy**. This is where the Government or the central bank seeks to control the price and the supply of money circulating in the economy. **Interest rates** represent the cost or price of money. The movement of base rate will affect other interest rates and thus can affect the demand for money in the economy.

    To encourage economic growth, the central bank may create or 'print' more money to stimulate spending and the economy but, if this is not controlled, it can lead to higher inflation. The Bank of England eased monetary conditions in 2009 and subsequently under the banner of 'quantitative easing'.

    The central bank can also seek to dampen the economy by taking money out of the system, for example to reduce inflation and raise currency values, although this risks leading to economic slowdown.

6.4 Inflation and interest rates

Inflation is an increase in the general price level over time. The term describes the situation where the prices of goods and services increase in a sustained manner.

Inflation can be measured by a range of indicators. The most commonly used measure in the UK is the **Consumer Prices Index (CPI)**. This is calculated by sampling the prices of various goods and services each month. As we all buy different baskets of goods and services from one another, and indeed our patterns of expenditure change over time, inflation has different effects on different people, as well as on our own situation over time.

Consider the effects of inflation on savers. If the amount of money we have is falling in value, theoretically we should save less and hold more in assets that will retain their value. This may or may not be the case:

- Those who hold savings for precautionary reasons, that is 'for a rainy day', may anticipate that their savings will no longer be able to cope with future needs and will therefore top up their savings.

- Those who hold savings in order to buy something in the future may save less and spend immediately, as they anticipate that they may not be able to afford the intended purchase later on.

Until 1977, successive UK Governments were committed to full employment in the economy. The UK came out of the Second World War with fresh memories of the great depression of the 1930s, so governments took it on themselves to ensure that the mass unemployment of those times would not recur.

However, during the 1970s the UK economy nearly collapsed due to problems of failing competitiveness, increasing industrial and social unrest, and rising inflation. The level of inflation during the 1950s had been typically 2% per year, but this rose to 24% in 1973 and peaked at 32% shortly afterwards. This destroyed the value of savings balances, created massive uncertainty and exacerbated the problems confronting the already ailing economy.

An economic crisis from 1975 to 1977 meant that the Government had to take a radically new approach to economic policy. Controlling inflation became the main economic target, and full employment as a primary goal was sacrificed. At the time of the general election of 1979, inflation remained at 18%. The 1980s saw a steady decline in the level of inflation but also a worrying rise in unemployment.

The shift in the focus of government policy away from full employment and towards controlling inflation is of direct relevance to financial institutions. Many of the products and services of financial institutions are priced by interest rates. In turn, the general level of interest rates in the economy is set by the Bank of England's Monetary Policy Committee on behalf of the Government: this has a direct impact on the prices that can be charged by financial institutions, or paid to investors.

Today, the Government sets a **target for inflation** and it is the role of the Monetary Policy Committee of the Bank of England to try to bring inflation close to the target.

- Currently, price stability is defined by the Government's inflation target of **2%**. The inflation target of 2% is expressed in terms of an annual rate of inflation based on the Consumer Prices Index (CPI). The remit is not to achieve the lowest possible inflation rate. Inflation below the target of 2% is judged to be just as bad as inflation above the target. The inflation target is therefore symmetrical.

- If the target is missed by more than **1 percentage point on either side** – ie, if the annual rate of CPI inflation is more than 3% or less than 1% – the Governor of the Bank of England must write an open letter to the Chancellor explaining the reasons why inflation has increased or fallen to such an extent and what the Bank proposes to do to ensure inflation comes back to the target.

Interest rate policy is particularly important in the UK because most savers and borrowers enter into contracts that are subject to variable rates. Even 'fixed rate' mortgages are fixed only for an initial period of time. By contrast, savers and borrowers in continental Europe and in the US are much more used to fixed rate products. This is one reason why the Government would be taking a significant political risk in joining the Eurozone, as control of interest rates would pass to the European Central Bank.

QUICK QUESTION

What is a common measure used to report the state of the economy?

Write your answer here before reading on.

Pause for thought ...

In what ways do changes in the inflation rate affect your daily living?

In what ways do changes in interest rates affect your daily living?

6.5 Gross domestic product (GDP)

One way of gauging the state of the economy is through the growth in gross domestic product (GDP). GDP is a measure of the market value of all the goods and services produced within a country during any given year. If GDP is growing, the economy is said to be expanding; on the other hand if GDP is falling, the economy is contracting. If an economy has two or more quarters of negative GDP growth it is said to be in recession. A sustained recession is called a depression.

GDP can be measured in total terms or total GDP may be divided by the number of people in a country to give GDP per capita. For example, in 2005, the US topped the global GDP charts with 28% of the world's total GDP. However, if we look at GDP per capita, then the US drops to eighth on the list, with Luxembourg topping the list.

The performance of an economy can be assessed by such indicators as:

- Unemployment – what percentage of the population is out of work?

- Payrolls – how many jobs are being created? Are these permanent, full time jobs or more temporary positions?

- Industrial production – are factories producing more or fewer products?

- Retail sales – are households more or less economically active and what are the reasons behind this?

- New housing developments – the building trade is an important indicator of economic activity. Usually the demand for new housing falls as the economy enters a recession (due to low levels of consumer confidence) and the subsequent recovery can be well advanced before demand for housing begins to pick up again.

- Trade deficit – do imports exceed exports?

- Budget deficit – is the Government overspending?

- Consumer confidence – do households plan to keep spending?
- Business confidence – do firms plan to expand?

7 Financial markets

A market is simply where buyers and sellers of goods and services come together. The world-famous street market in Portobello Road in London's West End is an example of a market, where buyers and sellers physically come together to trade in an eclectic range of goods. There are many markets today where the buyers and sellers do not normally conduct transactions while they are in the same physical location – examples would include the stock market, and eBay.

Financial markets provide for buyers and sellers of financial products come together to trade in financial securities. The players can be the Government, or institutions from the private sector, or individuals, all sharing a common interest in trading, whether to raise or buy capital, and thereafter to trade in them.

Within financial markets, there are two different types of market:

- Primary markets, and
- Secondary markets

A **primary market** is where new issues of shares or other forms of security are offered to the market for the first time. For example, if the Government is seeking to fund a road building project, it may choose to finance this project by borrowing the necessary funds on the market. To do this, they will issue Government securities. Perhaps you have heard of Treasury Stock or Exchequer Stock: these are examples of Government securities. These are often referred to as 'gilt-edged' securities or 'gilts'. The probability of the Government defaulting on their obligation to repay such stock is effectively nil, and so the risk of default is deemed to be negligible. This method of raising funds has been used since 1693. Similarly, if a business is seeking to raise capital, it may choose to do this by either issuing new shares (equities) or bonds to the market, usually by using the services of an investment bank or issuing house.

A **secondary market** is where these securities are traded after their initial issue. It is easiest to think of the secondary market as a 'second-hand' market, where securities that have already been issued through the primary market are traded in again. The Stock Exchanges in London, New York and Tokyo are all examples of secondary markets.

Pause for thought ...

In what ways does your bank interact with the UK financial markets?

8 The UK and the City of London in Europe

The UK – and the City of London in particular – is a key player in the global financial market. The City is host to a huge number of overseas banks and plays an important role in facilitating the flow of capital around the globe, in both the developed and the developing world.

There are a number of reasons why the UK has developed to play such a pivotal role, including its history of being an open market economy with a pool of talented people available. Its regulatory, accounting and legal frameworks have also contributed to this development, as well as the long term-stability and predictability of its tax regulations. Key sub-sectors include banking, insurance, and asset management. The fact that English has developed as the international language of business has also been a contributing factor.

While the UK is a significant player in the global financial market, it does not operate alone. In recent years global financial markets have grown considerably. As a result, a number of overseas companies raise capital in the UK and have this capital traded in London. On the other hand, some UK companies will choose to seek capital from overseas markets, for example, by raising Eurobonds.

Now that many trade barriers between European countries have been removed, individuals are free to choose the financial products and services from any providers in the EU. UK-based financial services providers can either set up European subsidiaries or market their products directly.

Much UK financial services regulation originates in the EU. The EU is also very active in developing rules for Europe's financial markets that are designed to deepen the internal market. Since the UK has to give effect to European law, active engagement with Europe is essential. Indeed, around 70% of the policymaking effort of the UK Financial Services regulators, currently the FCA and the PRA, is driven by European initiatives, including the Financial Services Action Plan (FSAP).

It is crucial that the standards developed in international forums are proportionate and informed by economic analysis. Otherwise, better regulation domestically would be more difficult to achieve.

There has been specific EU legislation promoting the single market since the 1980s. However, there was a step change when the FSAP was launched in 1999. It consists of 42 measures, including 24 EC Directives to be transposed into the law of each Member State, and Regulations, which apply directly in all Member States.

The FSAP has three specific objectives:

- To create a single European wholesale market
- To achieve open and secure retail markets
- To create state-of-the-art prudential rules and structures of supervision

These objectives are designed to promote Europe's wider economy by removing barriers and increasing competition among financial services firms, thereby making markets more efficient and reducing the cost of raising capital to industry generally.

Since 1999 the EU has adopted or updated requirements concerning, amongst others:

- The amount of capital which firms should hold
- The rules they must comply with when carrying on business with their customers
- The controls they must apply to counter the risk of money laundering and terrorist financing
- The tests to apply when assessing the suitability of new controllers or large shareholders
- The requirements they must impose to counter the risk of market abuse
- The disclosures which companies must make when seeking new capital

Completion of the FSAP within a tight deadline was accompanied by a new legislative approach to developing and adopting EU financial services legislation.

Pause for thought ...

In what ways does your bank interact with the EU and international markets?

KEY WORDS

Key words and phrases from this chapter are given below. Make sure you know what they mean and add any other words or phrases that you want to remember. You can use the space provided to write your own revision notes.

- Definition of a bank
- Commercial banking
- Investment banking
- Bancassurance
- Purpose and functions of a bank
- Financial intermediary
- Liquidity
- Profitability
- Other providers of financial services
- UK central bank
- Fiscal and monetary policy
- Gross domestic product
- Financial markets

REVIEW

To help you reflect on and review the content of this chapter, give some thought to the following questions.

- What is the difference between commercial banking and investment banking?

- What is the difference between retail banking and wholesale banking?

- What is meant by 'bancassurance'?

- What is the purpose of a bank for deposit customers?

- What is the purpose of a bank for credit customers?

- In what way does a bank function as a financial intermediary?

- In what way is there a conflict between the bank's duties to its savers and borrowers? (Consider the need for both liquidity and profitability.)

- What are three ways that a bank makes its money?

- What role does the bank play in society?

- How did banking in the UK develop?

- In reviewing the content of this chapter, and reflecting on your own role and experience, what do you consider to be key features of the business and economic environment in which your bank operates?

- Apart from banks, what other types of financial services organisations operate in the business environment?

- What are the main functions of the Bank of England?

- What role does government play in the economy?

- What is the difference between fiscal and monetary policy?

- What is meant by inflation?

- What impact might changes in interest rates have on savers?

- What is the significance of Gross Domestic Product in an economy?

- What are the key indicators that can be used to assess the performance of an economy?

- What is the difference between a primary and secondary financial market?

chapter 2

THE REGULATORY AND LEGAL ENVIRONMENT

Contents

Learning objectives

By the end of this chapter, you should be able to:

- Explain the role of financial services regulators in the UK

- Identify the key regulatory and legal requirements that apply to banking

- Explain how banking regulation and legislation influence culture, products and services

Introduction

This chapter is about the key regulatory and legal requirements that apply to banking and how these requirements influence the way a bank operates.

We begin with an overview of the regulatory reforms that were implemented in 2013. We explain the roles of the twin regulators of the financial services industry: the Financial Conduct Authority (FCA) and the Prudential Regulation Authority (PRA). Then we consider key regulatory and legal requirements, including those relating to consumer credit, payment services, anti-money laundering, data protection, and anti-bribery legislation. We also consider requirements for Treating Customers Fairly ('TCF'), banking conduct and corporate governance.

We conclude the chapter by considering legal aspects of the banker/customer relationship and different types of businesses.

1 The UK regulatory framework for financial services

1.1 2013 regulatory reforms

The financial crisis of the late 2000s had brought into focus the problems of financial instability affecting some banks and other financial sector institutions. There had been criticism of the regulator at the time, the Financial Services Authority (FSA), for failing to be aware of the weakness of banks such as Northern Rock, which required emergency assistance and had to be nationalised. The financial turmoil of the late 2000s stemmed in large part from excessive lending by banks, much of it to sub-prime borrowers, and from the 'securitisation' or packaging of mortgages by lenders for selling on to investors who were insufficiently aware of the risks attached to the securities.

In June 2010, with a new Conservative-Liberal Democratic coalition Government in power, it was announced that the UK's single-regulator system under the FSA would be abolished. There would be a sweeping increase in the powers of the **Bank of England**, which was given a new remit of preventing a build-up of risk in the financial system.

1.2 The two financial services regulators

With effect from April 2013, two regulators have overseen the financial services industry.

- The **Prudential Regulation Authority (PRA)** was established to oversee the stability of 'prudentially significant' firms, including deposit-taking institutions, insurers and investment banks: that is, the 'prudential' issues of safety and soundness of these firms.

- The regulation of conduct across the sector, including in firms that are PRA-regulated, and encompassing issues surrounding advice given to retail consumers, became the responsibility of the new **Financial Conduct Authority (FCA)**, which was formed out of the FSA legal entity.

Firms such as **banks, insurers, and major investment firms** are thus supervised by the two independent regulators – the PRA and the FCA, for prudential and conduct regulation, respectively. This is called **'dual regulation'**. The two regulators will work to different objectives and act separately with firms, but will coordinate internally to share information and data on dual-regulated firms. All other firms will be supervised by the FCA for both conduct and prudential issues.

1.3 Financial Policy Committee (FPC)

A new **Financial Policy Committee (FPC)** of the Bank of England took over the would-be functions of the Council for Financial Stability and the Bank of England's Financial Stability Committee. In common with the existing Councils, the new FPC has representatives from prudential regulators and from HM Treasury. Additionally, the 11-member FPC also has external representation and will meet four times annually and at times of crisis.

The FPC will address issues of financial stability and resilience at the 'macro' level – that is, at the level of the economy and the financial services sector and sub-sectors. These are referred to as **macro-prudential risks**, while risks at the level of the firm are **micro-prudential risks**.

The absence of an effective macro-prudential agency was considered to have been a major failing in the UK, EU and US before the recent financial crisis. This lack was highlighted with the inability of the authorities to deal with asset price bubbles, especially in the property market, and the accumulation of debt and leverage across the financial system.

1.4 Financial Conduct Authority (FCA)

The FSMA 2000 (as amended) gives to the FCA a single strategic objective of: **Ensuring that the relevant markets function well**.

FSMA 2000 supplements this strategic objective with three **operational objectives**:

- The **consumer protection objective**: securing an appropriate degree of protection for consumers

- The **integrity objective**: protecting and enhancing the integrity of the UK financial system

- The **competition objective**: promoting effective competition in the interests of consumers in the market for regulated financial services and for services provided by a recognised investment exchange.

The Authority also has a duty to address **financial crime**.

The FCA has a vision to make markets work well so that consumers get a fair deal. As an 'integrated conduct' regulator, the FCA must look across the whole financial services sector, not only in investment and capital markets but also in banking and wholesale insurance markets. Under its consumer protection remit, the Authority will define 'consumer' as including even the largest wholesale firms. This enables the FCA to exercise wide discretion over the interpretation of its objectives and to ensure high standards across the financial services industry in the service of its strategic objective.

The FCA is a private company limited by guarantee, and has direct reporting responsibility to the Treasury, to which it must submit a report each year.

Pause for thought ...

Which of the regulatory bodies is going to have the most direct impact on your role and in what ways?

UK regulatory architecture

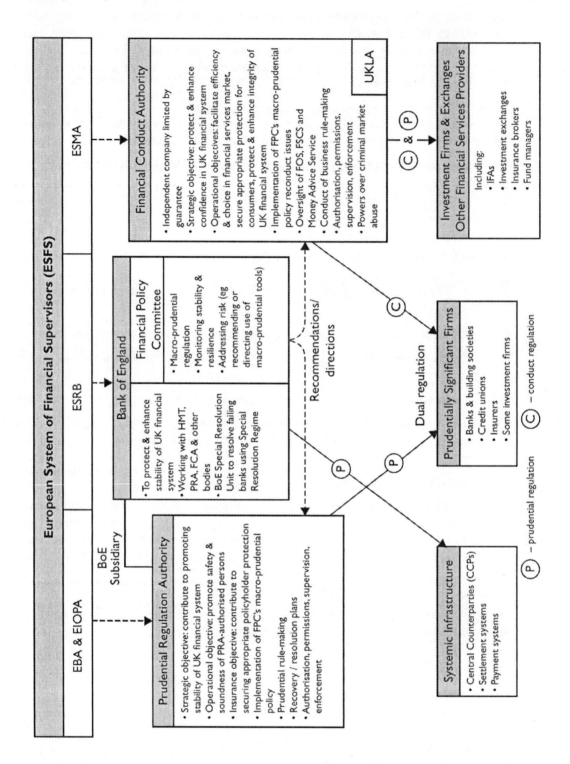

1.5 Risk-based approach of FCA

The FCA operates a **risk-based approach**, concentrating on the big risks and accepting that some failure cannot be avoided. Potential risks are prioritised, using impact and probability analysis, and an appropriate regulatory response is then determined, to establish what approach they will take and how much resource will be allocated to mitigating the risk.

Consumers must accept responsibility for the decisions they make when they are choosing investments. However, the regulator's publication entitled *'A new regulator for a new millennium'* identified a number of different risks within the financial services industry:

- **Prudential risk** – the risk that the company could collapse as a result of poor or ineffectual management

- **Bad faith risk** – caused by, for example, mis-selling, fraud, misinterpretation, failure to disclose important information

- **Complexity or unsuitability risk** – caused by a lack of understanding on the part of the consumer, leading to the wrong choice of product

- **Performance risk** – caused by investments failing to meet forecast returns.

The regulator makes clear that, while it can accept responsibility for regulating the first three risks, it cannot control performance risk.

1.6 Powers of the FCA

The **FCA's powers** include the following.

- Granting authorisations and permissions to firms in the industry
- Approving persons in the industry to perform in certain controlled functions
- The right to be heard in court on a banking or insurance transfer
- Imposing penalties for market abuse
- Taking disciplinary action
- Authorising unit trust schemes and recognising collective investment schemes
- Making rules
- Requiring information from authorised persons (mainly, firms)
- Conducting investigations with HM Treasury
- Instituting criminal proceedings where necessary
- Maintaining a public record of authorised persons, prohibited individuals and approved persons
- Initiating or participating in insolvency proceedings
- Cooperating with other regulators

1.7 Accountability of the FCA

The FCA is accountable or at least liable to give an explanation of its conduct in many different ways.

The organisations and individuals to whom the FCA is accountable include the following.

- Its governing body
- Its non-executive committee
- Parliament
- The public
- The courts
- The Treasury
- Practitioners
- Consumers
- The Complaints Commissioner

2 Key areas of regulation and legislation

2.1 Introduction

We will consider the following areas of law and regulation in this Section.

- Cross-border financial services and the Markets in Financial Instruments Directive (MiFID)
- Capital requirements
- Consumer credit
- Payment services
- Anti-Money Laundering (AML) and Counter-Terrorist Financing (CTF)
- Data protection
- Anti-bribery legislation

Many of these areas are influenced by European law and regulation.

2.2 EU directives and regulations

In addition to the rules and principles of the UK regulatory authorities, the banking industry is subject to **European Union (EU)** regulations.

EU regulations are the most direct form of EU law as they are binding throughout every member state in their entirety. No amendments can be made to the regulations and so they need to be relevant to all of the current member states. EU regulations become law as soon as they are passed and national governments do not have to take any further action to implement them.

European Directives are passed by the European Parliament and have a potential impact on all European member states. After a Directive is passed, it is up to member states to pass national legislation in order to comply with the provisions of the Directive, normally within a period of two years.

Thus, in the UK it is the responsibility of the UK Government to pass Acts of Parliament (**'primary' legislation**) and Statutory Instruments (**'secondary' legislation**) as appropriate to implement EU Directives in the UK. This implementation process will, for financial services, lead to the UK regulators changing their rules and guidance as appropriate to comply with the provisions of the legislation.

2.3 Markets in Financial Instruments Directive (MiFID)

The **Markets in Financial Instruments Directive (MiFID)** was adopted by the European Council in 2004 and is part of the European Financial Services Action Plan (FSAP), which is designed to help integrate Europe's financial markets. After delays, MiFID eventually became effective on 1 November 2007.

MiFID replaced the previous Investment Services Directive (ISD), and it applies to all investment firms, eg investment and retail banks, brokers, assets managers, securities and futures firms, securities issuers and hedge funds.

The idea of MiFID is to enable firms to use their domestic authorisation to operate not only in their Home State, but also in other Host States within the European Economic Area (EEA) (comprising EU countries plus Norway, Iceland and Liechtenstein). The aim is to **make cross-border business easier** as, under the MiFID '**passporting**' rules, investment firms only need to be authorised by the Member State in which their registered office is located (the Home State). MiFID sets out detailed requirements governing the organisation and conduct of business of investment firms, and how regulated markets operate.

Although MiFID extended regulation beyond what was regulated under the earlier ISD, a significant part of the retail financial services sector, relating to investment advice, falls outside the scope of MiFID. Other activities excluded from the scope of MiFID include insurance companies, pension funds, and collective investment schemes such as unit trusts and open ended investment companies (OEICs).

2: THE REGULATORY AND LEGAL ENVIRONMENT

2.4 Capital requirements directive and the Basel Accords

The original Basel Accord was agreed in 1988 by the Basel Committee on Banking Supervision. The 1988 Accord, now referred to as **Basel I**, helped to strengthen the soundness and stability of the international banking system as a result of the higher capital ratios that it required.

Basel II was a revised framework implemented in the European Union via the Capital Requirements Directive (CRD). The CRD first came into force in 2007. Basel II is a revision that affects banks and building societies and certain types of investment firms.

There are four main components to this framework, so that **Basel II**:

- Was more sensitive to the risks that firms face, including an explicit measure for operational risk and more risk-sensitive risk weightings against credit risk

- Reflected improvements in firms' risk management practices

- Provided incentives for firms to improve their risk management practices with more risk-sensitive weightings as firms adopt more sophisticated approaches to risk management

- Aimed to leave the overall level of capital held by banks collectively broadly unchanged, although there are tighter rules on the type and quality of this capital.

The framework of the **Basel II Accord** consists of three 'pillars':

- **Pillar 1** sets out the minimum capital requirements firms will be required to meet for credit, market and operational risk.

- **Pillar 2** focuses on an appropriate system of governance with firms and supervisors (ie, national regulators) having to take a view on whether a firm should hold additional capital against risks not covered in Pillar 1 and must take action accordingly.

- **Pillar 3** aims to improve market discipline by requiring firms to publish certain details of their risks, capital and risk management.

Subsequently, the Third Basel Accord (**Basel III**) was developed by the Basel Committee in response to the inadequacies of financial regulation revealed by the financial crisis that emerged during the late 2000s. Basel III is a comprehensive set of reform measures designed to improve regulation, supervision and risk management in banking. It introduces the first **global framework for bank liquidity regulation**.

Basel III is for implementation over the period 2013 to 2021 and addresses bank capital adequacy, stress testing and market liquidity risk, with the aim of strengthening bank capital requirements, and introduces new regulatory requirements on liquidity and leverage. ('Leverage' here is the ratio of Tier 1 capital to average total consolidated assets. Tier 1 capital comprises the bank's common shares and retained earnings.)

2.5 Consumer credit

2.5.1 Consumer Credit Directive

This EU Consumer Credit Directive came into effect in February 2011, and has the following key elements.

- The lender must provide adequate explanations about the credit on offer to the borrower.
- The lender is obliged to check creditworthiness before offering or increasing credit.
- There are requirements regarding credit reference databases.
- Consumers have a right to withdraw from agreements within 14 days without explanation.
- There are requirements to inform consumers when debts are sold on.
- Credit intermediaries are required to disclose fees and links to creditors.
- Consumers have a right to make partial early repayments of credit.

BPP
LEARNING MEDIA

45

2.5.2 Consumer Credit Act 2006

The **Consumer Credit Act 2006 (CCA 2006)** resulted from a three-year review of consumer credit law. CCA 2006 extended the scope of the **Consumer Credit Act 1974**, gave consumers the right to use the Financial Ombudsman Service, and allowed borrowers to challenge unfair debtor/creditor relationships in court.

CCA 2006 aims to protect the consumer and create a fairer and more transparent credit market by:

- Enhancing consumer rights and redress by empowering consumers to challenge unfair lending, and through more effective options for resolving disputes.

- Improving the regulation of consumer credit businesses by streamlining the licensing system, by requiring minimum standards of information provision to consumers, and through targeted action to drive out rogues.

- Making regulation more appropriate for different types of transaction by extending protections to all consumer credit and by creating a more proportionate regime for business.

The consumer credit legislation defines credit as any form of financial accommodation where goods and services are sold to a buyer without any immediate payment, which implies that there is trust and confidence on the part of the lender in the borrower's ability to repay in full at some future, agreed, time.

There are two types of credit agreement:

- **Restricted use** – applying to the acquisition of goods and services
- **Unrestricted use** – applying to obtaining cash loans that can be used for any purpose

A consumer credit agreement is established where the person granting the loan (the creditor) provides the person obtaining the loan (the debtor) with credit.

CCA 2006 redefined what is meant by an 'individual' in terms of consumer credit and the definition may be wider than you thought. The 1974 Act looked upon an individual in much the same way that you would probably recognise a consumer (although unincorporated associations and clubs were also included). CCA 2006 extended to credit obtained by the 'individual' to cover single-person businesses, and partnerships with two or three partners, although partnerships with more than this number are exempt.

There is no limit for the amount of a loan with an 'individual' for it to fall within the scope of the CCA 2006 (previously, there was a ceiling of £25,000 for an agreement to be regulated).

There are the following exemptions from consumer credit regulations:

1 Where the lending is to a **business** and the business has signed a declaration in a prescribed form.

2 Where the lending is to a **high net worth borrower** who has provided a valid declaration of their high net worth.

To qualify for exemption under **point 1**, the agreement must be entered into wholly or predominantly for the purpose of a business carried on.

Under **point 2**, if the borrower is claiming a high net worth exemption, they must supply the lender with a statement which evidences that:

- For the last financial year, either their net income after tax and National Insurance was more than £150,000, or

- Their net assets exceeded £500,000, but this cannot take into account the value of the borrower's house, certain life assurance policies or pension entitlements.

2.5.3 Charge for credit and the annual percentage rate (APR)

The **total charge for credit** is the total amount that the debtor is required to pay through the life of a loan. This includes repaying the loan, all interest, and any fees, but not insurance.

The **APR** is a measure of the true **cost of borrowing**. It is the total charge, expressed as a percentage, the method of calculation being laid down in the **Consumer Credit Act 1974**, with additional assumptions being added by the **EU Consumer Credit Directive**.

- The standardisation of the APR calculation gives consumers a way to compare different loan products.

- The APR demonstrates what the interest paid would be if the interest was compounded and paid annually instead of monthly (or any other period).

You will probably have seen publicity materials from banks and other financial services organisations quoting 'typical' APRs offered by them. A 'typical' APR quoted in an advertisement must be representative of the business that it is expected to generate. This means that the advertisement will have to quote the highest APR that at least 66% of the eventual number of consumers formally accepting a credit agreement in response to the advertisement are expected to be given.'

EXAMPLE

Someone borrows £100 at a monthly rate of interest of 1%. There will be no repayments during the first year. The APR is calculated as follows.

Loan amount	£100.00
January interest: £100 × 1% = £1 + £100	101.00
February interest: £101 × 1% = £1.01 + £101	102.01
March interest: £102.01 × 1% = £1.0201 + £102.01	103.0301
April interest: £103.0301 × 1% = £1.030301 + £103.0301	104.0604
May interest: £104.0604 × 1% = £1.040604 + £104.0604	105.101
June interest: £105.101 × 1% = £1.05101 + £105.101	106.15201
July interest: £106.15201 × 1% = £1.0615201 + £106.15201	107.21353
August interest: £107.21353 × 1% = £1.0721353 + £107.21353	108.28566
September interest: £108.28566 × 1% = £1.0828566 + £108.28566	109.36851
October interest: £109.36851 × 1% = £1.0936851 + £109.36851	110.46219
November interest: £110.46219 × 1% = £1.1046219 + £110.46219	111.56681
December interest: £111.56681 × 1% = £1.1156681 + £111.56681	112.68247

Therefore the APR is 12.68%

2.5.4 Aspects of credit agreements

The agreement

The law on consumer credit defines the form and content of a regulated agreement. If both the debtor and creditor do not sign the document, in its prescribed form, the agreement is not properly executed. However, agreements are no longer unenforceable simply because some mandatory information has been omitted. It is now at the discretion of the court what the effect of any omission will be. The agreement must include all of the terms of the agreement, including any cancellation rights. Once the agreement has been made, a copy of the executed agreement must be sent to the debtor.

Cancellation

The consumer has the right to cancel the regulated agreement within a short time after it has been executed, if any preliminary negotiations included legal representations. This period is called the **cooling off period**'.

This period does not apply if the unexecuted agreement is signed on the lender's premises or oral representations did not take place in the preliminary negotiations. If the customer chooses to exercise these cancellation rights, the agreement is treated as if it had never existed. Therefore, all monies that the customer has received as a result of the agreement are to be repaid to the creditor.

Other aspects

Other requirements are as follows.

- Customers must be required to sign a separate box if they want to take out additional insurance cover along with a loan or credit card, such as payment protection insurance.

- If an APR is included in an advertisement, it must be more prominent than all the other financial information.

- The charges for repaying a loan early are restricted to interest for one month and 28 days (ie, approximately two months).

- The borrower must be given a Pre-Contract Information sheet which documents the conditions of the loan. It is up to the borrower how long they wish to wait between receiving this information and signing the loan papers. They may choose to reflect on matters for a few days before signing, for example, or they may choose to sign the loan papers that day.

- An Unfair Relationships Test enables a court to make an order in relation to an agreement with an individual if it is unfair to the debtor.

- Post-contract transparency regulations provide that annual statements must be sent to borrowers.

2.5.5 FCA regulation of consumer credit providers

With the abolition of the Office of Fair Trading, on 1 April 2014 the **FCA** became responsible for **authorising firms who offer consumer credit**. The FCA Handbook includes the **Consumer Credit Sourcebook (CONC),** which sets out the detailed conduct standards and rules for firms carrying out consumer credit activities.

The FCA regulates more than 50,000 firms that offer credit, loans or debt services. Consumer credit firms include credit card issuers, credit brokers, payday lenders, log book lenders, peer-to-peer lenders, pawnbrokers, and debt management and debt collection firms.

- At least one individual in most consumer credit firms (with the exceptions of except most providers of not-for-profit debt advice, and some sole traders) must be **approved persons**, that is, approved by the FCA.

- As for approved persons in other firms, when considering a candidate's **fitness and propriety**, the FCA will look at: honesty (including being open regarding any self-disclosure); integrity and reputation; competence and capability; and financial soundness.

Pause for thought ...

In what ways does the consumer credit regulation and legislation affect your role at work?

2.6 Payment services

2.6.1 Payment Services Directive (PSD)

The **Payment Services Directive (PSD)** is broadly a harmonising directive. It introduces an authorisation and registration regime for a newly created category of firm called **payment institutions**

(PIs). All providers must meet conduct of business requirements for payment services providers. The FCA is the competent authority for most aspects of the Payment Services Directive (PSD). PIs must be either authorised by or registered with the FCA. The UK implemented the PSD through the Payment Services Regulations 2009.

The PSD has five main objectives:

- Achieving a single payment market in the EU
- Providing the regulatory framework for a single payment market
- Creating a level playing field and enhancing competition
- Ensuring consistent consumer protection and improving transparency
- Creating the potential for more efficiency of EU payment systems

The Directive therefore aims to remove legal barriers to the provision of payment services in the EU and to allow citizens and businesses to make all kinds of payment easily, safely, timely and cost efficiently. Types of information could include how long a payment will take to reach a beneficiary, what exchange rates are applicable and the level of charges that will be applied to the transaction.

The Directive applies to most payment transactions and includes placing, transferring or withdrawing funds. It also applies to the provision and operation of payment accounts. These regulations also stipulate customers' rights and responsibilities and set out the circumstances in which a bank will be liable. If any bank breaches these regulations, the FCA can impose penalties and censures. If a required term or condition is omitted from the documentation, then the bank concerned cannot enforce the missing term or condition.

The FCA met the requirements of the Directive for retail banks through the **Banking: Conduct of Business Sourcebook (BCOBS)** in the FCA Handbook.

A revised second Directive **PSD2** has followed, coming into force on 12 January 2016.

Elements of PSD2

- Standardising and improving the efficiency of payments in the EU

- Providing for better consumer protection

- Promoting innovation in payments, and reducing costs

- Incorporating and clarifying emerging payment methods such as mobile payments and online payments

- Levelling the playing field for payment service providers, enabling entry of new companies

- Harmonising pricing and improving security of payment processing across the EU

2.6.2 Payment Systems Regulator

Launched on 1 April 2015, the **Payment Systems Regulator (PSR)** is the economic regulator of the UK payment systems industry. The PSR is a subsidiary of the Financial Conduct Authority, but has its own objectives and governance arrangements.

The purpose of the PSR is to make payment systems work well for those that use them.

The systems regulated by the PSR are designated by HM Treasury, and comprise:

- Bacs
- CHAPS
- Cheque and Credit Clearing Company
- Faster Payments Service
- LINK
- MasterCard, and
- Visa Europe

The PSR's vision is that payment systems are accessible, reliable, secure, and value for money.

The **PSR's statutory objectives** under the FSMA 2000 (as amended) are, in summary:

- To ensure that payment systems are operated and developed in a way that considers and promotes the interests of all the businesses and consumers that use them

- To promote effective competition in the markets for payment systems and services – between operators, payment service providers (PSPs), and infrastructure providers

- To promote development of and innovation in payment systems, in particular the infrastructure used to operate those systems

The PSR has **regulatory and competition powers** to:

- Give directions to take action and set standards

- Impose requirements regarding system rules

- Require operators to provide direct access to payment systems

- Require PSPs to provide indirect access to smaller PSPs

- Amend agreements relating to payment systems, including fees and charges

- Investigate behaviour which is not consistent with its directions

- Act where the PSR sees anti-competitive behaviour, alongside the Competition & Markets Authority (CMA)

PSR oversight does not extend to the payment systems that are embedded in securities clearing systems and central counterparties and are **overseen by the Bank of England**.

2.7 Countering money laundering and terrorist financing

2.7.1 Introduction

The risk of having been found to be non-complaint with anti-money laundering (AML) rules is often viewed as a major risk faced by banks. This topic has moved up the political agenda in recent times because of issues such as the heightened terrorism threat worldwide and the ever-increasing focus on drug trafficking.

Some have expressed unease about the broadness of the regulations and have wanted to see a more focused approach supported by targeted requirements. In fact, for a number of years now, a **risk-based approach** has been the cornerstone of UK and international AML/CTF (Anti-Money Laundering/Counter-Terrorism Financing) measures.

The **risk-based approach to AML procedures** is, indeed, **mandatory** under MLR 2007. This type of approach acknowledges that money laundering and terrorist threats vary across customers, jurisdictions, products and delivery channels. With a risk-based approach, management are permitted to differentiate between their customers so as to match procedures with the risks in their business. The approach requires the full commitment and support of senior management, and the active co-operation of business units.

C A S E   S T U D Y

A bank account could be opened and the sum of £500,000 lodged every two or three weeks. This may at first glance seem good business for the bank, but if the funds are regularly being paid away to other parties or withdrawn by the customer, the bank could be facilitating money laundering. On the other hand, it may be perfectly normal for the account to be conducted in this manner – perhaps for a business where this type of transaction is perfectly normal, but the bank should be aware of the type of activities that the customer is involved in so that transactions that are likely to occur on the account can be anticipated.

In this case, if the bank had made initial enquiries and discovered that the customer acted as an agent for an overseas company to purchase computer software, it may be perfectly normal for large sums to be deposited in the account from time to time when the company funds its agent to make the necessary purchases, then for the funds to be paid away shortly after as the agent buys software for the company. However, if you were initially advised that the customer operated a small shop you would expect to see lodgements to and withdrawals from the account following a different pattern.

2.7.2 Stages of money laundering

There are three typical stages in the process of money laundering: **placement, layering,** and **integration**.

Placement is where the cash proceeds from criminal activity first enter the financial system, for example:

- Many small cash credits paid into an account which in total amount to a substantial sum
- Buying bank cheques (sometimes called 'drafts') may be bought with cash
- Many individuals may make deposits into one account.

Layering takes the form of a series of multiple transactions, designed to hide the original source of the 'dirty' money, for example:

- The purchase of valuables, such as property, gold, jewellery
- Early repayment of loans or credit cards which seems inconsistent with the customer's financial standing.

If layering has succeeded, **integration** allows the funds to be withdrawn without further suspicion, for example through:

- Redeeming for cash a single premium life assurance policy purchased with dirty money
- Sale of property and other valuables initially purchased with dirty money
- Frequent large cash withdrawals.

2.7.3 Terrorist activities

There is a considerable overlap between the movement of terrorist funds and the laundering of criminal assets. Terrorist groups are also known to have well-established links with organised criminal activity. However, there are two major differences between terrorist and criminal funds.

- Often only small amounts are required to commit a terrorist atrocity, therefore increasing the difficulty of tracking the funds.

- Whereas money laundering relates to the proceeds of crime, terrorists can be funded from legitimately obtained income.

2.7.4 Money laundering directives and regulations

Financial organisations, and indeed individuals working therein, have many duties under AML legislation and regulations, resulting in severe penalties, at both organisational and/or individual level, if compliance is found to be lacking. These range from duties of disclosure to assisting in the retention or control of the proceeds of criminal conduct.

The issue of money laundering was addressed by the **First EU Money Laundering Directive** in 1991 that was enacted into UK legislation via the **Criminal Justice Act 1993 (CJA 1993)**. The money laundering offences within CJA 1993 were repealed and replaced by the **Proceeds of Crime Act 2002 (POCA 2002)**.

In 2001, a Second EU Money Laundering Directive was adopted to cure some of the deficiencies in the first Directive. A Third Money Laundering Directive came into force on 15 December 2007. The Third Directive more fully incorporates into EU law the Forty Recommendations of the international Financial

Action Task Force (FATF). The latest Money Laundering Regulations 2007 (MLR 2007) repeal earlier regulations and implement the Third Directive.

In February 2013, the European Commission announced that it had adopted proposals for the framework of a **Fourth EU Money Laundering Directive (4MLD)**. As well as the Directive, there is a separate proposed regulation which sets out new information requirements for transfers of funds.

4MLD seeks to strengthen international co-operation and to harmonise the approach to compliance with anti-money laundering measures throughout Europe. The Directive stresses the risk-based approach that is the cornerstone of UK AML/CTF measures.

Most of the requirements implemented in the 4MLD proposals are included within the UK AML/CTF regime already, and so the changes will not be great for the UK. After the draft Directive is considered by the European Parliament and the Council of Ministers, changes to legislation can be implemented within EU member States.

2.7.5 Risk-based approach

A highly prescriptive approach formerly adopted by the financial services regulator was replaced by the provisions of a sourcebook, **Senior Management Arrangements: Systems and Controls (SYSC)**, now within the FCA Handbook. SYSC imposes a responsibility on senior management for having effective anti-money laundering and counter-terrorist financing policies in place. Whereas the once detailed regulations required all institutions to have exactly the same safeguards, SYSC acknowledges that the risks are different for the various types of financial institution, and even for common groups of organisations. The FCA expects all institutions to take a risk-based approach to formulating anti-money laundering (AML) policies, taking into consideration factors such as the size of the organisation, the products and services offered, channels to market and geographical scope of operation.

Financial services providers are expected to take into account the guidelines issued by the **Joint Money Laundering Steering Group**, as well as national and international intelligence made available by bodies such as the Financial Action Task Force (FATF).

As mentioned earlier, the money laundering rules require firms to employ a **risk-based approach**

- The risk-based approach needs to be part of the firm's philosophy, and as such reflected in its procedures and controls.

- There needs to be a clear communication of policies and procedures across the firm, together with robust mechanisms to ensure that they are carried out effectively, any weaknesses are identified and improvements are made wherever necessary.

2.7.6 Training in money laundering prevention and procedures

If you work in a role that is exposed to the risk of money laundering activities, you will need to attend regular training and awareness programmes to ensure that you are fully up to date with regulatory requirements and your organisation's policies. Your organisation has a statutory duty to provide such programmes. It is important to understand that under certain circumstances individual employees can be personally liable for breaches of the provisions of the legislation.

2.7.7 Risk assessment and 'Know Your Customer'

Firms are expected to 'know their customers'. The **Know Your Customer (KYC)** requirements:

- Help the firm, at the time customer due diligence is carried out, to be reasonably satisfied that customers are who they say they are, to know whether they are acting on behalf of others, whether there are any government sanctions against serving the customer, and

- Assist law enforcement with information on customers or activities under investigation.

Based on an **assessment of the money laundering/ terrorist financing risk** that each customer presents, the firm will need to:

- **Verify the customer's identity (ID)** – determining exactly who the customer is.

- **Collect additional 'KYC' information**, and keep such information **current and valid** – to understand the customer's circumstances and business, and (where appropriate) the sources of funds or wealth, or the purpose of specific transactions.

Many customers, by their nature or through what is already known about them by the firm, carry a **lower** money laundering or terrorist financing **risk**. These might include:

- Customers who are employment-based or with a regular source of income from a known source which supports the activity being undertaken; (this applies equally to pensioners or benefit recipients, or to those whose income originates from their partners' employment).

- Customers with a long-term and active business relationship with the firm.

- Customers represented by those whose appointment is subject to court approval or ratification (such as executors).

2.7.8 Due diligence

One of the most important ways in which money laundering can be prevented is by establishing the identity of clients, thus making it difficult for those trading under assumed names or through bogus companies to gain access to the financial markets. This emphasises, again, the obligation to '**know your customer**'.

In the context of **conduct of business rules**, the firm may generally accept at face value information which customers provide. The **money laundering regulations**, however, require that the firm takes positive steps to verify the information that they receive. The **JMLSG** Guidance Notes lay down some basic, but not exhaustive, procedures that can be followed.

2.7.9 CDD, EDD, SDD, and ongoing monitoring

MLR 2007 regulations require detailed **customer due diligence (CDD)** procedures and these are explained in the **JMLSG** guidance.

CDD involves:

- Identifying the customer and verifying his identity

- Identifying the beneficial owner (taking measures to understand the ownership and control structure, in the case of a company or trust) and verifying his identity

- Obtaining information on the purpose and intended nature of the business relationship.

A firm must apply CDD when it:

- Establishes a business relationship
- Carries out an occasional transaction of €15,000 or more
- Suspects money laundering or terrorist financing
- Doubts the veracity of identification or verification documents.

As well as standard CDD, there is:

- **Enhanced due diligence (EDD)** – for higher risk situations, customers not physically present when identities are verified, correspondent banking and **politically exposed persons** (**PEPs**). EDD measures include obtaining additional documents, data or information to those specified below, requiring certification by a financial services firm, and ensuring that an initial payment is from a bank account in the customer's name.

- **Simplified due diligence (SDD)** – which may be applied to certain financial sector firms, companies listed on a regulated market, UK public authorities, child trust funds, certain pension funds, and low-risk products. In practice, this means not having to identify the customer, or to verify the customer's identity, or, where relevant, that of a beneficial owner.

The category **'politically exposed persons' (PEPs)** comprises higher-ranking **non-UK** public officials, members of parliaments other than the UK Parliament, and such persons' immediate families and close associates. Prominent PEPs can pose a higher risk because their position may make them vulnerable to corruption. Senior management approval (from an immediate superior) should be sought for establishing a business relationship with such a customer.

As an obligation separate from CDD, EDD or SDD, firms must conduct ongoing **monitoring of the business relationship**. Ongoing monitoring of a business relationship includes scrutiny of transactions undertaken including, where necessary, sources of funds. **CDD** and **monitoring** is intended to make it more difficult for the financial services industry to be used for money laundering or terrorist financing, but also helps firms guard against fraud, including impersonation fraud.

Firms' information demands from customers need to be '**proportionate, appropriate and discriminating**', and to be able to be **justified to customers**.

2.7.10 Evidence of identity

How much identity information to ask for in the course of CDD, and what to verify, are matters **for the judgement of the firm**, based on its **assessment of risk**.

For **private individuals**, the firm should obtain full name, residential address and date of birth of the personal customer. Verification of the information obtained should be based either on a document or documents provided by the customer, or electronically by the firm, or by a combination of both. Where business is conducted face-to-face, firms should request the original documents. Customers should be discouraged from sending original valuable documents by post.

Firms should therefore obtain the following in relation to **corporate clients**: full name, registered number, registered office in country of incorporation, and business address.

The following should also be obtained for private companies:

- Names of all directors (or equivalent)
- Names of beneficial owners holding over 25%

The firm should verify the identity of the corporate entity from:

- A search of the relevant company registry, or
- Confirmation of the company's listing on a regulated market, or
- A copy of the company's Certificate of Incorporation

2.7.11 Reporting of suspicious transactions

All institutions must appoint an 'appropriate person' as the **Money Laundering Reporting Officer (MLRO)**, who has the following functions.

- To receive reports of transactions giving rise to knowledge or suspicion of money laundering activities from employees of the institution

- To determine whether the report of a suspicious transaction from the employee, considered together with all other relevant information, does actually give rise to knowledge or suspicion of money laundering

- If, after consideration, he knows or suspects that money laundering is taking place, to report those suspicions to the appropriate law enforcement agency, the National Crime Agency (NCA)

For the purpose of each individual employee, making a report made to the MLRO concerning a transaction means that the employee has fulfilled his statutory obligations and will have **no criminal**

liability in relation to any money laundering offence in respect of the reported transaction. If the MLRO considers it to be appropriate, she will make a report called a **Suspicious Transaction Report (STR)** to the **National Crime Agency (NCA)**.

QUICK QUESTION

What are your bank's procedures for verifying a person's identity?

Write your answer here before reading on.

QUICK QUESTION

Apart from verifying a person's identity, what other procedures does your bank have to protect it against money laundering?

Write your answer here before reading on.

2.7.12 Money laundering offences

The four main offences are:

- Assistance
- Failure to report
- Tipping off
- Failure to comply with the Money Laundering Regulations

If any person knowingly **assists** another person to launder the proceeds of criminal conduct, he or she will be committing an offence under ss327-329 of the **Proceeds of Crime Act 2002 (POCA 2002))**. The maximum penalties for assisting a money launderer are 14 years' imprisonment and/or an unlimited fine.

If a person discovers information during the course of his employment that makes him believe or suspect money laundering is occurring, but fails report it as soon as is reasonably practicable, he commits a criminal offence (ss330-332 POCA 2002). For those working in the regulated sector (for an authorised firm), this offence of **failing to report** covers not only where the person had actual suspicion of laundering (ie subjective suspicions) but also where there were reasonable grounds for being suspicious. This offence is punishable with a maximum of five years' imprisonment and/or an unlimited fine.

Even where suspicions are reported, the parties must generally be careful not to alert the suspicions of the alleged launderer since, within the regulated sector, this can itself amount to the offence of **tipping**

off under s333A POCA 2002 (as amended). This offence under 333A is punishable with a maximum of two years' imprisonment and/or an unlimited fine.

Failure to comply with any of the requirements of the **Money Laundering Regulations (MLR 2007)** constitutes an offence punishable by a maximum of two years' imprisonment and an unlimited fine.

2.8 Data protection

Under the **Data Protection Act 1998 (DPA 1998)**, where persons process personal data, whether electronically or manually, they must (unless exempt) be registered with the **Information Commissioner's Office (ICO)** (which maintains a **public registry of data controllers**) and must comply with the DPA provisions. The requirements apply to most organisations and cover all personal data about living persons, including for example clients and employees, or any other person. Failure to register is a criminal offence.

There are various data protection obligations for any organisation that keeps personal information, as follows.

- The organisation must have a **data protection policy**.

- **Personal data** must have been **obtained lawfully and fairly** and shall not be processed unless at least one of the **Schedule 2 conditions** is met (see below).

- In the case of **sensitive personal data** (eg, regarding racial or ethnic origin, religious or political beliefs, health, or sexual orientation), the data subject's explicit consent is normally required.

- Data must be **held and used** only for **lawful purposes**.

- Data should be used only **for the purposes for which it was originally obtained**.

- The data must not exceed what is **necessary** for the purpose for which it was obtained.

- Data must be **accurate** and must be **updated regularly**.

- Data must **not be kept longer than is necessary** for its lawful purpose.

- The person whose data is held is entitled to ask for **access** to that information (called a **subject access request**) and has the right to correct it where appropriate. The **data subject** may be charged a **maximum fee of £10 for access** to their records, with a **maximum fee of £2** in the case of credit reference agency records. The person is also entitled to be told the source, purposes and recipients of the data. The 1998 Act requires **subject access requests** to be dealt with 'promptly' and, in any event, within **40 days** of the request (along with any fee) being received.

- The data must be **protected** by appropriate technical and organisational measures against unauthorised or unlawful access and against accidental loss, destruction or damage.

- Personal data must not be transferred outside the European Economic Area unless to a country or territory that ensures an adequate level of protection for the rights and freedoms of data subjects in respect of processing of personal data.

The **Schedule 2 conditions** (see above) are that:

(a) The data subject has given consent to the processing of the data.

(b) The processing is necessary in connection with a contract entered into by the data subject.

(c) The processing is necessary for the data controller to comply with legal obligations.

(d) The processing is necessary for public functions exercised in the public interest.

(e) The processing is necessary in pursuing the data controller's legitimate interests, provided that the processing does not prejudice the data subject's rights, freedoms or legal interests.

The ICO can serve an **enforcement notice** (or 'stop now' order) if it considers a data controller to be in breach of any of the data protection principles. Failure to comply with such an enforcement notice is an offence. The ICO can serve a monetary penalty (fine) of up to **£500,000** for serious breaches.

Pause for thought ...

In what ways does the data protection legislation affect your role at work?

2.9 Law against bribery

2.9.1 Overview

The **Bribery Act 2010 (BA 2010)** has replaced previous anti-corruption legislation, introducing a new offence for commercial organisations of negligently failing to prevent bribery. Organisations and individuals will face heavy penalties if prosecuted and convicted under BA 2010.

Only firms with a **'demonstrable business presence' in the UK** will be subject to BA 2010, and a 'common sense approach' will be adopted in interpreting this.

The **FCA** does not have responsibility for enforcing the criminal offences in BA 2010 for authorised firms. Where the FCA finds evidence of criminal matters, it will refer them to the SFO, which is the UK lead agency for criminal prosecutions for corruption. However, authorised firms who fail to address corruption and bribery risks adequately remain liable to regulatory action by the FCA.

2.9.2 Bribery offences

There are four **main offences** under BA 2010:

- **Section 1: Active bribery** – offering, promising or giving a bribe.

- **Section 2: Passive bribery** – requesting, agreeing to receive or accepting a bribe (passive bribery).

- **Section 6: Bribing a foreign public official** – a breach of this section may also breach s1 BA 2010, and prosecutors will need to decide which is the more appropriate offence for the case.

- **Section 7: Failure of firms to prevent bribery** – failure by a commercial organisation to prevent persons associated with it from bribing another person on its behalf.

Note that, as well as a company's agents and consultants in overseas countries potentially being **'associated persons'** under BA 2010, a company's own employees are also associated persons, and so their actions could make a company criminally liable. Firms should take this into account in establishing their anti-bribery policy or code of conduct.

Note also that a **'facilitation payment'** is a type of bribe: the Serious Fraud Office (SFO) asserts that they should be seen as such. A common example is where a government official is given money or goods to perform (or speed up the performance of) an existing duty. Facilitation payments were illegal before the Bribery Act came into force and they are illegal under the Bribery Act, regardless of their size or frequency.

2.9.3 Adequate procedures as a defence

An organisation has a defence against the s7 offence (failure to prevent bribery) if it can prove that, despite a particular instance of bribery having occurred, the organisation had **adequate procedures** in place to prevent persons associated with the organisation from committing bribery.

Associated persons include anyone performing services for the commercial organisation, but suppliers of goods are not necessarily 'associated persons'. The legal relationship between a joint venture entity and its members does not automatically mean that they are associated: this would depend on the degree of control the joint venture has over a bribe paid by its employee or agent.

Under s9 BA 2010, the **Minister of Justice** is required to publish **Adequate Procedures Guidance** on the defence. The final Guidance was published in March 2011, and is supplemented by a Quick Start Guide aimed at smaller businesses, which does not form part of the statutory guidance.

- The guidance seeks to reassure senior management of properly organised businesses that BA 2010 is not intended to bring the force of the criminal law to bear on businesses that experience isolated incidents of bribery on their behalf. The guidance seeks instead to assert the importance of the matter of bribery and to encourage effective procedures to be established.

- The guidance also seeks to define the circumstances in which bribery may or may not have been committed. For example, genuine client hospitality or entertainment, for example at sporting events, that has a legitimate business aim and is appropriate and proportionate, would not be caught by the legislation.

2.9.4 Ministry of Justice Guidance: principles

The **Ministry of Justice's Guidance** sets out **six principles** to help firms, which can be summarised as follows.

- **1: Proportionate procedures.** Procedures should be proportionate to the risks faced by the organisation, with tailored procedures based on a **risk assessment**.

- **2: Top-level commitment.** Senior management in the organisation need to help create a **culture of integrity** with a **commitment to zero tolerance to bribery**.

- **3: Risk assessment**. The organisation's assessment of the risks it faces should be periodic, informed and documented.

- **4: Due diligence.** In alignment with the requirement for a **proportionate** and **risk-based** approach, the extent of due diligence for different relationships will vary greatly depending on the particular relationship and the associated risks.

- **5: Communication (including training)**. Internal communications should include a clear **statement of the policies and procedures** of the organisation, and of how concerns about instances of bribery can be raised.

- **6: Monitoring and review**. An organisation must be able to demonstrate that it regularly monitors and reviews the adequacy and suitability of policies and procedures and adapts them to reflect organisational changes.

2.9.5 Penalties

Under BA 2010, the **maximum penalty** for a bribery offence committed by an **individual** is 10 years' imprisonment and an unlimited fine. A **company** that is convicted of failing to prevent bribery is subject to an unlimited fine.

Pause for thought ...

What impact does the Bribery Act have on your role at work?

BPP
LEARNING MEDIA

2.10 Regulatory influences on banks

The legal and regulatory requirements that apply to banking subject banks to certain restrictions and provide constraints and guidelines for the way they do business. In general, the regulatory structure is designed to create transparency between banks and the people and companies with whom they do business.

Common aims are to:

- Protect depositors (the bank's creditors) and reduce the level of risk to which they are exposed
- Lend responsibly
- Provide customers with the best service
- Protect customer information and maintain confidentiality
- Reduce the risk of banks being used for criminal purposes
- Reduce the risk of disruption and bank failure resulting from adverse trading conditions for banks

The requirements influence, for example:

- How much of its deposits the bank lends to customers
- The investment decisions it makes
- The bank's policies and procedures
- How the bank deals with customer complaints
- How the bank deals with customer information
- How the bank operates customer accounts
- How it manages risk
- How it markets its products and services
- How it discloses and reports financial information
- How the bank is governed and managed

Pause for thought ...

Think about your own role at work.

Which regulatory and legal requirements most affect the work that you do?

In what ways do these requirements influence the way that you and/or your team operate?

3 FCA principles and rules

3.1 Treating Customers Fairly (TCF)

The section of the FCA Handbook called **PRIN** contains the eleven high-level **Principles for Businesses**, which underlie the regulatory approach and state in broad terms how banks and other financial services firms are expected to conduct their business.

Principle for Businesses 6 states: **A firm must pay due regard to the interests of its customers and treat them fairly**.

Treating Customers Fairly (TCF) is an initiative that was introduced to the regulatory framework in 2008, aimed at improving the customer experience when dealing with financial services providers. Clearly linked to **Principle for Businesses 6**, TCF was set up in response to growing concerns about customers being mis-sold financial products and services. It extends to all customer interactions, and so affects branches, agencies, call centres, written material, website content and marketing materials.

On its website, the FCA states that 'TCF is central to the delivery of our retail regulatory agenda as well as being a key part of our move to more principles-based regulation'. Fundamentally, the concept of TCF is that banks should carry out their business in a way that ensures that the customer receives fair treatment.

Before looking at what TCF is, it is worthwhile considering what TCF is not.

- TCF is not about creating a satisfied customer – the customer may be unhappy about a decision by the bank not to grant them credit facilities, but the customer may well have been fairly treated.

- TCF is not about each bank providing an identical level of service – all banks are different and have different levels of resources, so they will go about providing their customer service in their own way.

- TCF is not about taking customers' decision-making powers away from them, nor is it about removing the responsibility for decision making away from the customer. What banks are expected to do is ensure that customers have enough information to make an informed and educated decision.

The FCA has provided examples of both good and bad TCF, but it has not dictated how TCF should be applied in a bank; rather it is each individual bank's responsibility to decide how to apply it. The regulator has however identified six behavioural drivers which are considered to have a significant effect on whether or not a bank will meet the requirements of TCF.

- **Leadership**. Senior management should provide middle management with sufficient direction and ensure that adequate controls are in place to monitor. A bank's business plan should provide for the ongoing development of policies, management information and procedures.

- **Strategy**. TCF should be incorporated into any changes made to the business; for example, by inclusion in the mission statement that the bank will treat its customers fairly. Procedures can also be instigated to ensure that all the changes implemented by the bank have had an earlier analysis of TCF, such as when designing a new complaints procedure or implementing new documentation. It is expected that, before a change is delivered, whoever in the bank has responsibility for the final sign off of this change should ensure that TCF requirements have been embedded.

- **Decision making and challenge**. The bank should encourage staff to challenge anything they see which contradicts TCF. This could involve the establishment of focus groups to review both new and existing processes and procedures to question and challenge how they meet TCF expectations. Banks should communicate to their staff that each individual has the responsibility to ensure that TCF is being considered in everything that the bank does. An approach of this kind will ensure that a **TCF culture** is embedded throughout the bank or other firm.

- **Controls**. Banks should identify, interpret and use relevant management information which will allow them to monitor TCF effectively and show that the bank is indeed treating its customers fairly. Relevant management information could include customer surveys, mystery shopper results, complaints returns and so on. Any issues or concerns that emerge from this management information should be investigated fully and any necessary actions taken. This kind of information can also be used to demonstrate compliance with TCF. For example, customers could make an increasing number of enquiries about how long it should take for a cheque to clear and, as a result, the bank may include a clearing timetable on its website.

- **Performance management**. Employees should receive performance management objectives that demonstrate what TCF means for their particular role, both in terms of what they should do (their actions) along with the way in which they should do this (their behaviours).

- **Reward**. Banks should consider how targets can be met while still treating the customer fairly. This requirement will guard against the likelihood of an employee treating a customer unfairly simply to achieve a performance management objective; for example, selling a customer a credit card for which they have no need in order to meet a sales target.

Pause for thought ...

How do we know if we are treating our customers fairly?

The FCA has defined six **customer outcomes** that they expect banks to demonstrate when they have achieved the aims of treating customers fairly:

- **Outcome 1: Customers can be confident that they are dealing with firms where the fair treatment of customers is central to the corporate culture.** Therefore TCF should be incorporated into the bank's business plan and strategic plan. Policies and procedures should reflect TCF and the concept of TCF should be present in staff training. Management information that relates to TCF should be scrutinised and appropriate corrective action taken.

- **Outcome 2: Products and services marketed and sold in the retail market should be designed to meet the needs of identified customer groups and targeted accordingly.** Therefore all products must consider the needs of TCF before they are signed off and offered by the bank to its customers.

- **Outcome 3: Customers should be provided with clear information and are kept appropriately informed before, during and after the point of sale.** Banks should ensure that all customer documentation adheres to TCF (for example, plain English should be used throughout).

- **Outcome 4: Where customers receive advice, the advice is suitable and takes account of their circumstances.**

- **Outcome 5: Customers should be provided with products that perform as firms have led them to expect and the associated service should be of an acceptable standard and as they have been led to expect.**

- **Customers should not face unreasonable post-sale barriers imposed by firms to change product, switch providers, submit a claim, or make a complaint.** Adhering to Banking Conduct of Business Standards will help banks to be compliant in this respect, as well as adherence to other codes and guidelines, such as the FCA timescales for dealing with complaints.

Compliance with TCF is monitored and regulated as part of the FCA's routine assessments.

3.2 Banking Conduct of Business rules

The FCA Handbook contains various sets of rules relevant to:

- Specific groups of organisations, such as building societies and credit unions
- Certain activities and policies, such as money laundering
- Specific products and services, such as investments, insurance and mortgages.

The regulations are set down in sourcebooks, which are intended to amplify eleven high level principles that all financial services providers should observe.

You may be familiar with some of the sourcebooks. Mortgages are regulated under MCOB (Mortgage Conduct of Business rules) while insurance is regulated under ICOB (Insurance Conduct of Business rules).

Until fairly recently, the regulatory framework did not apply to some of the core products offered by most banks, including retail savings and deposits, debit cards and loans. The reason for this is that it was generally accepted that the products and services were relatively simple and that banks were generally very safe.

There had been some concerns about the services provided by financial institutions to personal and business customers in the 1990s, so a voluntary regime was created under the auspices of the Banking Code Standards Board. This body created the Banking Code and the Business Banking Code as **voluntary codes** of best practice.

Nearly all retail banks signed up to these codes, which set out core principles and then declared the minimum standards that customers can expect in relation to various areas, such as deposits, loans, plastic cards, how arrears will be managed and so on. The Codes were freely available to all customers.

As the Codes were voluntary, they had no regulatory force, although this did not mean that contravening the Codes had no consequence as the Financial Ombudsman Service (FOS) could take undertakings in voluntary codes into account when deciding on complaints referred to them. The FOS can make awards of up to £150,000 to customers whose complaints are upheld.

In spring 2009, the FSA announced that it would be introducing rules relating to retail banking (Conduct of Business Standards). These regulate many of the areas previously covered by the Banking Code. As the new rules have force of law, the regulator can fine organisations that contravene them. Since the abolition of the Office of Fair Trading in 2014, FCA regulation has extended to **credit agreements under the Consumer Credit Acts**.

In its consultation paper, the regulator acknowledged the important role the Banking Code Standards Board has played in setting and monitoring standards in the industry. However, it concluded that it was somewhat anomalous for the regulator to oversee certain areas of banking activity while having no similar rules in place for core products and services. It was also considered that the regulator would focus more on customer outcomes, incorporating those stated in the 'Treating Customers Fairly' material, rather than setting detailed rules: this is the essence of the '**principles-based approach**', which expects firms to establish many of their own detailed rules, which must accord with the regulator's high-level **Principles for Businesses**.

In putting together the BCOBS rules, the regulator has stated that the following two of the **Principles for Businesses** would be of particular importance.

- **Principle for Businesses 6: A firm must pay due regard to the interests of its customers and treat them fairly.**

- **Principle for Businesses 7: A firm must pay due regard to the information needs of its clients, and communicate information to them in a way which is clear, fair and not misleading.**

The **Banking Conduct of Business Sourcebook (BCOBS)** – part of the **FCA Handbook** – sets out the rules and guidelines by which the FCA regulates retail banking (or, more specifically, banking for consumers and small businesses and charities) under an approach that is primarily a **principles-based approach**.

BCOBS:

- Provides guidance on financial promotions and communications with banking customers throughout the lifetime of their relationship with a bank.

- Specifies how and when communications should be entered into with customers depending on the type of account held and what the information being provided relates to, for example, pre-notification of charges.

- Covers changes to the charging structure, interest rates and terms and conditions of an account as well as a number of other areas previously covered by the Banking Code.

Some of the **key rules in BCOBS** are summarised in the following paragraphs.

Communications. Firms must pay due regard to the interests of their customers and treat them fairly. They must also pay due regard to customers' information needs and communicate information to them in a way that is **clear, fair and not misleading**.

Customer information. Customers must receive full information on the product or service up-front so that they may make an informed decision. For example, at the outset of the banker/customer relationship, the prospective customer has to be given the terms and conditions of the contract for the bank account, in good time before the customer is bound by them.

Banks and building societies must provide reasonable advance notice of changes to key terms and conditions. This is especially important where a change in the service will be to the disadvantage of the customer. For example, customers must be given at least two months' prior notice of any disadvantageous interest rate changes in respect of current and instant access accounts. This requirement is not applicable, however, if the account explicitly tracks a reference rate, for example 1% above the Bank of England base rate, or the change is an explicit part of the contract.

Post-account opening, the customer must be provided with sufficient 'appropriate information' to enable them to continue to make informed decisions. This includes information regarding interest rates, charges, rights to cancel, complaints and compensation arrangements and cheque clearing cycles.

Statements of account. Statements of account must be provided to customers, although of course where a passbook is provided this is not necessary, nor where the service is provided at a distance, ie internet banking, where statements can be viewed/accessed online. No charges can be made for such statements but, where a copy statement is requested, an agreed charge can be made, with the statement being sent within a reasonable period after the request.

Post-sale requirements. The general requirement here is that the service provided to customers must be prompt, efficient and fair. This can take many shapes and forms, but there is an absolute requirement to deal fairly with a banking customer who is in financial difficulty.

Moving accounts. For many years, one of the reasons why customers appeared to be indifferent to poor service offered by some banks and building societies was the seemingly interminable time and extraordinary hassle involved with switching their accounts to a new provider. This was to a large extent tackled by provisions within the now-defunct Banking Code. These provisions have now been included within the regulations and, for example, where a bank customer wishes to move their banking business and there are arrangements between their bank and the bank that they wish to move to, the existing bank must provide a prompt and efficient service, for example by closing any accounts, transferring the account balances and making arrangements in respect of any direct debits or standing orders.

Dormant accounts. Many people forget about, or lose track of, small deposits of money in bank and building society accounts. The Dormant Bank and Building Society Accounts Act 2008, when fully implemented, will enable banks and building societies to transfer money held in dormant accounts for reinvestment in the community, and also provides account holders with a right to repayment.

Before that stage, however, BCOBS requires firms to make it easy for customers to trace and, if appropriate, to have access to their deposits. This applies even if the customer cannot provide the firm with sufficient information to identify the account concerned easily, or where the customer may not have carried out any transactions for an extended period of time.

Unauthorised payments. A common complaint from customers relates to phantom cash machine or other unauthorised withdrawals. In these situations, BCOBS now fairly and squarely places the onus on the account provider to prove that the payment was authorised. If it cannot do so, it must, within a reasonable period, refund the amount of the unauthorised payment to the customer and, where applicable, restore the customer's account to the state it would have been in had the unauthorised payment not taken place.

A firm may require a customer to be liable for **up to £50** for losses in respect of unauthorised payments arising from the use of a lost or stolen card/cheque book or where the customer has failed to keep their personalised security features safe from misappropriation, such as their **personal identification number (PIN)**. Even this amount may not be deducted if the loss occurred after the firm was notified of the loss, theft or misappropriation.

A customer may be liable for all losses in respect of unauthorised payments where they have acted fraudulently or where they have intentionally, or with gross negligence, failed to comply with their obligations under the agreement in relation to the issue or use of the card/cheque book, or to take all reasonable steps to keep any PINs safe.

Right to cancel. A retail bank customer has a right to cancel a contract (including a cash deposit ISAs), without penalty and without giving any reason, within **14 calendar days**. The cancellation period begins either from the day the contract is concluded, or from the day on which the customer receives the necessary contractual terms and conditions, if that is later.

There is no right to cancel a contract (other than for a cash deposit ISA) where:

- The interest payable on the deposit is fixed for a period of time following conclusion of the contract

- A contract whose price depends on fluctuations in the financial market outside the firm's control that may occur during the cancellation period, or

- The service is a cash deposit Child Trust Fund (other than a distance contract).

A firm may provide longer or additional cancellation rights voluntarily but, if it does, these must be on terms at least as favourable to the customer as described above, unless the differences are clearly explained.

3.3 Accountability of individuals

3.3.1 Approved persons regime

Before the FSMA 2000, individuals in senior management functions were subject to general legal provisions dependant on the type of firm. For example, most banks are public limited companies or private limited companies, and so officers were (and remain) accountable under the Companies Acts 2006. By contrast, building societies have their own separate legislation, with officers governed by additional provisions in the Building Societies Acts 1986 and 1997.

Up to March 2016, an 'approved persons' regime has applied generally to regulated financial services firms under FSMA 2000. An **approved person** is an individual who has been approved by the regulator to perform one or more **'controlled functions'** on behalf of an authorised firm.

In order to become an approved person, the individual must:

- Satisfy the regulator that he or she can meet and maintain the criteria for approval (the 'fit and proper test', or FIT), and

- Perform the controlled function in a manner that is consistent with the **Statements of Principle and Code of Practice for Approved Persons**

The main criteria for assessment, as set out in the FIT Sourcebook, are:

- Honesty, integrity and reputation
- Competence and capability
- Financial soundness

Approved persons have been categorised in various ways since these regulations were introduced. The functions are now grouped as:

- Significant influence functions, which in turn are sub-divided into governing functions, required functions and systems and control functions

- Significant management functions, and

- Customer functions

As explained in the following Section, from **7 March 2016**, the approved persons regime will no longer apply to deposit-taking firms (banks, building societies, and credit unions) and PRA-regulated investment firms. In those firms, a new **Accountability Regime** will apply. The approved persons regime will continue to apply in other regulated firms, until around 2018, when the new Accountability Regime will apply across all regulated financial services firms.

3.3.2 New Accountability Regime: from 7 March 2016

Rule changes on 7 March 2016 have implemented recommendations of the **Parliamentary Commission on Banking Standards (PCBS)** through the establishment of a new **Accountability Regime**, comprising the **Senior Managers Regime**, the **Certification Regime**, and **Conduct Rules**.

- The new Accountability Regime aims to remedy the perceived errant behaviour and culture within banks that played a major role in the late 2000s financial crisis and in conduct scandals such as the manipulation of the benchmark interest rate, LIBOR.

- Initially, the new regime applies only to deposit-taking firms (banks, building societies, and credit unions) and PRA-regulated investment firms.

- In other cases, the existing approved persons rules will still apply, and the two regimes will operate in parallel, until around 2018, when the accountability regime will be rolled out to all regulated firms.

Part 4 of the **Financial Services (Banking Reform) Act 2013** set out new regimes to be applied by the financial regulators (the FCA and PRA) in order to provide for **accountability of individuals in the banking sector**. Proposals for the new regimes were published in a 395-page joint FCA/PRA consultation paper, alongside another joint consultation paper dealing with **alignment of risk and reward in remuneration structures** in the banking sector.

3.3.3 Transforming the culture of banks

The **shift of focus** by regulators to **individual accountability** was a response to challenges such as the uncovering of manipulation of the multi-trillion dollar currency markets within banks, six of which were fined a total of $4.3 billion by US and UK regulatory authorities. These events showed that financial institutions' governance and control structures were prone to potential rogue behaviour which could present serious challenges to the firms' financial objectives and reputation.

Purposes of the changes

- To increase and to **define more clearly the responsibilities of those at the highest levels of the management of relevant firms**

- To extend the class of individuals subject to sanctions for misconduct to all of an institution's **staff who pose a risk of significant harm to the firm or its customers**, and

- To make it easier for the **regulators to hold individuals accountable** for breaches

In view of these three new aims, both the FCA and the PRA will be granted wider powers to tackle misconduct. A regulator will be able to take individual enforcement action against any senior manager.

Enforcement action could arise in any of **three ways**: a breach of the **conduct rules** (outlined later), being 'knowingly concerned' in a breach by the firm, or breach of regulatory rules applying in the area of the firm's activities for which the senior manager is responsible.

Senior managers could also face prosecution under the **new criminal offence** of **taking, or failing to prevent, a decision causing a financial institution to fail**, where the person is aware of the risks and their conduct fell 'far below what could reasonably be expected'.

The changes have the potential to transform the culture of **banks, building societies, credit unions and PRA-designated investment firms** in the UK, and probably of other financial institutions to which the measures are likely to be extended, including UK branches of foreign banks, resulting in decreased reputational risks, greater market efficiency, and transparency. Appropriate processes, talent retention, and robust management plans, will be key to reforming firms' culture and to ensuring their competitiveness.

3.3.4 Senior Managers Regime

Under the new **Senior Managers Regime (SMR)**:

- The **regulators** (not the firm) will pre-approve senior individuals with specific **Senior Management Functions (SMFs)**
- The relevant **bank or other firm** will need to monitor continuously the propriety and fitness of the individuals who carry out **SMFs**

An **SMF** is a function that 'requires the person performing it to be responsible for managing one or more aspects of the relevant firm's affairs' which 'involve, or might involve, a risk of serious consequences for the authorised person, or for business or other interests in the UK'.

This regime will replace the existing Approved Persons Regime (APER), covering a narrower range of individuals than APER. The SMR replaces the Significant Influence Function (SIF) in the existing APER and will apply to individuals holding a **Senior Management Function (SMF)**.

Which individuals are senior managers under the SMR? Between them, the FCA and PRA have identified the following seventeen **SMFs** in relevant firms which will require approval. (The scope of the SMR is complicated by the two regulators taking different views on how important responsibilities and functions are allocated to regulated individuals.)

FCA

Executive functions	SMF3: Executive Director SMF16: Compliance Oversight SMF17: Money Laundering Reporting SMF18: Significant Responsibility
Non-executive functions	SMF13: Chair of the Nominations Committee SMF15: Non-Executive Director

PRA

Executive functions	SMF1: Chief Executive SMF2: Chief Finance Function SMF4: Chief Risk Function SMF5: Head of Internal Audit SMF6: Head of Key Business Area SMF7: Group Entity Senior Manager SMF8: Credit Union Senior Manager

Non-executive functions	SMF9: Chairman
	SMF10: Chair of the Risk Committee
	SMF11: Chair of the Audit Committee
	SMF12: Chair of the Remuneration Committee
	SMF14: Senior Independent Director

The **PRA** proposes to create rules establishing a set of additional **Prescribed Responsibilities (PRs)** that firms must allocate to senior managers. There are 20 PRs, and examples of them are: '1. Performance by the firm of its obligations under the senior management regime, including implementation and oversight. 2. Performance by the firm of its obligations under the Certification Rules'.

The **Significant Responsibility SMF** has been created by the **FCA** in order to bring non-board members with significant responsibilities within the scope of the SMR. The regulator has indicated that the test to be applied in order to determine whether an individual performs a **Significant Responsibility SMF** is whether the board has delegated to them overall responsibility for a particular function and whether they are primarily responsible for reporting to the board regarding that function. To help with this, the FCA has set out a list of **key functions** that are likely to apply to most firms. Firms need not necessarily appoint a single individual as an SMF for each function in the list. There are 27 key functions, and examples of them are: '1. Establishing and operating systems and controls in relation to financial crime. 2. Safekeeping and administration of assets of clients. 3. Payment services. 4. Settlement'.

The FCA and the PRA plan to issue rules requiring firms to prepare and keep updated a **Responsibilities Map**, which will be a single document describing the firm's management and governance arrangements.

When **applying for an individual to be approved** for an SMF, a firm will be required to submit to either the FCA (for FCA SMFs) or to the PRA (for PRA SMFs):

- A **statement of responsibility** – 'a statement setting out the aspects of the affairs of the authorised person concerned which it is intended that the person will be responsible for managing in performing the function'

- A **responsibilities map**, to show how the various responsibilities have been allocated, and to ensure that there are no gaps in accountability, and

- **Other information**, such as organisation charts, CVs, job descriptions and development plans

Handover arrangements. The regulators will also require firms to take reasonable steps to ensure that newly appointed senior managers are made aware of all necessary information and risks of regulatory concern in order to perform their responsibilities effectively.

3.3.5 Certification Regime

The new **Certification Regime (CR)** requires the **bank** or other **firm** (not the regulator) to assess and to certify annually that individuals who could pose significant risk to the firm or its customers are fit and proper. Such individuals are said to be carrying out **significant harm functions** (also known as **certification functions**).

The **CR does not overlap with the SMR**: an individual who is covered by the SMR does not require certification under the CR.

This requirement will apply to a wider range of individuals than under the existing APER, but certified persons will no longer be approved by the regulator: the relevant firm will have responsibility for certifying these individuals.

- Under the **PRA**, a **certified person** is a **material risk-taker**, unless their functions are unrelated to the firm's regulated activities.

- Under the **FCA**, a wider population of individuals is subject to the CR. Under the FCA regime, as well as material risk-takers, **individuals formerly classified as performing significant-**

influence functions, such as proprietary traders and benchmark submission functions, are included. Also included will be employees in **customer-facing roles** who are subject to Training and Competence Sourcebook qualification requirements, and those who supervise or manage a certified person.

An employee who performs **multiple CR functions** must be assessed by their firm as **fit and proper** for each function, but all of the individual's functions may be covered by a single certificate. It is envisaged that the standards of fitness and propriety will be similar to those applying under the existing regulatory regime.

3.3.6 Conduct Rules

Conduct Rules apply to all individuals within the relevant firms who are in a position to have an impact on the PRA's and FCA's statutory objectives. For FCA-regulated firms, the new rules will extend further, to cover all staff except for ancillary staff roles. The individuals who will not be subject to the rules will be staff performing a role that is not specific to the financial services business of the firm – in other words, to those whose role would be fundamentally the same if they worked in a non-financial services business. Such roles would include security, catering, or cleaning.

These rules are included in the FCA Handbook within the **Code of Conduct for Staff Sourcebook (COCON)**. The new rules replace the existing Statements of Principles and the Code of Practice for Approved Persons.

The **Conduct Rules** – set out in the following Table – will comprise **first tier** and **second tier** rules. Firms will need to provide tailored training programmes for Senior Managers and Certified Persons. Firms must notify breaches to the regulators.

	Senior managers	Certified staff and other non-ancillary staff
Individual Conduct Rules: first tier		
Rule 1: You must act with integrity	✓	✓
Rule 2: You must act with due skill, care and diligence	✓	✓
Rule 3: You must be open and co-operative with the FCA, PRA and other regulators	✓	✓
Additional Individual Conduct Rules: FCA-only first tier		
Rule 4: You must pay due regard to the interests of customers and treat them fairly	✓ [FCA]	✓ [FCA]
Rule 5: You must observe proper standards of market conduct	✓ [FCA]	✓ [FCA]
Senior Management Conduct Rules: second tier		
SM1: You must take reasonable steps to ensure that the business of the firm for which you are responsible is controlled effectively	✓	✗
SM2: You must take reasonable steps to ensure that the business of the firm for which you are responsible complies with relevant requirements and standards of the regulatory system	✓	✗

	Senior managers	Certified staff and other non-ancillary staff
SM3: You must take reasonable steps to ensure that any delegation of your responsibilities is to an appropriate person and that you oversee the discharge of the delegated responsibility effectively	✓	✗
SM4: You must disclose appropriately any information of which the FCA or PRA would reasonably expect notice	✓	✗

QUICK QUESTION

Which entity is responsible for each of the following in a bank?

(a) Pre-approval of individuals carrying out senior management functions (SMFs)
(b) Ongoing monitoring of the propriety and fitness of individuals carrying out SMFs
(c) Certification of individuals

Write your answer here before reading on.

(a)
(b)
(c)

4 Corporate governance

4.1 Overview

Corporate governance is the term used to describe the ways in which organisations are directed and controlled and how their affairs are handled both by the Board of Directors and the employees.

- In the past, the needs of shareholders were at the forefront of corporate governance initiatives, but now governance encompasses the organisation's obligations to the wider society in which it operates.

- Institutional shareholders have abandoned their traditional 'back seat' role and show an increasingly proactive approach to holding directors of the company to account. The change in attitude has been fuelled by some notable corporate failures and the perception that directors may be improving their own pay and conditions at the expense of the shareholders.

Corporate governance is concerned with issues such as:

- Effectiveness and efficiency of its operations
- Reliability of financial reporting
- Compliance with laws and regulations
- The safeguarding of assets

4.2 The UK Corporate Governance Code

The **Financial Reporting Council (FRC)** is the UK's independent regulator responsible for promoting high-quality corporate governance and reporting. The FRC promotes high standards of corporate governance through the **UK Corporate Governance Code**. This code sets out standards of good practice in relation to board leadership and effectiveness, remuneration, accountability and relations with shareholders.

Effective corporate governance should contribute to better company performance by helping a Board discharge its duties in the best interests of shareholders and other stakeholders. If it is ignored, the consequence may well be vulnerability or poor performance. Good governance should facilitate efficient, effective and entrepreneurial management that can deliver shareholder value over the longer term.

4.3 Financial reporting and disclosure requirements

The **British Bankers' Association** has published a **Disclosure Code for Financial Reporting** as part of their efforts to ensure that banks continue to provide the market with high quality, decision-useful information about their financial positions.

These key principles are as follows.

- UK banks are committed to providing high quality, meaningful and decision-useful disclosures to users to help them understand the financial position, performance and changes in the financial position of their businesses.

- UK banks will continue to keep under review and are committed to ongoing re-evaluation and enhancement of their financial instrument disclosures for key areas of interest.

- UK banks acknowledge the importance of good practice recommendations and similar guidance issued from time to time by relevant regulators and standard setters and will assess the applicability and relevance of such guidance to their disclosures.

- UK banks will seek to enhance the ability to compare financial statement disclosures across the UK banking sector.

- UK banks should clearly differentiate in their annual reports between information that is audited and information that is unaudited.

5 The banker/customer relationship

5.1 Introduction

What is meant by a bank customer? Case law can help us here to define a customer. One case determined that the term 'customer' implied a course of dealing, or a habit of calling at the bank from time to time; another that some sort of account must be maintained. This seems straightforward enough, but what about someone who has just opened an account with the bank? How often must this person call at the bank before being classed a customer? It would seem obvious that as soon as someone has opened an account with a bank, they immediately become a customer.

CASE STUDY

This view was confirmed in the case of *Ladbroke and Company v Todd 1914*, the judgement of which decreed that the relationship of banker and customer begins as soon as an account is opened and the first cheque is paid in and accepted by the banker for collection and not merely when the cheque has been paid. In *Great Western Railway Co v London and County Banking Co 1901*, it was held that a person is not a customer unless he has some sort of an account, either a deposit or current account or some similar relation with the bank. In *Taxation Commissioners v English, Scottish and Australian Bank 1920,* it was held that a person becomes a customer as soon as he opens an account, and in the case of *Woods -v- Martins Bank 1959,* it was held that a person could become a customer even before he had opened an account, if it was his intention to open one and he subsequently did so.

The banker/customer relationship, therefore, is deemed to begin:

- In respect of an **account holder** – as soon as the bank opens an account for someone (with the intention that the relationship be permanent)

- In respect of **any other banking service** – as soon as the bank agrees to provide that service.

Early thinking on the relationship between a bank and its customer was that a banker is a custodian of the customer's funds. This thinking implies, however, that the customer will receive the same notes and coins as they paid in initially and if correct, would restrict the banker's ability to deal with the customer's funds as they saw fit and to on-lend the funds to other customers.

It was eventually agreed that the basic relationship between a banker and customer is that of debtor and creditor. In the case of *Royal Bank of Scotland v Skinner 1931*, it was held that the banker is not merely the custodian of money, as when money is paid in it is used by the bank for the purposes of its business and that the bank undertakes an obligation to repay an equivalent amount. The relationship between banker and customer is one of contract, although when an account is opened, no formal contract is entered into.

5.2 The banker's duties

The **bank's principal duty** is to honour customers' cheques on demand.

The bank must honour its customers' cheques provided that:

- There are sufficient available funds in the account of the customer who has issued the cheque

- The cheque is technically in order (that is, it has been signed, and the amount in figures is the same as the amount in words)

- There is no legal or other impediment preventing the banker from making payment.

Bankers would be in breach of their basic duties to customers if they wrongfully dishonour cheques (in other words, return a cheque unpaid). It is therefore the duty of the banker to ascertain beyond any doubt that a customer has insufficient funds before refusing payment of a cheque or returning a cheque unpaid.

Another duty is that of secrecy which is a vitally important element in the banker's relationship with the customer. A bank must not disclose any details of its dealings with a customer, even after the customer no longer maintains an account with that bank.

The duty of secrecy applies just as much to an account in the name of an individual vis-à-vis his or her spouse as with any other account. Therefore, if a banker is faced with a request from a customer to be advised of the balance on his wife's account, that request should be politely declined; otherwise the bank could be liable to the husband in an action for damages.

There are four circumstances when a bank is permitted, and in some cases compelled, to divulge information concerning its customers' affairs. The circumstances which impinge on a banker's duty of confidentiality were set out in the judgement in the case of *Tournier v National Provincial and Union Bank of England 1924* and are:

1 Where disclosure is under compulsion by law
2 Where there is a duty to the public to disclose
3 Where it is in the interests of the bank to disclose information
4 Where the disclosure is made with the consent of the customer.

QUICK QUESTION

What can a customer do to ensure that their cheques are not easily altered?

Write your answer here before reading on.

5.3 The customer's duties to the bank

The customer owes certain duties to the bank. The customer should ensure that, when cheques are issued, there are sufficient funds in the account or that a suitable overdraft has been arranged in advance to enable the cheques to be paid when presented to the bank.

If a bank pays a cheque on which the signature of the customer is forged, it will be unable to debit the customer's account. Similarly, if a cheque has been altered and the alteration has not been authenticated by the customer, then in some circumstances the bank will not be able to debit the customer's account. The customer has a duty, however, to ensure that cheques are issued in a manner which does not facilitate alteration and that, in the event of the customer becoming aware that their signature is being forged on cheques, they must take all possible steps to minimise the bank's loss.

The customer could, for example:

- Not leave any spaces between words when writing the amount of the cheque

- Draw a line between the last word and the amount box

- When inserting the figures in the amount box, use a long line between the pounds and pence figures in order to use the full width of the box

6 The compliance function and risk teams

6.1 Compliance department

Banks have had the task of managing compliance for as long as they have made loans. In modern times, expanding expectations of compliance have expanded the scope of programmes of compliance.

Every bank will have a **compliance function or department**, the main purpose of which is to ensure that policies and practices are consistent with the provisions of law, codes of practice and in-house policies. Generally, larger institutions have large product ranges and often offer more complex products. The size and structure of the compliance function must reflect this.

It is a requirement of the FCA that adequate resources be devoted to compliance, and also that the department should be headed by a suitably senior individual. Some organisations now **outsource** some or all of their compliance functions. This does not enable accountability to be delegated to a third party. The organisation remains responsible for ensuring compliance, even if third parties are involved in carrying out compliance duties.

The compliance department is an integral part of the internal control function, and as such should have a direct communication line to senior management. In most organisations, it reports – or has the ultimate power to report – to the Audit Committee, which is a standing committee of the board of directors.

Reporting lines are particularly important as the FCA sourcebook Senior Management Arrangements: Systems and Controls (SYSC) lays down as best practice the need for short and direct communication lines in respect of critical control activities. In some organisations, compliance and internal audit are dealt with under the same functional head, while in others they are completely separate functions.

The compliance department must ensure that the organisation's policies and practices are compliant with numerous sets of laws, regulations and codes, including:

- **Money laundering** – it is a statutory requirement for financial institutions to appoint a Money Laundering Reporting Office or other nominated person.

- **Consumer credit** – financial institutions that offer loans regulated under this legislation must ensure full compliance with the requirements of CCA 1974 and CCA 2006. This is especially important, as failure to comply with some of the rules may render credit agreements unenforceable.

- **Security** – all organisations must safeguard their assets as well as their employees and customers. The compliance department must regularly evaluate the security arrangements that are in place.

- **High level principles** – the organisation's policies and practices must comply with the requirements of the FCA sourcebooks. These rules are especially relevant to advertising and promotion of products, the sales cycle, how prices and interest rates are presented and complaints management.

- **Data protection** – the organisation has to comply with the eight principles of data protection as laid down in the 1998 Act, and must have rigorous systems in place to defend the integrity of personal data held.

- **Human resource management** – the organisation must comply with various laws affecting employees as well as prospective recruits. There are many relevant laws, including those relating to discrimination, equal opportunities, diversity and so on.

- **Codes of practice** – the department should examine systems that should ensure compliance with financial services industry codes to which the organisation has subscribed.

6.2 Risk teams

Many banks have a **risk team** that integrates compliance and operational risk programmes, recognising that greater efficiency and effectiveness may be gained by centralising the overseeing of these functions. The Credit Risk Officer is also likely to be a member of the risk team.

- **Operational risk** relate to matters that can go wrong on a daily basis while the organisation is carrying out its business operations.

- **Compliance risk** is the risk of legal sanctions, material financial loss, or loss to reputation that the organisation may suffer as a result of its failure to comply with laws, regulations, codes of conduct, or standards of best practice.

- **Credit risk** is the risk that an obligation (such as a loan) might not be repaid.

We consider risk management in more detail in Chapter 5 of this Study Text.

CASE STUDY

The parent organisation of Clydesdale Bank plc is CYBG plc. CYBG plc is a holding company that owns Clydesdale Bank and Yorkshire Bank in the UK. It was formed by National Australia Bank in February 2016, in advance of the divestment of its UK business through a stock market flotation.

The diagram below shows the structure of the risk team of Clydesdale Bank.

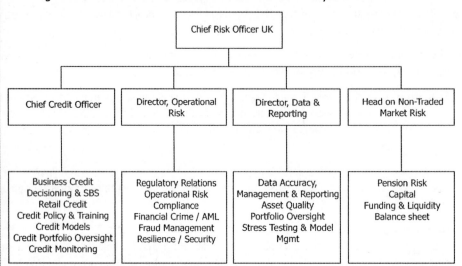

The remit and accountabilities of management risk governance committees was reviewed in 2012. The number of risk governance committees was reduced to simplify the risk governance structure.

The remit of the Risk Committee, appointed and chaired by the Chief Executive Officer, was reviewed and the key areas of focus for that committee include: risk appetite; risk performance and control environment; regulatory environment; risk culture, capability and capacity; and risk policies, frameworks and tools. An annual operating schedule guides the agenda for committee meetings aligned to these responsibilities.

The membership of the committee was changed to include the directors from each business unit who report to the committee on the risk profiles for their areas. Committee members from the Risk function provide challenge and oversight, and attendees from Internal Audit give an independent assurance perspective. The duration of committee meetings was extended to incorporate the wider agenda.

Each major business area established a Management Assurance Committee (MAC) to support the oversight and governance of risk at a business unit level. Each MAC is chaired by the relevant business unit director.

Business unit directors attend and report to the Board Risk Committee on business unit risk profiles. The Chief Risk Officer provides challenge and oversight from a Risk perspective and the Head of Internal Audit attends the Board Risk Committee from an independent assurance perspective.

7 Law of contract

What is a contract?

Write your answer here before reading on.

7.1 How is a contract formed?

Working in financial services, it is important for you to have an understanding of the **law of contract** particularly because, when you are dealing with a contract, you must ensure that it is enforceable. The law of contract is wide ranging and is derived in the main from **common law** – this is, by case law, established by precedent through court cases that relates to contractual matters. However, there are some areas of contract that are regulated by **statute** –that is, by laws passed by Parliament.

A **contract** is **an agreement that is enforceable by law**. This definition is important, as not all agreements will create a contract. It is important to establish whether or not an agreement is a contract, as contracts give rise to rights and obligations (or duties) that a court will enforce; for example, if a dispute arose between a bank and a customer regarding the conditions of a loan. From the moment that a contract is formed, one or both parties to the contract will be required to perform some duty. If they should fail to carry out this duty, the other party will be entitled to a remedy for this 'breach' of contract.

A court may order the completion of a contract or, if it is not practical to do so, order that some form of **compensation** be paid to the injured party. Compensation is also known as '**damages**'.

7.2 How is a contract formed?

A contract is formed when one or more parties voluntarily agree (or consent) to enter into an agreement to perform certain obligations and intend that the agreement will be enforced by law if necessary.

What are the essential features that create a legally binding and valid contract?

- Firstly, the parties must be in full agreement on all of the material aspects of the contract, that is, there must be *consensus in idem* which means that there is agreement about the same thing – in other words, the offer and acceptance made to create the contract must match.

- The parties must give consent to contract, that is, they must intend to be legally bound by the contact, therefore a contract that is formed by force or by fear is unenforceable.

- The parties must have capacity to enter into contracts; for example, insane persons cannot enter into contracts – they are said to have no capacity to contract; also children have no capacity to contract, although certain contracts may be permitted where the circumstances dictate that it is normal for a child to enter into the transaction.

- The contract must conform to any formality; contracts may be created orally or in writing; there is no usual requirement for a contract to be set out in any special form or to be witnessed; there are, however, some contracts that must be formally created in writing, such as contracts creating or transferring interests in land (which means real property, which may comprise land and/or buildings).

- The agreement must not be illegal or impossible.

In England and Wales, there must be also be some consideration (or patrimonial interest) for the contract to be enforced. The parties must be able to show that they have suffered some material injury, measurable in money terms, due to a breach of contract, if they are to pursue damages.

If an agreement does not meet these essential features, it is not a contract.

In Scotland, consideration is not an essential feature of a contractual obligation. Whereas in England and Wales contracts must create obligations on the part of both parties (a **bilateral obligation**), in Scotland it is possible for a contract to create an obligation on the part of only one party. This is known as a unilateral (or one-sided) obligation. For example, a promise by one party to make payment to another party, without the second party having to perform some task, is binding on the first party.

7.3 Validity of a contract

An agreement that at first appears to create a valid contract may not become binding on all of the parties if there is some flaw in the agreement. Flaws may result from:

- Lack of capacity
- Lack of formality, or
- Misunderstanding.

Flaws may result in the contract becoming void, voidable, or in some circumstances it may remain valid.

A **void contract** is one where the flaw is serious (material) and as such, the contract is treated as if it had never existed. Since it never existed, no rights or duties have been created and none can be enforced. In effect, neither party is bound because no agreement has been reached.

A **voidable contract** is one where the flaw is less serious. The contract is initially valid, but one party can rely on the flaw and ask the court to have the contract set aside. If neither party takes action, the contract will continue to be a **valid** contract.

7.4 Offer

A contract is formed when one party makes an **offer** and the other party accepts this offer, subject to the conditions mentioned earlier being met. Offers can be created verbally or in writing and may also be formed by implication – that the contract is created by the actions of the offeror.

Some things that may appear to be 'offers' are not actually offers from the point of view of contract law. For example, goods on display at a supermarket or in a shop window are not offers to sell to the public, but are invitations to treat – that is, indications of a willingness to do business. A consumer takes the goods from a shelf and makes an offer to a supermarket which then either accepts or rejects the offer.

Offers last until they are accepted, rejected or after a time limit set on the offer expires without acceptance having taken place. Some offers may have no time limit set for acceptance. The offer then ends after a reasonable time has elapsed. Offers also end if the other party comes back with a 'conditional acceptance' (one that differs from the terms of the offer). Such conditional acceptances are known as 'counter-offers' and have the effect of cancelling the original offer.

In life assurance, the proposal form makes up the offer which the life assurance company can either accept at standard rates or on special terms, or reject. If the assurance company accepts on special terms, it is effectively rejecting the proposal and making a counter-offer, which the proposer then either accepts or rejects.

7.5 Acceptance

Acceptance of a contractual agreement can generally take any form, unless expressly stated otherwise, but usually the form of acceptance will mirror the offer, such as a written offer is usually accepted in writing. Acceptance of an offer takes place as soon as the offeror is advised of it and this creates the contract. If the acceptance is sent by post, the contract is formed as soon as the acceptance is posted – not when it is received.

If the offeror wishes to withdraw the offer, they must ensure that the withdrawal (or 'revocation') must reach the other party before the acceptance is posted. However, an acceptance, once posted, can be revoked if a cancellation (or revocation) reaches the offeror before the acceptance. An example of an acceptance is when the customer accepts the terms laid down in the bank's offer/facility letter when they are borrowing funds.

QUICK QUESTION

What can make a contract invalid?

Write your answer here before reading on.

7.6 Errors in contracts

The term '**error**' relates to Scots law. In England, Wales and Northern Ireland, the term '**mistake**' is more commonly used. If an error has been made in the formation of a contract, this may affect the validity of the contract, depending on the type and seriousness of the error. For the contract to be invalidated, it must be an essential error and material to the contract – that is, an error which, had it been known before the contract was formed, would have led to the contract not being entered into.

Some errors automatically result in the contract being declared as void, while others will make the contract voidable. In some cases, the contract will remain valid; for example, a contract which both parties enter into with the same mistaken belief (a '**bilateral common error**').

If an error in a contract is deemed to be an '**error in the substantials**' this would automatically result in the contract being declared void and might occur because of:

- Price
- Identity of a party to the contract
- The nature of the contact
- The subject matter of the contract
- Quality, quantity or extent of the subject matter

If the same situation occurred for any other reason (an '**error concomitans**') then the contract would be valid.

Errors may be induced (caused) by something that the other party has said or done. This is known as '**misrepresentation**', and may be accidental ('innocent misrepresentation') or deliberate ('**fraudulent misrepresentation**'). Both types of errors cause contracts to be void if the error relates to an error in the substantials, and voidable if an error is concomitant. With innocent misrepresentation, the aggrieved party can only have the contract set aside and be returned to the position that they were in before the contract was formed.

Any additional losses cannot be reclaimed. Under fraudulent misrepresentation, as there was a civil wrong, the aggrieved party can seek damages in addition to having the contract set aside. Fraudulent misrepresentation does not even require that the person making the statement knows it to be false.

7.7 Relevance of contract law to financial services

All financial service agreements are contracts, whether we are talking about, for example:

- Opening a bank or building society account
- Insurance policies
- Loan agreements
- Finance company agreements, or
- Credit union services

All require offers to be made and acceptances to be made to the offers.

The creation of a contract provides the customer with rights that their chosen financial institution is required to fulfil. However, each customer also has duties to the financial services provider. For example, when a bank account is opened, the bank has the duty to accept deposits to the account from the customer and the customer has the corresponding right to make deposits. The bank has the right to make reasonable charges for the provision of its services and the customer has a duty to pay.

Contract law arising out of common law applies equally to financial services contracts as it does to other contracts; however, there are several statutory rights and obligations, set out in various Acts of Parliament, which impact on the provision of services and contracts. Some of these have provided additional protection for consumers.

QUICK QUESTION

Who or what is an agent?

Write your answer here before reading on.

8 Agency

8.1 Who is an agent?

Agency can be defined as:

> ... the relationship between two parties, one of whom – the principal – empowers the other – the agent – to act on his behalf and undertakes to be bound by the agent's acts as if they were his own.

If you work in a bank you are acting as agent, in many ways, each day. You are, in fact, contracting for the principal – your customer. Thus it is important that you understand the concept of agency and how the relationship is formed.

8.2 Who is an agent?

An **agent** can best be described by function.

- It is the function of an agent to bring the principal into contractual relations with third parties.

- An agent is empowered by the principal to enter into a contract on their behalf, with another person or organisation – his is contractual capacity and the agent is deemed to have the same contractual capacity as the principal.

- As a banker you act as agent. For example, when you pay a cheque drawn by your customer, the principal, you are acting as the customer's agent.

8.3 Constitution of agency

The relationship between a principal and agent can be created in a variety of ways.

- **Express consent.** Agency may be expressly constituted by verbal or written contract. Where the contract is in writing, it may be formal or informal. A common formal method is that of a power of attorney – an instrument by one person authorising another to do certain acts for them. Such a power is strictly construed; the agent is only held to have the powers expressly given to him in the formal writing or those necessarily implied. Alternatively, the appointment of the agent may be informal even if the agent is to make contracts which by law must be expressed in writing and there is no restriction on the method by which such an oral appointment may be proved.

- **Implied consent.** If an appointment is by implied consent, the relationship of principal and agent is constituted, not in writing or verbally, but by inference from the conduct of the parties. For example in a partnership, every partner is an agent of the firm and the other partners for the purpose of the business of the partnership, and at common law a director is implied to be an agent of the company. Another example is where a person is permitted to take charge of an office or a business or is in some way placed in a supervisory position.

- **Holding out.** The concept of holding out arises if a principal has had an agent conducting business on their behalf on a regular basis in the normal course of business. In this situation the principal cannot decide to subsequently withdraw from any transaction the agent has entered into with this third party.

- **Ratification.** When a person has acted on behalf of another when in fact he has no authority, express or implied, to do so, the party for whom the act was done may later ratify the act. This has the effect of creating rights and liabilities as at the date of the contract between the principal and the agent and the principal and the third party. The question of ratification may arise where the agent has exceeded their authority or where another person who did not at any time have authority to contract for the alleged principal has contracted for them.

  Before the alleged principal can ratify, the following conditions must be satisfied:

  - The contract must have been made expressly on behalf of the principal

  - The principal must have been in existence at the date of the contract: for example, contracts made on behalf of a limited company before its incorporation cannot be ratified

  - The principal must be fully aware of all the circumstances at the time of ratification

  - Ratification must be made within the required time, if time is essential to the validity of the contract

  - The whole contract must be ratified

  - The act to be ratified must not have been void at its inception

- **Necessity.** Agency of necessity arises in an emergency when a person becomes justified in appropriating to themselves the powers of an agent, and the person on whose behalf these powers are assumed is bound. The rule is of very limited application and is generally confined to carriers of goods by sea or land. The principle applies where an emergency arises and it is not possible for the agent to obtain instructions from their principal and the agent takes action to protect the principal's interests and not merely for the convenience of the agent.

QUICK QUESTION

What is a negotiable instrument?

Write your answer here before reading on.

9 Negotiable instruments

A **negotiable instrument** is a transferable, signed document that promises to pay the bearer a sum of money at a future date or on demand. Examples are:

- Bills of exchange
- Cheques (provided they are not marked 'not negotiable')
- Promissory notes

In accordance with the **Bills of Exchange Act 1882**:

1   A **bill of exchange** is 'an unconditional order in writing, addressed by one person to another, signed by the person giving it, requiring the person to whom it is addressed to pay on demand, or at a fixed or determinable future time, a sum certain in money to or to the order of a specified person, or to bearer'.

2   A **cheque** is 'a bill of exchange drawn on a banker payable on demand' (known as a 'check' in the USA).

3   A **promissory note** is 'an unconditional promise in writing made by one person to another, signed by the maker, engaging to pay on demand, or at a fixed or determinable future time, a sum certain in money to or to the order of a specified person or to bearer'.

The term 'negotiable' has a special meaning within the context of banking. Transferability is different from negotiability. Transferability means that a person to whom the bill is transferred gets only the original payee's rights and if these are defective in any way, the subsequent holder gets no better title.

EXAMPLE

- Smith owes Crawford £500
- Crawford owes Jones £500

Crawford could pay Jones by getting Jones to agree to accept payment in the form of Crawford transferring the debt of £500 owed by Smith which would leave Jones to demand payment of the £500 from Smith and, if Smith doesn't pay up, then Jones could sue him. This might all seem straightforward, but there are potential problems.

Crawford might have a defect of title in respect of the debt owed to him by Smith. This can happen if the debt owed by Smith to Crawford arose as a result of Crawford selling goods to Smith on credit. If the goods turned out to be substandard, Smith may refuse to pay Crawford the £500 or only offer to pay a smaller sum. So the £500 owed by Smith to Crawford may be disputed.

If Crawford transfers the debt to Jones, Jones only gets the rights that Crawford had and in this case he may not receive the full £500 if Smith is successful in his claim against Crawford and does not have to pay the full price for the sub-standard goods.

Another problem is the procedural one of dealing with the assignation of the debt from Crawford to Jones. In order to ensure that Smith does not pay Crawford or that Crawford does not transfer the same debt to another of his creditors, Jones should write to Smith explaining that Crawford has transferred the debt to him.

This procedure involves either the debtor giving the creditor a signed piece of paper promising to pay (a promissory note) or the creditor giving the debtor a signed piece of paper ordering the debtor to pay (a bill of exchange) and the debtor signing this, thus accepting the obligation.

Using Smith, Crawford and Jones as an example, Crawford could hold either a promissory note signed by Smith or a bill of exchange accepted by Smith and could transfer the instrument to Jones. Jones in turn could transfer the instrument to one of his creditors who would acquire full rights for repayment of the debt against Smith (and also against Crawford if he had signed the instrument).

These instruments (promissory notes where the debtor promises to pay and bills of exchange where the debtor is ordered to pay) enable a debt to be transferred from party to party without any transferee having to worry about any defect of title the original creditor may have had and also without requiring intimation of the transfer to the debtor.

In the banking sense, this is what is meant by a negotiable instrument. In other words, anyone who is a party to a negotiable instrument and who is neither the drawer nor the payee is not affected by other claims to the money it represents. This person can enforce payment of the instrument even if the title of the person who negotiated it to them is defective. The person who negotiated the instrument to them could not enforce payment.

Certain conditions must be satisfied to enable the third party or holder to get a perfect title free of defects in the title of the person from whom they acquired the bill.

To achieve a perfect title:

- The holder must have acted honestly and be unaware of any defect in the transferor's title

- The holder must have paid for the bill in some way, that is, given value for it, which is why the words 'value received' appears on some bills

- The bill is not marked in a way as to stop the holder getting good title, for example marked 'not transferable' or 'not negotiable'

- The bill is not overdue, and

- There is nothing on the bill to arouse suspicion.

10 Forms of business organisation

10.1 Introduction

A bank's business customers may be of a number of different types. There are three main ways in which a commercial business enterprise may be set up – as a **sole trader**, as a **partnership** or as a **limited company**. Most of the businesses that you deal with will be structured in one of these three ways.

10.2   Sole traders

As the term implies, a **sole trader** (or 'sole proprietor') is an individual who is carrying on a business in their own name. You may have come across business bank accounts that are named something like 'Karen Smith T/A Kaz Cycle Repairs'. In this case, Karen is trading on her own account as a cycle repairer. ('T/A' denotes 'trading as'.) Although she may employ people, her employees do not have a share in the business. In order to set up as a sole trader, all that an individual needs to do is open a separate business bank account and inform HM Revenue & Customs.

- A sole trader has the advantage of being in complete control of their business.
- The main drawback is that they have unlimited liability for the debts of the business, and this liability can extend to their personal assets as well.

10.3   Partnerships

A **partnership** is where two or more people come together to conduct business with the aim of making a profit. The main advantage that a partnership has over a sole trader is that the more partners there are in the business, the more expertise the business can call on. A partnership is also advantageous from the point of view of shared responsibility.

Three **essential elements** must be present for a partnership to exist. The partnership must be (1) a **business**, (2) **conducted for profit**, (3) **by or on behalf of its partners**.

The more partners there are, the greater the capacity of the business to raise capital to finance operations – either at the start of the business, or when the business has been operating for some time and needs an injection of more capital. It may well be cheaper for the partnership to raise funds in this way, rather than having to pay the market rate from a commercial lender such as a bank.

Partnership was traditionally the normal organisation in the professions as most professions prohibit their members from carrying on practice through limited companies, and the **Partnership Act 1890 (PA 1890)** set out law governing this form of business organisation.

- 'Partnership is the relation which subsists between persons carrying on a business in common with a view of profit' (Section 1, PA 1890).
- 'Person' includes a corporation such as a registered company as well as an individual living person.

In a partnership governed by the PA 1890, a partner is personally liable for all the debts of the firm (incurred while he is a partner and sometimes even after he has ceased to be a partner). The partnership thus shares the main disadvantage of a sole trader – **unlimited liability**. The partners are personally liable for the debts of the partnership, even if that debt has been created by another partner.

A further disadvantage is that, as with any situation where there is more than one person involved, disagreements may occur. Therefore when a partnership is established, the partners should draw up an agreement outlining the rules of the partnership. This will help to avoid the situation where disagreements occur due to misunderstandings between the partners.

A partnership is created as a result of a contract between two or more parties, where the contract may be **in writing**, by **oral agreement**, or **inferred from the facts and circumstances**. A partnership which is formed by oral agreement or by implication may create problems for any third party dealing with the partnership and also for the partners themselves if there is a dispute between them at a later date. It is more usual for the agreement to be in writing, as this has the advantage of providing a permanent record of the rights of the partners amongst themselves. Where there is a simple handwritten agreement the document is known as the **Articles of Partnership**. Where there is a partnership agreement in the form of a deed, this is the **Deed of Partnership**.

For trading purposes, a partnership must conform to legalities concerning the naming of the firm and the number of partners involved. In law the terms 'partnership' and 'firm' are synonymous and can be freely interchanged. However, the terms 'firm' and limited company' cannot be interchanged as 'firm' relates to a partnership and 'limited company' refers to a limited liability company, yet it is common for the media to refer to businesses generically as 'firms'.

A partnership is permitted to trade using all the surnames of the partners with or without initials or forenames. It may also trade under a business name. If it does so, must comply with the provisions of the **Business Names Act 1985** which sets out the requirements for business names and prevents certain words that could cause confusion from being used in business names. If the word 'company' or any abbreviation of it such as '& Co' is used in a business name, it is a partnership. However, should the word 'company' be followed by the word 'limited', or any abbreviated version, then it is a limited company.

- Smith, Jones & Co – a partnership
- Smith, Jones & Co Ltd – a limited company

10.4 Limited Liability Partnerships (LLPs)

The LLP structure was introduced by the **Limited Liability Partnership Act 2000** and came into effect in 2001. The idea was to combine the organisational flexibility and tax benefits of a partnership, but without the unlimited liability associated with the partnership. LLPs are popular with those professions that are precluded either by law or by professional arrangements from forming a limited company, and they can also be attractive to the small business that allows the business person to protect their investment in the business.

In many ways, the LLP is more like a private limited company than a partnership. It is a separate legal entity from the people who make up the partnership. It is also possible for an LLP to hold property in its own name and its existence can continue even after changes in the partners. The partners subscribe to an incorporation document and this is filed with the Registrar of Companies. Each member of the LLP is able to bind the LLP subject to some limitations that are set out in the legislation. Every member of an LLP is an **agent** of the LLP. As such, where the member has authority, the LLP will be bound by the acts of the member.

Lending to an LLP is treated the same way as lending to a limited company. As the LLP has a separate legal personality to its members there is no recourse against the members of the LLP. An LLP and any negligent members are liable for the full extent of their assets. The rights and duties of the members to one another and to the LLP are covered by a confidential agreement between the members, which need not be in writing.

Profits made by an LLP are shared amongst the members and each member is liable to pay income tax on this. In most cases the members will be self employed, so will include their share of profits on their individual self assessment tax returns. Each member is also responsible for paying their own National Insurance Contributions and should register with HM Revenue & Customs as self employed.

QUICK QUESTION

How do limited companies differ from sole traders and partnerships?

Write your answer here before reading on.

10.5 Limited companies

10.5.1 Features of limited companies

Limited companies have the following features.

- A limited company is formed under the Companies Act 2006, which is the main statute governing companies in the UK. Many companies were formed under the provisions of previous legislation. Some provisions of the Companies Act 1985 remain in place, including a section relating to the creation of charges over the assets of Scottish companies.

- Once a company is incorporated by registration with the Registrar, the company has a distinctly separate legal identity from its shareholders (members) and its directors (the managers).

- A company is said to have 'perpetual succession' which means simply that the company lives on and on despite even the death of all of its members.

- In any limited company, a member's liability is limited to any amount which remains unpaid on their shares. If shares have been fully paid up, then the member has no further liability for the debts of the company.

- A company is managed by the directors, so that those ordinary shareholders who are not directors have no management rights.

- Shares in a company are usually freely transferable, although there may well be a restriction on members of a private limited company from transferring shares to outsiders.

- A minimum of one shareholder and one director is required to form a private limited company. These may be the same individual. A private company does not have to appoint a company Secretary. A public limited company must have a minimum of one shareholder and two directors, of which at least one must be a natural person. A public limited company must appoint a Company Secretary.

- Unless a company is registered as being unlimited, which would be unusual, the company must file its annual accounts with the Registrar of Companies. Since this register is open to public inspection, privacy and secrecy relating to business matters are forfeited. (One of the main advantages of operating as a sole trader or partnership is that business affairs can be kept secret.)

- A company can grant a security over its whole assets and undertaking by way of a floating charge which can increase the borrowing potential of a company. A floating charge is a security over the assets of a limited company, but can only be realised when the company is wound up.

10.5.2 Corporate personality

One of the main advantages of incorporation as a limited company is that the process involves the creation of a **separate legal person**. A company, as a separate legal entity, may have liabilities in tort (e.g. to pay damages for negligent acts) and crime.

Criminal liability of companies is a topical area following events such as the Paddington train disaster.

It is difficult to prosecute a company on criminal charges, as it is necessary to show a *'mens rea'*, or controlling mind.

Unless a company is very small, it is problematic to show that the mind controlling the company was connected with the criminal act. However, the Law Commission has issued proposals which include a charge of killing by gross carelessness, which it would be easier to charge companies with. There is, at present, no such criminal offence in the UK.

10.5.3 Types of limited company

You will probably be aware that there have been many major issues of shares to the general public, for example by previously Government-owned businesses such as Railtrack and Powergen. Such allotments of shares are preceded by the issue of a Prospectus, a document containing information about securities to be offered which is submitted to an approved stock exchange for approval.

The essential difference between a **public company** and a **private company** lies in the fact that only public companies may issue a prospectus. Therefore private limited companies will not have issued a prospectus.

You may also have heard the term '**quoted company'**, in which 'quoted' refers only to public companies and means that the company applied for a stock exchange quotation and was granted permission to have its shares dealt on the exchange. Such companies may also be referred to as **listed companies**.This means that the shares of such companies are freely transferable and quoted daily. Not all public limited companies are 'quoted'.

10.5.4 Formation procedures

A limited company is formed by the completion of designated registration procedures which involve the drawing up of various documents including a Memorandum of Association and Articles of Association. Both these documents, and others, must be filed with the Registrar of Companies in Edinburgh for a company registered in Scotland, or Cardiff for companies registered in England or Wales. There are fees which must also be paid.

It is also necessary for the new company to submit details of the founding directors and shareholders to the Registrar. New public companies must also submit the name of the company Secretary.

A further document that must be submitted is the Statement of Capital and Initial Shareholding. This sets out the number, classes (usually ordinary or preference) and nominal value of the shares issued on formation, and the extent to which they will be paid up (it is possible for the company to defer calls for capital contributions, although a public company must have minimum capital of £50,000 or alternatively 57,100 euros, of which 25% must be paid up).

When the Companies Registrar is satisfied that the requirements of the **Companies Act 2006** have been complied with, the company is granted an Incorporation Certificate.

10.5.5 Memorandum of Association

The Companies Act 2006 radically revised the requirements in relation to this document. The Memorandum of Association must now include only two clauses:

- A statement that the company has been formed

- A statement that the subscribers (the founding shareholders) have taken at least one share of specified value in the new company.

Prior to the 2006 Act, the Memorandum was more significant. It set out the name of the company, its location within the UK, its objects (or objectives), its authorised capital (the maximum that it would be able to raise) and a declaration of the subscribers. Companies founded before the implementation of the 2006 Act will continue to have these clauses in the Memorandum. However, the 2006 Act states that these clauses will now be regarded as forming part of the Articles of Association.

10.5.6 Articles of Association

The **Articles of Association** form the basis of the members' relationship with the company and also govern the relationship of the members with each other. The Articles form a contract between the shareholders and the company.

The government has published model Articles of Association in standard form for three different types of company. A company can choose to adopt these as they stand, adopt them and alter any Articles as appropriate, or prepare their own Articles of Association. Before the Companies Act 2006 came into effect, the model Articles were commonly referred to as 'Table A', which was the relevant appendix to the Companies Act 1985. Some writers and businesses continue to use this term.

The Articles of Association set down clauses relating to, for example, share capital, share certificates, transfers of shares, alterations of capital, company meetings, voting, directors, accounts and audit.

10.6 Joint and several liability

Joint and several liability may apply when we are dealing with more than one person; for example it could be a partnership, or it could be a couple who operate a joint current account.

- If parties have **joint liability**, then each is liable for the full amount of a debt or obligation.
- With **several liability**, the parties are liable only for their respective obligations.

Under joint and several liability, a claimant may pursue an obligation against any single party as if they were jointly liable. It is then the responsibility of the defendant parties to settle among themselves their respective liabilities.

The concept of joint and several liability is most relevant where a plaintiff is seeking damages from any of a number of defendants, whatever is their individual share of the liability.

Where two or more persons in a partnership have joint and several liability for a debt, a creditor is able to sue any one of the partners if the debt is not repaid. If business partners enter into a contract for which there is joint and several liability, and the contract is breached, then one of the partners may be sued and could be required to pay all of the damages due. It is up to that partner then to claim from the other partners their share of the liability.

KEY WORDS

Key words and phrases from this chapter are given below. Make sure you know what they mean and add any other words or phrases that you want to remember. You can use the space provided to write your own revision notes.

- Financial Conduct Authority (FCA)
- Prudential Regulation Authority (PRA)
- Markets in Financial Instruments Directive
- Capital Requirements Directive
- Consumer Credit Directive
- Consumer Credit Acts
- Payment Services Directive
- Money Laundering Regulations
- Data Protection Act
- Bribery Act
- Treating Customers Fairly
- BCOBS
- Senior Managers Regime
- Certification Regime
- Corporate governance
- The banker/customer relationship
- Contract
- Agency
- Negotiable instrument
- Sole trader
- Partnership
- Limited liability partnership
- Limited company

REVIEW

To help you reflect on and review the content of this chapter, give some thought to the following questions.

- What does the Financial Services Authority do?

- What are the respective roles of the Prudential Regulation Authority and the Financial Conduct Authority?

- What are key regulatory and legal requirements that apply to banking?

- How does the regulator seek to make senior individuals in banks accountable for their actions?

- What is the aim of Basel III?

- In what ways does consumer credit legislation influence the way a bank operates?

- In what ways do money laundering regulations influence the way a bank operates?

- In what ways does data protection legislation influence the way a bank operates?

- In what ways does anti-bribery legislation influence the way a bank operates?

- What is a banker's responsibility for Treating Customers Fairly?

- What is the purpose and scope of the FCA's Banking: Conduct of Business sourcebook?

- What is meant by corporate governance?

- What is the nature of the banker/customer relationship?

- Who are typical members of a bank's risk team?

- What is a contract?

- What is the significance of a contract for the practising banker?

- What does 'agency' mean?

- What is the significance of agency for the practising banker?

- What is a 'negotiable instrument'?

- What is the significance of a negotiable instrument for the practising banker?

- What are the key differences between a sole trader, a partnership, and a limited company?

chapter 3

SERVING CUSTOMERS

Contents

Learning objectives

By the end of this chapter, you should be able to:

- Understand the bank customer categories, typical life stages and needs
- Understand banking products and services and how these appropriately meet customer needs

Introduction

A sustainable and successful banking industry is built on solid foundations of high ethical and professional standards. Banks deal with money that belongs in the main to their customers, and they take risks to generate income and create wealth. Trust is therefore a vital element of the relationship between a bank and its customers. The extent to which the public trusts its banks will be influenced largely by what banks do and how they do it and the values and principles that guide their actions.

The aim of this chapter is to increase your awareness and understanding of the range of products and services offered by UK banks and how they are matched to the needs of different customers so that you can meet the financial needs of customers professionally and responsibly. As you study this chapter about serving customers, keep in mind the concept of Treating Customers Fairly from Chapter 2.

1 Types of customer

1.1 Introduction

Typically, a bank serves a wide range of customers. Although each customer will have their own particular financial needs, it is useful to classify them into certain types.

Banks aim to serve the financial needs of:

- Personal customers
- Business and corporate customers

1.2 Personal customers

Typically, personal customers are looking for a bank to:

- Provide a safe place for depositing excess money
- Lend them money when required
- Make payments on their behalf

Personal customers usually conduct business with their bank through a variety of channels, including:

- A local branch
- Contact centre
- Online
- Mobile phone

Personal accounts can be categorised as follows:

- Sole account
- Joint account
- Account for minors
- Trustee account

Type of personal account	Who it is for?
Sole	One account holder
Joint	Two or more account holders
Account for minors	Under 18s
Trustee (may also be a business account)	People who are holding money in trust for someone else

1.3 Business customers

Like personal customers, corporate (company) and other business customers are looking for a bank to:

- Provide a safe place for depositing excess money
- Lend them money when required
- Make payments on their behalf

The sums involved will usually be larger than for personal customers, with more complex transactions and for different purposes.

Business customers can usually conduct business with their bank through the same channels as personal customers. Additional communication channels are:

- Business support centre
- Relationship manager

Each relationship manager is likely to have a number of business or corporate customers in their portfolio to serve.

Business accounts can be categorised as follows:

- Sole trader
- Partnership
- Company
- Clubs and societies
- Trustee

Type of business account	Who it is for?
Sole trader	One account holder
Partnership	Two or more people who join together to run a business with a view to making a profit
Company	Corporate customers (incorporated limited companies owned by shareholders). Companies have a separate identity to their owners and managers
Clubs and societies	Unincorporated bodies run by a committee
Trustee (may also be a personal account)	People who are holding money in trust for someone else

2 Products and services

2.1 Introduction

Banks offer products that allow customers to:

- Deposit or save and invest money
- Borrow money

Deposits, savings and investments	
Current account	To deposit money and finance routine transactions. Small amount of interest usually paid
Deposit/savings account	For cash savings. Interest paid at regular intervals. Term savings accounts are cash savings. Customers required to give the bank available for longer term notice of any withdrawals. Higher rates of interest usually paid
Individual Savings Account (ISA)	Pays tax-free interest on cash savings up to a maximum limit in each tax year. The savings can be invested as deposits, or as stocks and shares
Pension plans & investment-based life assurance products	These are further forms of investment offered through many banks

Borrowing	
Overdraft	Set credit limit on a current account. Usually subject to annual review
Personal loan	For a range of purposes, e.g. a car or home improvements. Fixed monthly repayments
Mortgage loans	Typically for house purchase and secured on the property
Credit card account	Set credit limit. Minimum monthly repayment required. Once repaid, the credit becomes available again

2.2 Deposits and savings

2.2.1 Current accounts

A **current account** is sometimes called a **money transmission account**. Many people in employment have their salary paid directly into a current account by their employer. Customers use their current account to finance their routine transactions. Banks may pay the customer interest for the credit balance on a current account, although the rate of interest tends to be much lower than that paid on a designated savings account.

A wide range of current accounts is available, from a basic account with just a debit card to accounts with overdraft facilities. Some offer additional features such as free travel insurance.

To allow customers to keep track of their spending, they can receive regular statements of account (usually monthly), or they can check their transactions by going online, phoning the bank's contact centre, or visiting an automated teller machine (ATM). Customers can also opt to receive their account balance by text message.

QUICK QUESTION

What types of current account does your bank offer?

Write your answer here before reading on.

2.2.2 Deposit and savings accounts

While a current account is used for the customer to pay for their day-to-day expenses and perhaps to help manage any short term shortfall in funds, many customers will want to keep their savings in a different account.

QUICK QUESTION

For what reasons might a customer want to save?

Write your answer here before reading on.

Customers will have different reasons for wanting to save, such as:

- Future expenditure – saving for a holiday, a deposit on a house, or a wedding
- Emergencies – saving for a 'rainy day'
- Saving money to give their children or grandchildren when they get older
- Saving money to earn interest and generate wealth
- Saving for retirement

Savings accounts are usually used for holding medium to long term surpluses of funds. They are usually operated by way of a plastic card or, in a few cases, by a passbook. Interest is paid by the bank, based usually on the amount of money lodged in the account. The payment of this interest will vary from product to product. For example, some savings accounts pay interest monthly to provide the customer with some form of monthly income, while other accounts pay out interest quarterly, six monthly or even annually. Also, depending on the particular account chosen by the customer, the account into which the interest is paid can also vary.

The level of interest rate varies depending on both the balance of the account and the terms of the account. Generally, the higher the balance of the account, the higher the rate of interest that will be paid. The terms of the account will also affect the level of interest paid. For example, if there is a limited number of withdrawals permitted each year, the account will tend to pay a higher rate of interest than an account that allows the customer to make an unlimited number of withdrawals.

Another condition that can affect the rate of interest paid is the notice required on withdrawals. An account that allows customers to withdraw funds without giving any notice at all will tend to pay a lower rate of interest than an account that requires the customer to give notice of withdrawals (the notice period could be seven, thirty or even ninety days).

2.2.3 Individual Savings Accounts (ISAs)

An ISA is a tax-free savings account.

- They can consist of cash or stocks and shares
- There is no tax liability
- There are maximum annual limits set for the amount that can be paid into an ISA and these are reviewed by the government annually
- Stocks and shares ISAs can be opened by anyone over the age of 18 who is resident in the UK for tax purposes
- A cash ISA can be opened by anyone over the age of 16 who is ordinarily resident in the UK for tax purposes

QUICK QUESTION

What types of savings accounts does your bank offer?

Write your answer here before reading on.

2.3 Overdrafts and personal loans

2.3.1 Overdrafts

An overdraft is a negative balance on a current account. The amount of the overdraft should be agreed in advance between the bank and the customer. Customers use an overdraft when they spend more money than they have in their bank account.

There are two kinds of overdraft.

- **Authorised overdraft**. This is where a customer has a set overdraft limit that has been pre-arranged with the bank. Although some banks provide interest-free overdrafts, usually customers will be required to pay interest or a fee in return for making use of the overdraft.
- **Unauthorised overdraft**. This is where the customer has not agreed an overdraft facility with their bank in advance and where they have withdrawn more money than they have available in their account or where they have taken out more than their authorised overdraft limit. Unauthorised overdrafts are usually subject to charges and fees, which can be expensive.

Key term

An overdraft that is agreed in advance between the bank and the customer is an **authorised overdraft**.

An overdraft that has not been agreed in advance between the bank and the customer is an **unauthorised overdraft**.

2.3.2 Personal loans

Personal loans are used by a large number of personal customers to finance the purchase of major assets such as:

- Cars
- Holidays
- Domestic appliances like fridges, freezers, washing machines
- Home improvements, and
- Personal computers

To apply for a personal loan, the customer completes an application. The application can be made either by completing a form, calling a customer contact centre, or online. Once the application is received, the lender completes a credit assessment process – usually using some form of credit scoring. If the application is approved, an agreement form is drawn up, and the customer and the lender sign it. The funds can then be released to the customer, usually by transferring the money from the personal loan account into the customer's current account.

Typically, the customer repays the loan monthly by direct debit. This is for a fixed amount over an agreed number of months.

Interest is usually charged at a **flat rate of interest** over the life of the loan, with the total amount of interest being added to the capital sum (amount borrowed) at the start of the loan. The true rate of interest, the Annual Percentage Rate (APR) will also be advised to the customer.

2.4 Mortgage loans

2.4.1 Introduction

A mortgage loan – that is, a loan that is secured on property – is usually used for buying a house. Traditionally, mortgages, or house purchase loans, were widely offered only by building societies. Now they are offered by banks as well.

- A mortgage is usually taken over a long period of time for a large sum.

- Security is generally taken over the property being purchased.

- There are two ways in which a mortgage can be repaid: making regular payments covering capital and interest; or repaying the interest only, then making a large one-off payment at the end of the loan to cover the capital sum.

A residential mortgage can be made available to a customer in order to buy a residential property in which they will be living. A **'buy-to-let' mortgage** is made to enable the borrower to buy a house that they will be renting to tenants. A buy-to-let owner faces the risk that they may not be able to find tenants to occupy the property. To reflect the greater risk involved, a buy-to-let mortgage is likely to carry a higher rate of interest than a residential mortgage that is provided to an owner-occupier.

Key term

Mortgagee. The person or business making a loan that is secured by the real property of the person (mortgagor) who owes money to the mortgagee.

Mortgagor. The person who has borrowed money and has pledged real property as security for the (mortgagee).

2.4.2 Capital and interest mortgage (or 'repayment mortgage')

This type of mortgage requires the borrower to repay part of the capital borrowed and an interest payment charged on that capital every time an instalment is made. The balance of the account should therefore be zero at the end of the loan period. Thus the interest repayment element makes up a larger part of the repayment than the capital element in the early stages of the loan. It is only later in the life of the loan – when these small reductions of capital are beginning to reduce the total amount of capital outstanding – that the amount of interest accrued reduces and the capital amount of the repayment becomes more dominant. The amount of the monthly repayment will vary as the interest rate varies.

When the Monetary Policy Committee (MPC) of the Bank of England changes the base interest rate, there are illustrations in the media of how this change will affect a typical loan. Generally, financial institutions change their interest rates when the MPC announces a change following its monthly meeting. However, many institutions decide their own internal reference rate, and this may or may not be changed by the same percentage as that announced by the MPC.

2.4.3 Interest-only mortgage

With an interest-only loan, there are no repayments to the loan account of any capital at all during the life of the loan, so that the loan is repaid in its entirety at the end. Therefore the monthly payments made by the customer to the lender cover only the accrued interest on the capital balance. Like a capital and interest loan, the only occurrence that will cause this amount to change is if there is a change in Base Rate. The customer should be confident that they have the funds available at the end of the loan period to make a full repayment. Although a customer may have amassed savings over the period of the loan that would allow them to do this, it is more common to have some form of **repayment vehicle** set up to allow these funds to be available.

Financial advisers may be involved in helping clients with mortgage choices and, if an interest only option is being considered, the choice of an appropriate repayment vehicle for the mortgage will be a part of this. However, with the implementation in April 2014 of the **Mortgage Market Review (MMR)** (discussed further later), the requirement on intermediaries to assess **affordability** has been removed, with this responsibility now falling on **lenders**.

There are three commonly encountered **repayment vehicles**:

- An endowment policy
- A personal pension plan
- An ISA

The proceeds of any of these products are used to provide the customer with a lump sum from which to make the capital repayment. The main problem is that there is no guarantee that there will be sufficient funds to make the repayment in full. If there is a shortfall forecast, the customer may be advised to do one or more of the following four things:

- Increase the level of payments that they pay into their repayment vehicle

- Arrange to set aside additional funds to meet the shortfall

- Extend the term of the loan and/or the repayment vehicle

- Convert all or part of their loan to a capital and interest loan – by so doing, the amount of the loan now outstanding could be reduced to the projected return from their investment

2.4.4 Current account mortgage

With this type of mortgage, the customer's house purchase loan and current account are amalgamated into one account. The main advantage is that, as each month's salary is credited to the account, the total amount outstanding is reduced. As a result, the interest that is accruing on the outstanding balance is slightly lower. The cumulative effect of this over the years of the mortgage can produce savings for the

BPP
LEARNING MEDIA

customer, so that they can repay their loan earlier and more flexibly than if the home loan and current account were maintained separately.

2.4.5 Islamic mortgage

Mortgages are interest-based and this is something that does not conform to the Islamic **Sharia law**. Therefore Muslims in the UK seeking to comply with Sharia law have found themselves in a difficult position as a mortgage contravenes their faith and, due to the nature of the financial services industry, if they wish to own their home, they have had no choice in many cases but reluctantly to take out a mortgage. However, some lenders do now provide Sharia-compliant mortgage products.

Sharia-compliant products currently available in the UK are based on Ijara and Murabaha methods. Under an Ijara finance plan, the customer chooses the property and agrees a price with the vendor in the normal way. The property is then purchased by the financier, who takes its legal title. The property is then sold on to the customer at the original price, with payment spread over an agreed period of time. During that time, the customer also pays the financier rent for the use of the property. Once the agreed period of time has elapsed, ownership of the property is transferred to the customer. By following this arrangement, the lender makes money from the rent that the customer pays to them. As rent is not another name for interest, it is seen to be a fair payment for living in a property that is owned by the financial institution, rather than being a charge for borrowing money.

Under a Murabaha plan, the customer chooses the property and agrees the price with the vendor in the normal way. Similarly, the financier then purchases the property from the vendor, but on the day of completion it is immediately sold on to the customer at a higher price. The higher price is determined by the value of the property, and the number of years that the financier allows the purchase price to be paid over and the amount of the first payment. The customer then makes regular monthly payments until the purchase price is paid.

2.4.6 Equity release products

The term 'equity' in this context refers to the difference in value between the market value of a property and the total value of the mortgage and other loans secured on the property. **Equity release** enables a customer to borrow some proportion of this equity, freeing up capital that is otherwise 'locked in' until the property is sold.

Equity release can be facilitated in various ways:

- **Conventional mortgage or remortgage**. This entails the customer making a conventional application for the amount required, which the lender then assesses against its lending criteria. For example, an applicant who owes £50,000 on a home valued at £200,000 would typically be able to raise up to £130,000, assuming that the lender is prepared to make a 90% loan available and that the applicant's financial circumstances confirm that the new level of debt can be afforded. Under the FCA's conduct of business rules for mortgages (MCOB), the lender must take account of both affordability and suitability.

- **Second mortgage**. The customer may take out a second mortgage with a lender other than the current mortgagee. This can be an unwise step, as it is usually more expensive to do so, but it may reflect the current mortgagee's reluctance to lend more and perhaps the borrower's pressing need to release equity due to other financial commitments.

- **Lifetime mortgage**. Older borrowers may consider a lifetime mortgage. Generally, these mortgages are designed for those over 55 years of age. Most are taken out by those who have no current outstanding mortgage commitments. There will be restrictions on the amount that can be borrowed in this way. Most lifetime mortgages have no expiry date but are repaid on death or when the property is sold or permanently vacated.

- **Home reversion plan**. The customer may consider a home reversion plan, which involves selling all or part of the property to the finance provider. The occupant then becomes a tenant for life, or until the property is sold or permanently vacated. It is therefore not a loan. Although a home reversion plan enables the owner of the property to raise more cash than under a lifetime mortgage, the amount raised will be significantly less than the market value of the property. Conventional equity release mortgages, lifetime mortgages and home reversion plans are regulated under the MCOB rules. Most second mortgages are regulated by the Consumer Credit Acts 1974 and 2006.

2.4.7 Bridging loans

A **bridging loan** is a short-term loan used to cover the situation where a customer has to pay for a major purchase before receiving the proceeds of a major sale. The most frequently encountered example of a bridging loan is when a customer is involved in the purchase and sale of property.

Imagine the situation where a customer has agreed to purchase a house on 1 July, intending to finance this purchase from the sale of their present home as well as taking out a house purchase loan. However, it is extremely rare to buy and sell two homes on the same date. Therefore, if they have agreed with the purchaser of their old home that settlement of this transaction will take place on 7 July, they will be substantially out of pocket for the period 1 – 7 July. This is where they would use a bridging loan.

The bridging loan is used to cover the period when the customer has paid for the new house, but is still waiting to receive the sale proceeds of the old house. Interest is charged on a daily basis and is applied to the bridging loan account. The lender will also require that the customer provides an irrevocable mandate in the form of a letter addressed to the customer's solicitor informing them to remit the free sale proceeds to the bank. It is called an irrevocable mandate as part of this letter will state that the customer cannot revoke, or cancel, this instruction. Once these proceeds are received, they are credited to the bridging loan account, which then has the interest applied to it before being closed off. Normally a bridging loan is only required for a matter of days. Bridging loans are now becoming less popular products for banks to provide.

2.4.8 Mortgage Market Review: lenders' responsibilities

Proposals for major reforms of the domestic mortgage market were issued in 2009 and 2010, as part of the regulator's **Mortgage Market Review (MMR)**. Most of the changes came into effect on **26 April 2014**. The changes reflect the regulator's move to a more intrusive style of supervision and seek to reform a market whose weaknesses formed an underlying cause of the financial crisis of the late 2000s.

The FCA has stated: 'It had become clear by the height of the market in 2007 that, while the mortgage market had worked well for many people, it had been a cause of severe hardship for others. The regulatory framework in place at the time had proved to be ineffective in constraining particularly high-risk lending and borrowing. The MMR package of reforms is aimed at ensuring the continued access to mortgages for the great majority of customers who can afford it, while preventing a return to the poor practices of the past.'

Lenders had already been responding to the problems arising from the financial crisis by applying more stringent checks in the mortgage application process. Because of this, the MMR changes are not likely to result in major changes to lenders' practices.

MMR: changes for lenders

- Lenders are now **fully responsible for verifying the income of a mortgage applicant**, and for scrutinising their finances, in order to assess whether the customer will be able to afford the repayments over the first five years of the loan. Lenders can still choose to use intermediaries in this process, but lenders remain responsible. (Intermediaries such as financial advisers were previously responsible for assessing affordability.) Less stringent affordability checks apply to high net worth borrowers.

- New affordability guidelines include '**stress testing**', which checks **how mortgage applicants would manage with a rise in interest rates**. Lenders have flexibility in deciding the interest rate to apply for the test. Many lenders are already using 7% as a yardstick in this test.

- Lenders are still allowed to grant **interest-only loans**, but only where there is a **'credible strategy' for repaying the capital**. Placing reliance on anticipated house price rises will not be sufficient.

- There are **transitional provisions** in the MMR that allow lenders to provide a new mortgage or deal to customers with existing loans who may not meet the new MMR requirements for the loan. The borrowing is not able to exceed the amount of their current loan, unless funding is required for essential repairs. The decision on whether or not to lend in these cases remains with the lender.

2.4.9 Mortgage Credit Directive

This EU Directive on credit agreements relating to residential property came into force on 20 March 2014. Member States have two years to implement this Directive into national law. Although the Directive accords fairly closely with the **MMR rules**, some changes may result from the implementation of the Directive.

QUICK QUESTION

What types of loans and mortgages does your bank offer?

Write your answer here before reading on.

2.5 Credit card accounts

A **credit card** account allows the customer to buy goods and services and pay for them at a later date using a credit card.

The two main **brands** of credit cards are **MasterCard** and **Visa**. MasterCard and Visa are multinational corporations that process transactions on behalf of merchants and card issuers, but these corporations do not themselves issue cards. Various financial services organisations issue their own branded versions of one or other of these types of card.

To obtain a credit card account, the customer must complete an application form which is credit scored by the bank as part of their credit assessment process. If the application is successful, the customer will be issued with a credit card and advised of their credit limit. This is the maximum balance that the customer may have on their credit card account.

The customer receives a **statement** from the credit card company monthly and has the option of either paying the entire balance or making a payment towards the balance. The **minimum payment** that the customer may make is generally 5% of the outstanding balance or £5, whichever is the greater. The period of time that the customer has to make this payment varies from card to card and is between 15 days and 25 days.

Should the customer choose not to repay the entire balance of the account, they will be charged interest by the credit card company. As the rates of interest tend to be relatively high, credit cards are usually considered to be an expensive form of consumer credit.

3 The customer life cycle

As we all have different financial needs at different stages of our lives, the products and services offered by a bank will be aimed at personal customers in a particular life stage, or businesses and companies at a certain stage in their development.

Taking personal customers as an example, a couple raising children may look for efficient ways of borrowing money for a car or home improvements. Once the children have grown up and left home, the couple's needs are more likely to be focused on saving as they should have more money to invest than they did when the children were at home.

The five main **life stages** identified by marketers are:

- Youth
- Independent
- Family
- Empty nesters
- Retirement

Youth. This is an attractive market as once an individual commences a relationship with a bank they are likely to stay for a long time. It is also easier for the bank to develop business with existing customers than it is to go out to the market and win new customers. A number of banks offer bespoke products aimed at this market.

Independent. These are young people who are likely to be earning, but have no dependants. They represent the transition between youth and family and are likely to have some short term savings goals, such as saving for a car, holidays or a deposit for house purchase.

Family. It is unlikely that this group will have much additional income to set aside in a savings account. If they do save, it will probably be for short term expenses like holidays. Some may have a longer term savings goal to fund their children's education.

Empty nesters. This is the stage where a couple can still be earning, but where their children have left home. As a result of this transition, their disposable income will be greater than in the last stage and they are likely to have the greatest opportunity to focus on savings and investments. Some of their additional disposable income may go on holidays and entertainment.

Retirement. This is the stage where savings are generally used as a source of income and this group would be interested primarily in gaining a good return on these savings. By using the life cycle approach, a bank can build and nurture relationships with its customers over a long period and maximise opportunities to keep these customers and obtain referrals from them.

Pause for thought ...

Which life stage are you at?

What do you want from your bank?

Now think about other people you know. Which life stage are they at? What do you think they might want from their bank?

What products and services does your bank offer? Who is each product or service aimed at? What does having this product or service allow the customer to do or have? What does it give them? Write some examples in the table below.

Product	Who it is for?	What it gives them

4 Other services

4.1 Foreign exchange

Most retail banks offer foreign exchange services. Customers may consider these services when planning to travel abroad on holiday or business.

The larger banks maintain a stock of notes for the most widely used **currencies**, eg US dollars and euros, in their branches, and can order other currencies to be delivered at reasonably short notice.

Travellers' cheques are much less common than they used to be as credit and debit cards can be used in most countries, but they may still be used by those travelling to certain destinations. These can be used for foreign exchange or to purchase goods and services, although relatively few businesses now accept them in most places. Banks may offer travellers' cheques issued by major providers such as American Express and Thomas Cook.

Financial institutions can also facilitate transactions in foreign currencies by offering **SWIFT** (Society for Worldwide Interbank Financial Telecommunication) electronic transfers and by issuing foreign currency drafts. Business customers making large volumes of transactions in foreign currencies may use the services of an International Division of a major bank, which will invariably offer a comprehensive service, including bills of exchange, letters of credit and documentary credits.

Key terms

key term

A **bill of exchange** is a document demanding payment.

A **letter of credit** is a document issued by a bank on behalf of a customer authorising payment to a supplier when the conditions specified in the document are met.

A **documentary credit** is a credit document used in export trade, when a bank issues a letter of credit against shipping documents.

4.2 Insurance services

Insurance business is a natural extension of deposit-taking and lending services, and many customers find it convenient to arrange all their financial requirements in one place.

Insurance services can be provided by banks in two ways.

- Banks who own insurance companies operate them as subsidiaries within their banking group.

- Banks may sell the products and services of other companies, in which case they receive a commission based on sales and the level of administration undertaken.

As we discovered in Chapter 1 of this Study Text, there are the following two types of insurance.

- **General insurance** is concerned with the probability of specified events occurring, such as damage to the home from fire, car accidents, business interruption due to flooding, and so on. These events may occur once, several times, or never.

- **Life assurance** is concerned with certainty. Life assurance contracts envisage only two possibilities: either the policyholder will survive the period in which the policy is in force, or will die.

Some companies offer only general insurance and some offer only life assurance. Companies that offer both are called composite companies. It is no longer possible to form a composite company in the UK, although it is possible for one company to own separate subsidiary companies within its group.

As the need for protection against sickness, accidents and unemployment is usually reviewed alongside the need for life cover, many companies that offer life assurance policies also offer policies for income protection and critical illness, for example. Life assurance companies may also offer personal pensions and life assurance investment funds.

4.2.1 General insurance

Key general insurance products available are:

- Household insurance
- Payment protection insurance
- Income protection insurance
- Travel insurance
- Car insurance
- Pet insurance

Household insurance. Most home owners need a mortgage in order to purchase the property, and continuous buildings insurance for full reinstatement value of the property is generally a minimum requirement in the mortgage deed. This requirement helps to protect the value of the lender's security against the loan. Reinstatement value covers rebuilding of the property in the event of destruction, for example by fire. Reinstatement value may be greater, or less than, the market value of the property, and is generally calculated from tables of typical rebuilding costs per square metre. Mortgage providers usually offer a package, combining buildings and contents cover. The insurance value is uplifted on an annual basis, with premiums index-linked to provide for this. Most financial institutions are also prepared to offer these policies to customers who have mortgages elsewhere, or no mortgage at all.

Payment protection insurance. When a customer takes out a loan, it can be desirable that the repayment is protected should the customer suffer sickness or accident, or becomes unemployed. Payment protection policies can provide for the repayments due on loans to be covered for up to two years should any of these misfortunes arise. These policies are run in tandem with personal loans, credit cards and mortgages. However, providers are no longer allowed to offer this type of protection at the time of sale. Instead, there must be a gap of at least **seven days** between the credit facility being provided and the payment protection insurance being offered. This type of cover is particularly important for new mortgage customers to consider, as claims for Income Support are subject to a waiting period. Policies are sometimes referred to as Mortgage Payment Protection Insurance (MPPI) and should not be confused with term life assurance which could be to pay off a mortgage in the event of the borrower's death.

Income protection insurance. This type of insurance used to be referred to as permanent health insurance. It provides income replacement in the event that the insured person cannot work due to illness. Cover is usually expressed as a percentage of regular income. The cover is permanent in the sense that any number of claims can be made. Related to this is critical illness insurance, which provides for a cash sum to be paid if the policyholder is diagnosed with a specified serious illness, such as heart disease, cancer, kidney disease or a stroke. The customer is often made aware of these policies during a fact find interview when considering other needs such as life assurance and pensions.

Travel insurance. Many families take holidays abroad and travel insurance provides protection in the event that medical and other costs are incurred. Policies vary widely in the scope of cover, but most include protection against flight delays and cancellations, repatriation in the event of serious injury and illness, loss of plastic cards and theft. Some companies offer specialised policies covering winter sports and other hazardous pursuits. A further product that some financial institutions make available is vehicle breakdown cover for those travelling abroad on driving holidays.

Car insurance. Unless a motorist is prepared to place a surety of £500,000 with the Accountant General of the Supreme Court, third party liability car insurance is mandatory for drivers. Many banks offer car insurance, mainly through agency arrangements.

Cover can be arranged at the following main levels:

- Third party only
- Third party, fire and theft
- Comprehensive

Pet insurance. Pet insurance is designed to mitigate the sometimes significant costs of veterinary treatment for pets. Policies can be purchased to cover illness and injury to most popular types of pet, such as cats and dogs.

Business customers may require advice on additional general insurance products, including business interruption, key person, professional indemnity and commercial property insurances.

4.2.2 Life assurance

The main life products available are:

- Term assurance
- Whole of life assurance, and
- Endowment assurance

Term assurance is the least expensive form of life cover as it provides for a cash sum (or, less commonly, a regular income) to be paid in the event of death if death occurs during the contracted term. Most mortgage borrowers take out a term assurance in order to ensure that the mortgage is paid off if the borrower dies. This is one of the simplest types of term assurance. If the loan is a capital and interest mortgage, the sum assured reduces as the capital is gradually paid off and for this reason is called **decreasing term assurance**. Other types of term assurance include level term assurance, increasing term assurance and family income benefit assurance. For all types of term assurance, if the policyholder survives the term, nothing is payable, but it is possible to take out a new policy subject to underwriting acceptance. For an extra premium, it is possible to purchase renewable term assurance which ensures that the policy can be renewed on expiry (subject to certain conditions).

Whole of life assurance provides for a cash sum on death, whenever the death occurs. As everyone has to die eventually, the policy is certain to pay out provided the premiums are maintained. These policies are generally more expensive than term assurances. Whole of life policies became popular during the Industrial Revolution, with policyholders contributing small regular premiums, often to doorstep collectors. The policies provided funds necessary for funeral expenses and perhaps a sum to help the family in the short term following bereavement. These policies were referred to as industrial insurances. Many of the 'over-50' plans advertised are types of whole of life assurance. Some financial institutions offer packaged whole of life products, such as funeral prepayment plans, but the majority of whole of life sales are concluded following a fact finding interview where each customer's needs are considered on an individual basis.

Endowment assurance combines long term investment with life assurance. A death benefit is decided in advance, and this is guaranteed to be paid should the policyholder die during the term of the policy. However, endowment policies also include an investment element designed to provide a cash sum on expiry. Endowment policies were once popular for borrowers taking out interest only mortgages, but disappointing investment performance during the 1990s had an adverse effect on the finances of many investors. For this reason, endowment mortgages are rarely considered by borrowers today.

QUICK QUESTION

What types of insurance services does your bank offer?

Write your answer here before reading on.

5 Pension plans

It is highly desirable for those who do not invest in an occupational pension through their employers to consider pension provision as early as possible. The life and pensions subsidiaries of financial institutions offer defined contribution plans that enable a pension fund to be built up, usually over 30 - 40 years. The investment objectives are to provide for a tax-free cash sum on retirement and a regular (taxable) pension thereafter.

A specific variation on the personal pension plan is the **stakeholder pension plan**. This concept, involving capped charges, low minimum contributions and easy transfers, was introduced by the government in order to encourage those in lower income groups to make some provision for retirement.

These products offer no guarantee of a minimum pension, but are a reasonably tax-efficient method of investing, as the Government provides tax relief on contributions at the investor's highest marginal income tax rate (subject to lifetime investment limits). Against this, it should be borne in mind that, after a 25% tax-free lump sum is normally taken, the pension income drawn down is taxable.

Pension needs are usually considered during a broad-based fact-find interview. Business customers may consider setting up group arrangements for life assurance and pension products on behalf of their employees. However, pension plans are only one way of saving for retirement: saving through **ISAs**, for example, is an alternative.

In spite of the Government's wish for people to make their own retirement provision and not to rely wholly on State provision, there are still many who have not made any private pension arrangement.

Auto-enrolment, which is being phased in over the period 2012-2017, means that employees will be automatically enrolled into a qualifying pension by their employer, unless the worker opts out.

QUICK QUESTION

What payment systems do you use and for what?

Write your answer here before reading on.

6 Payment methods

Over the years, banks have devised and delivered a range of payment methods to enable them to deal with customers' transactions. There are three key parties to a payment system:

- The customer
- The trader or retailer
- The bank

Payment systems include:

- Cash
- Cheques
- Debit cards
- Credit cards
- Automated payments, eg standing orders, direct debits

6.1 Cash

Cash is the oldest method of payment and is used mainly for smaller amounts.

6.2 Cheques

A **cheque** is a written instruction that orders the bank to pay a third party the amount stated from a bank account. The person writing the cheque, the **drawer**, usually has a current account where their money was previously deposited. The drawer writes on the cheque the details required, including the monetary amount, date, and a payee. The **payee** is the person or company to whom the money is to be paid. They then sign it as an order to the bank (the drawee) to pay that person or company the amount of money stated.

When a cheque is issued, it can take some time to reach the bank account on which it was drawn, so how does a cheque find its way from the customer's cheque book to their bank account?

The method of clearing cheques may vary from bank to bank but the basic principles are the same. When a cheque is issued, typically, the payee of the cheque takes it to their bank and has their account credited. The cash paid in does not need to clear or be confirmed by anyone.

Cheques paid in fall into two categories:

- Those that have been drawn on the same branch of the bank as the one where the payee is making the lodgement (sometimes called house cheques)

- Those that have been drawn on other branches and other banks

Cheques that have been drawn on the branch of the bank where the payee is paying it in should not be too difficult to deal with. The banker decides whether they will be paid or dishonoured; if a cheque is to be paid, it will be debited to the drawer's account. If any cheque is to be dishonoured, it will be returned to the person making the deposit, or lodgement. As soon as a house cheque has been paid, the payee can have full credit for its proceeds.

Cheques drawn on other banks and branches are not quite as straightforward. Such cheques must be directed to the account-holding banks and branches so that they can be paid (or not). There is a potential problem here for both the payee and the payee's bank because:

- The payee has provided goods or services but even when the cheques received from customers are lodged to their account, it is still not certain that they have been paid.

- The bank has permitted funds to be credited to the account in the name of the payee, but has no guarantee that the account will not have to be debited at a later date should the cheques not be honoured when they are presented to the respective account-holding banks.

The proceeds of cheques that have not yet been paid by the drawee bank are known as uncleared funds or uncleared effects. Banks will accept uncleared funds for lodgement into an account and the amount will immediately be added to the balance of the customer's account. Whether or not the customer can withdraw any uncleared funds will depend on the terms and conditions of their account.

Most retailers no longer accept cheques as a method of payment due to the delay in payment caused by the clearing cycle and the cost of processing.

Some banks have wanted to replace this rather labour-intensive method of payment. However, a plan to phase out cheques has been abandoned and they will continue to be provided for as long as they are needed.

6.3 Debit cards

Debit cards can be used to:
- Guarantee payment of a cheque
- Pay for goods and services
- Obtain cash from an account from some retailers when making purchases
- Withdraw cash and access other services from an automated teller machine (ATM)

When the customer is paying with their debit card, they may also obtain cash from their account from the retailer. This is called 'cashback'. This facility is available mainly from supermarkets.

There are two main advantages for the retailer.

- As they make cashback payments to customers, they are reducing the cash held in their tills which is an added security measure.

- As the retailer's cash holdings are reduced, they will have less physical cash to pay in to their bank, thus reducing the cash handling aspect of any service charge that their bank will charge them.

A debit card can also be used for ATM cash withdrawals, where the card is used in conjunction with a personal identification number (PIN).

A number of additional services are available from most ATM machines, including:

- Balance enquiries
- Make a deposit
- Mini statements

- Cheque book requests
- Alteration of PIN number
- Top up a mobile phone

6.4 Credit cards and other payment methods

A credit card allows the customer to buy goods and services and pay for them at a later date.

Credit card issuers generate income from:

- Commission charged to retailers who accept the card as a method of payment

- Interest charged to cardholders who do not repay their balance in full within a certain number of days of their credit card account statement date

Cardholders can choose whether to repay the full balance on their statement or to repay only 5% of it. Interest is charged monthly on the outstanding balance and is calculated from the date of each transaction.

Electronic funds transfer

Key terms

Electronic funds transfer (EFT) is the electronic exchange, transfer of money from one account to another, either within a single financial institution or across multiple institutions, through computer-based systems. When customers use a payment card to pay for goods and services at the point of sale, this is a form of EFT. Examples are a credit card, debit card, or electronic purse.

The card is swiped through a card reader and the customer is required to input their personal identification number (PIN) on a keypad. The transaction is then debited from the customer's account, credit card or electronic purse to complete the transaction.

An **electronic purse** is a plastic card with a small amount of money stored electronically on it, which can be used instead of cash to pay for things. Money is credited to the card via an electronic reader. A Transport for London Oystercard is an example of an electronic purse. As the card is used, the sum of money is reduced, until it comes to zero, when it needs to be topped up again.

The main benefits of an electronic purse are that:

- Customers can only spend what is on the card

- If the card is lost or stolen, the maximum exposure to loss is the balance on the card at that time

- There is no need for a live link to the customer's bank account at the time that the card is used – the amount spent is deducted from the card

6.5 Automated payments: standing orders and direct debits

Automated payments include standing orders and direct debits. Standing orders and direct debits are payments that the customer arranges to be made in advance. They are usually used for regular payments from an account. They are therefore called pre-authorised payments. Once set up, the payments are made automatically from the account, provided the customer has sufficient funds available to meet the payments.

With a **standing order**, the bank, acting on behalf of the person making the payment, will initiate the payment and will remit it directly to the bank account of the beneficiary (the person or company receiving the payment).

With a **direct debit**, the process happens almost in reverse where the beneficiary's bank initiates the payment and raises a claim against the payer's bank account. The end result is the same in that a payment is made from the payer's account into the beneficiary's account. In order for this to happen, the original instruction for a direct debit to be made must be signed by the payer to authorise the debits from their account.

Standing orders are used for regular payments for fixed amounts (for example, a subscription). An important difference between standing orders and direct debits is that a direct debit can be set up for a variable amount on an unspecified date. This allows the beneficiary to decide on the amount of the payment and also on the date on which the payment will be made.

The main advantage of an **unspecified** or **'variable direct debit'** is that, if the amount or payment date needs to change, this can still happen within the terms of the direct debit instruction, or mandate, although the beneficiary is required to give the payer notice of any changes. Having such a system means that the payment does not need to be amended, although, when using a standing order, it does have to be amended if the amount changes. Such an arrangement is ideal for mortgage payments which may alter in line with interest rate changes.

6.6 Faster Payments

Most banks now offer customers the **Faster Payments** service where it is possible to make automated payments that will reach the beneficiary's account quickly. The instruction may be made through the internet or by telephone.

Although banks have offered same-day payments services in the past (through the Clearing House Automated Payments System), these have been targeted at high-value transactions, such as in the settlement of house purchases and sales. With Faster Payments, up to £2,500 can be sent per transaction, although individual banks may impose lower limits, typically of £100,000 or less.

Faster Payments was launched in 2008. By the end of 2011, over 85% of phone and internet payments were being processed through Faster Payments.

The types of payments that can be processed through the Faster Payments service include:

- Single immediate payments, where the customer instructs the payment using online or telephone banking, or from a branch

- Forward-dated payments, where the customer sets up a payment to be made at a future date, eg to pay a credit card bill

- Standing orders

Single immediate payments made using Faster Payments must be made available in the receiving customer account within two hours, but generally is available within minutes.

7 Customer contact centres and internet banking

7.1 Overview

Customer contact centres are centralised service units that deal with customers mainly by telephone. They typically employ large numbers of people in a number of customer service teams.

The traditional organisational model of a bank had a head office at its hub, with departments configured on functional lines. For example, a bank would have an investment department, a credit department, an insurance department, and so on. More decentralised organisations maintained smaller head office departments and branch offices with large numbers of staff.

During the 1980s and 1990s, banks began to take a more holistic view of customer needs in an attempt to build multiple product relationships over longer periods of time. The fragmented approach to different types of product that existed at the time meant that it was necessary for customers to deal with different parts of the organisation, often having to make numerous calls or write numerous letters. The contact centre emerged as a way of servicing customer requirements irrespective of the nature of enquiry or need. In turn, banks benefited by no longer having to maintain large, specialised departments in head offices and branches. Customers could deal with their needs in one interaction and providers could save costs and other resources.

Some banks have set up their contact centres overseas to take advantage of lower labour costs. This has been particularly beneficial to the economies of countries that have highly educated workforces with a strong tradition in spoken English. It is generally accepted, however, that this has created some cultural difficulties, to the extent that some organisations now openly advertise that their centres are located in the UK. Other banks have outsourced their contact centres to external organisations.

The early contact centres dealt with routine transactions and provided telemarketing services. Today they provide a much wider range of services, as in the following examples.

7.2 Transactions

Customers who do not wish to visit a branch or use the internet can often carry out transactions by calling the contact centre. The service provided is no longer confined to routine transactions, as contact centres are organised so that they can deal with most types of business referred to them.

7.3 Information

The customer service advisers in contact centre teams have access to most of the information required to answer most types of query and deal with most types of problem. Furthermore, advances in telephony have enabled contact centre systems to install predictive models that can identify the incoming call number and, using data gathered from previous calls from the same number, direct the call to the team most likely to be able to deal with it.

Contact centres are now used by providers of quite complex products, such as long-term investments, shares and pensions, in order to provide information to customers and facilitate access to expert advice.

7.4 Automated responses

Most contact centres deploy a menu-driven answering facility which enables the caller to select the most appropriate service. In this way, customers can obtain information about, for example, their current balance, recent transactions, and credit available, without the need to speak to a person. Alternatively, customers may select the menu option to speak with a customer service adviser.

7.5 Telemarketing

Contact centres have access to vast databases, enabling their people and systems to anticipate and predict customer needs. Products and services can therefore be matched to customer profiles based on the information held. This helps to ensure that relevant products and services are flagged as being of potential interest to a particular customer. As it is generally more profitable to sell to existing customers than to recruit new customers, the contact centre is an important marketing resource for certain products and services.

7.6 Telemarketing to non-customers

FCA rules impose restrictions on cold calling (unsolicited calls to individuals who are not customers). Such calls must be made at an 'appropriate' time of day. The caller must identify himself and his firm, and make his purpose clear. The caller must clarify whether the client wants to continue or terminate the communication, and terminate it on request at any time.

7.7 Arrears management

Contact centres are used by some banks to contact customers who have missed a loan repayment and whose loan accounts have therefore fallen into arrears. This enables the adviser to work with the customer to deal with the problem if it is a short-term one, and to provide basic advice on how to deal with it.

7.8 Internet banking

Internet banking is perhaps the most important technological innovation from the 1990s. It enables most types of interaction with a bank to be carried out online instead of having to visit a branch or phone a contact centre.

Although the internet was 'invented' in the late 1950s, it was the late 1980s when it began to be exploited commercially. The first mass-marketed personal computers were launched in 1985, and the cost of the hardware was prohibitive until the early 1990s. Although internet banking was envisaged as a possibility, there were several impediments to its development:

- The costs of hardware fell very slowly
- Software was not especially user-friendly until Windows-based systems were developed
- There were major concerns about security and integrity of data
- Early internet systems relied on dial-up which was slow and inconvenient
- Customers were used to the more traditional ways of doing things

The major developments that rapidly accelerated the growth of internet banking were:

- Significant reductions in prices of hardware and software from the mid-1990s onwards

- Massive investment in new systems by banks and software suppliers

- Development of new security systems which gradually led to an increase in consumer confidence

- A general growth in computer literacy, especially among the young

- The introduction of broadband

- The development of new ways of accessing the internet, such as smart phones, tablets and netbooks

Banks quickly learned that the internet could provide a robust business model that would operate alongside (or sometimes instead of) conventional channels to market, lowering costs and relieving pressure on management time currently consumed by routine matters. Internet banking is advantageous to the customer in the range of facilities available online to:

- Access balances
- View transactions
- View/amend standing orders and direct debits
- Request payments to be made from their account
- Apply and receive approval in principle by completing applications for products and services online

Most types of transaction can be carried out, with the notable exception of being able to access instant cash. This problem has been overcome to some extent by the ability to transfer funds in real time or at very short notice, so that money can be transferred to an account that is accessible by ATM.

Banks can also use the internet to provide information for customers and shareholders, and some use e-voting for their general meetings. As databases have become more sophisticated, products and services can be targeted more precisely and more quickly to respond to customer needs, or even anticipate their needs. E-mail has taken over much of the role that the Royal Mail once routinely performed. With these exciting developments in technology, new challenges have arisen for both customers and service providers.

The greatest problems are concerned with security. Just as those using cheque books and bank guarantee/ATM cards had to learn new safeguards, such as keeping the cheque book and card separate and not revealing the PIN to anyone, those using internet banking services have to be fully aware of the possibility of fraud and theft.

For this reason, banks have had to devote considerable resources to educate the public on matters such as:

- The need to keep the username and password secret

- The importance of not storing confidential information on the hard disk

- The need to take extra care when using a laptop in less secure facilities, such as wi-fi networks in airports and hotels

- The dangers of spam mail through which 'phishers', purporting to be service providers, request that the user confirms usernames and passwords, often in the guise of security alerts

- The problems of other menaces such as 'pharming', through which fraudsters attempt to clone official sites and overlay them with bogus pages

It is generally accepted that, just as service providers continue to develop systems that will thwart criminals, the criminals themselves are becoming more sophisticated. For example, it was once assumed that chip and PIN technology would solve many problems of using cards at the point of sale, but there have been many cases of criminals successfully overcoming the security systems.

The advances in technology mean that there are various ways in which customers can do business with their bank; in other words, many different delivery channels, including branches, contact centres, ATMs and the internet. One of the ways of providing excellent service to customers is by increasing their awareness of the options available so that they can choose the most convenient methods for them.

Pause for thought ...

In what different ways do you interact with your bank? What different delivery channels do you use and for what?

7.9 Financial technology (FinTech) sector

7.9.1 Overview

The **financial technology**, or '**FinTech**', sector is an industry comprising enterprises that create innovation in in financial services. The applications range from front-end consumer product providers, to new entrants competing with existing players, and even to the digital currency Bitcoin. Service areas within the FinTech sector encompass personal and business lending including peer-to-peer (P2P), payment services, currency exchange, investment management, and wealth management. Given its reliance on technology rather than 'bricks and mortar' institutions, FinTech offers opportunities for delivering genuinely global services.

The FinTech sector has seen rapid growth in recent years. Globally, investment in financial technology increased from $930 million in 2008 to more than $12 billion in 2014. $1.5 billion was invested in financial technology companies in Europe in 2014, and $540 million of this was invested in London-based FinTech companies.

The emerging sector is broad, with players including start-ups, existing banks, and major technology companies. Banks have for a long time been innovative in the use of technology and, while the sector is arguably ripe for disruption, the established banks are generally willing participants in FinTech innovations rather than being 'tech-shy dinosaurs'. This willingness is reflected in the various FinTech partnerships and acquisitions that are occurring.

Innovate Finance seeks to champion the UK as a global centre of FinTech innovation, raising awareness globally of the innovations emerging from the UK financial services sector, and cultivating opportunities for established financial services firms as well as for start-ups.

FinTech and data security. As well as established competitors, FinTech companies face challenges from financial regulators concerned about data security. There is the threat of hacking as well as the need to protect sensitive financial data on customers and corporate financial data. The online financial sector is increasingly a target of distributed denial of service extortion attacks. Any data breach can have a severe adverse effect on the reputation of a FinTech company. Nonetheless, many of the same security challenges face the traditional banking sector, which has moved extensively into internet banking services.

The future of FinTech is unclear, but it is likely that any distinction between traditional banking channels and Fintech developments will become increasingly blurred, resulting in a major shift in how finance will serve customers over time.

7.9.2 Examples

Among the most well-known FinTech companies based in London are FundingCircle, Nutmeg, and TransferWise.

- FundingCircle is a peer-to-peer (P2P) lending service that enables savers to lend money directly to small and medium sized businesses. Set up in 2010, it now operates in both US and UK markets.

- Nutmeg is an online discretionary investment management company. It is seeking to shake up the world of private banking by offering to manage personal wealth 'for a small, transparent fee' (ranging from 1% for funds investing as little as £1,000 down to 0.3% for those investing over £500,000). By 2015, in its first 3 years of operation, Nutmeg had reportedly attracted over 40,000 users.

- TransferWise is an Estonian-developed and UK-based peer-to-peer money transfer service that is headquartered in London, with offices in Tallinn and New York. TransferWise supports more than 300 currency routes across the world.

There are also many FinTech startups in the US, including Money.Net, Betterment, Lending Club, Behalf, Prosper, SoFi, Square, and Stripe.

7.9.3 Crowdfunding and its regulation

Online **crowdfunding**, or peer-to-peer (P2P) lending, is one of the main innovations fostered by the FinTech sector.

- **Crowdfunding** is a way in which people, organisations and businesses, including business start-ups, can raise money through online portals (called crowdfunding platforms) to finance or re-finance their activities. Money is subscribed mainly by individuals but also by institutions. Some crowdfunding activity is unregulated, some is regulated, and some is exempt from regulation.

- **Loan-based crowdfunding platforms** enable people to lend money to individuals or businesses in the hope of a financial return in the form of interest payments and a repayment of capital over time (this excludes some business-to-business loans). Such platforms raised £749 million in business loans and £547 million in consumer loans in 2014 (Source: Nesta). The most commonly cited reasons for personal loans are for buying a vehicle (46%), making home improvements (26%), and consolidating debt (25%). The average business loan was £73,000 (2014) and an emerging trend is secured lending for real estate mortgages and developments, with some platforms specialising in this type of business.

BPP
LEARNING MEDIA

The FCA is responsible for regulating loan-based crowdfunding platforms. As well as core consumer protection requirements such as minimum capital standards and client money protections, the regulator seeks to protect investors in the loan-based crowdfunding market by ensuring that consumers interested in lending to individuals or businesses have access to clear information. This allows them to assess the risk and to understand who will ultimately borrow the money. The FCA also requires firms running these platforms to have resolution plans in place so that, if the platform collapses, loan repayments will continue to be collected so that those lending money do not lose out.

- **Investment-based crowdfunding platforms** enable people to invest in unlisted shares or debt securities issued by businesses. These instruments (termed 'non-readily realisable securities') are not listed on regulated stock markets and can carry significant risks.

   The FCA also regulates investment-based crowdfunding platforms. The regulator requires that firms may only make direct offer promotions to retail consumers who: take regulated advice; or who qualify as high net worth or sophisticated investors; or who confirm they will invest less than 10% of their net assets in this type of security.

- **FCA supervision** of investment-based crowdfunding platforms has included engaging with firms' senior management, monitoring their websites and reviewing monthly management information (MI). This approach has resulted in a number of regulatory interventions that have been mainly to ensure the protection of consumers. The FCA has taken a similar approach with loan-based crowdfunding platforms. However, additional forward-looking supervisory visits were undertaken to assess the governance, management and controls of five market participants to understand the risk that the sector poses to the regulator's statutory objectives.

CASE STUDY

Established financial services companies have linked up with FinTech startups. For example, in the US, Fidelity Investments and TD Ameritrade have partnered with FutureAdvisor, which was acquired by BlackRock.

The FutureAdvisor service offers to manage the investor's retirement accounts, taxable accounts, and other investment accounts. The service automatically monitors, re-balances, and tax-manages current investments, adding low-fee index funds where necessary to 'bolster the portfolio'. If the customer's accounts are already with Fidelity or TD Ameritrade, FutureAdvisor is a 'management layer you add over your existing accounts'. If the accounts are held elsewhere, FutureAdvisor processes the paperwork to transfer them to Fidelity or TD Ameritrade.

8 Providing a high quality service

8.1 Introduction

When thinking about customer service it is useful to consider what we personally regard as being good and bad service.

Pause for thought ...

Think of a time when you received really great service from someone.

What specifically was it about the experience that made it great?

How did you know you were getting great service?

How did you feel as a result of this experience?

As a result of this experience, would you do business with that person or company again?

Would you recommend this person or that company to others?

The reasons you perceived this experience as great will be unique to you.

Here are some factors that may contribute to a great service experience:

- Welcoming environment
- Was dealt with quickly and efficiently
- Person was pleasant, attentive, and helpful
- Person was knowledgeable and competent
- Person listened to me and was interested in finding out what I needed
- Left with the right product at the right price
- Expectations were exceeded
- Felt good about the experience

Now think about a time when you received really poor service.

What specifically was it about the experience that made it so poor?

How did you know you were getting poor service?

How did you feel as a result of this experience?

As a result of this experience, would you do business with that person or company again?

Would you recommend this person or that company to others?

The reasons you perceived this experience as poor will be unique to you.

Generally, here are some factors that may contribute to a poor service experience:

- People who appear unhappy or miserable
- People being rude or grumpy
- Untidy or dirty environment
- Long queues
- Unavailability of products
- Someone stopping their conversation with you to answer the phone
- Being ignored
- People chatting to each other when you're waiting to be served
- Over-promising and under-delivering
- People making commitments that they did not follow through
- Being offered an inappropriate product
- Technology not working as it should
- Unsuitable opening hours.

8.2 What is good service?

When we buy a tangible product, there is usually an intangible experience associated with our purchase. It is this experience that leaves us with our impression of the service – what we think and how we feel about our interaction with the service provider.

We, as customers, can react differently to what appears to be the same service. Furthermore, the same customer can react differently to the same service in different circumstances. How we perceive service could be influenced by a variety of factors, for example, our previous experiences, our expectations, our thoughts – even our mood, that is, how we are feeling at the time. Service is therefore subjective.

Good service is based on perception. As such, providing great service to all customers at all times is a challenge for any service provider.

QUICK QUESTION

For what reasons is providing great service important to you and your bank?

Write your answer here before reading on.

Some good reasons for providing great service are that:

- It makes people feel good – customers and the people providing the service
- It's good for business
- It's good for team morale
- Customers will keep coming back
- Customers will recommend the bank to others
- Customers will buy other products and services from the bank
- It can give the bank a competitive advantage

Pause for thought ...

In what follows, there are some statements and aphorisms about customer service. Read them, think about them, and mark the one that appeals to you most. Or, visit some quotation websites (some of which attribute quotations inaccurately, it should be noted) and select your favourite quote from those.

What was your reason for choosing that particular quote?

If you are not serving the customer, your job is to serve someone who is.

Jan Carlzon, ex-CEO SAP Group

If you do build a great experience, customers tell each other about that. Word of mouth is very powerful.

Jeff Bezos, CEO Amazon.com

Make a customer, not a sale.

Katherine Barchetti

A customer is the most important visitor on our premises, he is not dependent on us. We are dependent on him. He is not an interruption in our work. He is the purpose of it. He is not an outsider in our business. He is part of it. We are not doing him a favour by serving him. He is doing us a favour by giving us an opportunity to do so.

Attribution uncertain – possibly Kenneth B. Elliott

We see our customers as invited guests to a party, and we are the hosts. It's our job every day to make every important aspect of the customer experience a little bit better.

Jeff Bezos, CEO Amazon.com

In our way of working, we attach a great deal of importance to humility and honesty; with respect for human values, we promise to serve our customers with integrity.

Azim Premji

Every company's greatest assets are its customers, because without customers there is no company.

Michael LeBoeuf, author of: How to Win Customers and Keep Them for Life

Service, in short, is not what you do, but who you are. It is a way of living that you need to bring to everything you do, if you are to bring it to your customer interactions.

Betsy Sanders

Every contact we have with a customer influences whether or not they'll come back. We have to be great every time or we'll lose them.

Kevin Stirtz

Here is a simple but powerful rule: always give people more than what they expect to get.

Nelson Boswell

There is only one boss. The customer. And he can fire everybody in the company from the chairman on down, simply by spending his money somewhere else.

Sam Walton, Founder of Wal-Mart

Revolve your world around the customer and more customers will revolve around you.

Heather Williams

The customer's perception is your reality.

Kate Zabriskie, author of: Customer Service Excellence:
How to Deliver Value to Today's Busy Customer

When the customer comes first, the customer will last.

Robert Half

Under-promise and over-deliver.

Toby Bloomberg

The purpose of a business is to create a customer who creates customers.

Shiv Singh

You are serving a customer, not a life sentence. Learn how to enjoy your work.

Laurie McIntosh

It starts with respect. If you respect the customer as a human being, and truly honour their right to be treated fairly and honestly, everything else is much easier.

Doug Smith

Customer service is not a department, it's everyone's job.

Anonymous

What main themes about customer service emerge from these quotes?

Factors that contribute to the provision of a quality service include:

- The desire to provide great service
- Treating customers as individuals
- Treating customers fairly and with respect
- Being ethical, professional and responsible
- Being accurate, reliable and courteous
- Being effective (doing the right things) and efficient (doing things right)
- Listening to customers and responding to their needs
- Knowing what customers want, need and expect from the bank's products and services
- Knowing what great service looks, sounds and feels like
- Knowing what your bank's products do for customers
- Knowing how your bank's products work
- Knowing how your bank's products compare with other banks' products
- Providing customers with products and services that meet their financial needs
- Designing and implementing efficient processes and delivery mechanisms
- Having the right number of people with the right skills in the right place at the right time

Pause for thought ...

Considering the factors in the list above, which ones are about:

- Knowing something?

- Doing something?

- Being a certain way when interacting with customers?

As you can see, providing great service is a combination of knowledge, skills and a way of being with customers.

Thinking about your role at work, which of the these factors do you have control over?

Which ones do you have no control over?

Depending on your role, you may have no or little control over the terms and conditions of your bank's products, the design of delivery mechanisms, bank policy or regulatory requirements. What you do have control over is the development of your own knowledge and skills and how you are with customers. You may also be able to influence the design of processes and procedures that support delivery of products and services to customers by looking for opportunities to improve service within the context of your role, perhaps through your bank's continuous improvement initiatives or by sharing your ideas with colleagues.

Pause for thought ...

Who are your customers at work? (Consider internal customers or colleagues as well as external customers.)

Think about a time when you provided great service to a customer.

What was the situation?

What did you do?

What was the outcome?

How did you feel at the time?

How do you know you provided a great service?

Put yourself in your customer's shoes. If they were asked what is was like doing business with you, what would they say?

Think about your role at work. What could you do to improve the service you personally provide to customers? For example:

What could you do to manage queues if you work in a branch?

What could you do to show that you respect and value your customer?

What could you do to handle complaints effectively?

8.3 Queue management

Customers are busy people and waiting in a long queue at a branch or on the telephone can be frustrating.

Queues can be managed more effectively as follows.

- During busy periods, having more colleagues available to serve customers, for example by reallocating resources in a branch or ensuring sufficient advisers in a contact centre are available at peak times.

BPP
LEARNING MEDIA

- In a branch, having someone approach each customer to find out what business they would like to transact and to ascertain if they actually need (or want) to wait in the queue for this or if there is an alternative solution. For example, if a customer wants to pay a credit card bill by cheque, the person 'walking the queue' could take this transaction and process it later.

- Educating customers about other delivery channels that suit their needs, such as the ATM, a Drop Box facility to make deposits, or online banking.

Some customers may be entirely aware of alternative delivery channels yet be quite happy to queue on the basis that they will get to interact with a person – and perhaps they prefer this to other forms of interaction with the bank.

8.4 Showing respect

We can show respect to customers by, for example:

- Feeling respect for customers
- Greeting them with a 'hello' or 'good morning/afternoon/evening'
- Smiling, whether face-to-face, or on the phone – we can hear a smile as well as see it
- Using the customer's name at the start and end of the conversation
- Giving the customer our name
- Being attentive – listening to the customer, making eye contact, giving them our full attention
- Answering calls quickly, eg after three rings at most
- Explaining what we're doing, especially if we need to leave them or put them on hold while we deal with their enquiry
- Providing privacy and maintaining confidentiality
- Asking, at the end of the conversation, if there is anything else we can help them with
- Thanking them at the end of the interaction

8.5 Transferring calls

When transferring a call to a colleague, explain this to the customer and, where possible, let them know the name of the person with whom they will be dealing. Give your colleague all the relevant information so that the customer does not have to repeat what they have just told you.

8.6 Providing the customer with privacy and confidentiality

When working in a bank, we are dealing with customers' financial affairs day in, day out. It can therefore be easy to fall into the trap of looking at our customers' financial affairs as being routine. However, customers will rightly expect their financial affairs to be kept confidential.

If the customer has called into the branch, be particularly aware of your duty to maintain the confidentiality of the information you are giving them. For example, if a customer has called in to request their account balance, the first thing you need to do is to verify that the customer is actually who they say they are. Once this has been checked, either print off the balance or note it on a slip of paper, fold it, and hand it over to the customer. Similarly, the customer may request this information over the phone. If it is your organisation's policy to give information in this way, you again need to verify the caller's identity before you do so.

You should always be aware that when working in an office that has customers visiting, you must take steps to ensure that when discussing other customers' details with colleagues or over the phone, this information cannot be overheard. This is one way of demonstrating professionalism and is a key component of customer service.

Confidentiality is key when conducting an interview with a customer. Taking them away from a public office and giving them the privacy of an interview room will help put the customer at ease, as they know that other customers will not overhear confidential information. It is also useful for you as you are more likely to have a better quality conversation with the customer. The more information you have about the customer, the easier it is for you to identify their needs and be able to meet those needs.

Another factor to consider is ensuring that confidential information is not left in sight of other customers. This is particularly important if, for example, you are working at a desk that is in the front office of a branch. Also, if you have been speaking to a customer in an interview area and are about to see another customer, always ensure that your desk is clear of confidential information before the next customer comes in. Any paper that has customer information on it should be carefully disposed of – preferably shredded. You should also be aware of the requirements of the *Data Protection Act 1998*.

Customers' affairs must not be discussed outside the office, nor with anyone outside the organisation. This is part of a banker's duty of confidentiality.

8.7 Image and presentation

One of the first and most lasting impressions of any organisation is the condition, tidiness and cleanliness of its premises. This is something we can all easily relate to as customers. Think of a time when you have thought about entering a shop and been put off by its untidy appearance.

The smartness and tidiness of a bank is a key way of communicating the organisation's image to current and potential customers. If a branch office is untidy, with the desks overflowing with paper, this may suggest to a potential customer that they are dealing with an inefficient organisation. An important aspect of customer service, therefore, is the presentation of your office.

8.8 External environment

The first impression that every current and potential customer has of your office is the external environment, therefore for this impression to be positive, the outside of the office must be clean, free of graffiti and any lit signs should be operational.

8.9 Internal environment

Make sure that:

- All publicity material on display is up to date and smartly presented
- Leaflet dispensers are full and neatly stocked
- Posters are hanging straight
- The office is well lit and all light bulbs operational
- There is adequate stock of customer stationery neatly displayed
- Pens for customer use are working
- Signage is clear
- Clocks and calendars are at the right date/time
- Any machinery for customer use is clean, eg ATMs, night safes, drop boxes
- The customer area is clean, tidy and litter-free
- Desks are tidy, with any excess papers and files stored out of sight

8.10 Serving customers who are vulnerable or who experience difficulty

8.10.1 Introduction

In February 2015, the FCA published an Occasional Paper No. 8 *Consumer vulnerability*. Much of this sub-section draws on material in this Occasional Paper.

The FCA recognises that many **consumers in vulnerable circumstances** are not receiving fair treatment from their financial services providers. While there are examples of good practice in some firms, some people find communicating with providers or accessing products difficult. They may find that they cannot get a flexible, tailored service that meets their needs from banks and other financial services firms. **Customers who experience difficulties** may find that providers seem ill-equipped with the skills and procedures that could help them. The regulator wants to help firms identify consumers in potentially vulnerable circumstances, and the FCA wants to try to identify what 'good' looks like in serving those consumers. The FCA emphasises that **fair treatment of all customers is central to core conduct**.

Much consumer protection legislation is underpinned by the **notion of the average or typical consumer**, and what that typical consumer might expect or understand, or how they might behave. However, consumers in vulnerable circumstances may be significantly less able to represent their own interests, and more likely to suffer harm than the average consumer. Regulators and firms need to ensure these consumers are adequately protected.

Financial services need to be able to **adapt to the changing circumstances** that real life throws at people, rather than being designed for the mythical perfect customer who never experiences difficulty. Vulnerability can affect people's interaction with any consumer market, but it is particularly challenging in the context of financial services due in part to the long-term nature of commitments, and the complexity of products and information.

The FCA has developed the following **definition** to guide its work in this area.

Key term

Vulnerable consumer. 'A vulnerable consumer is someone who, due to their personal circumstances, is especially susceptible to detriment, particularly when a firm is not acting with appropriate levels of care' *(FCA).*

8.10.2 Types of vulnerability

Vulnerability can come in various forms; it can be temporary, sporadic or permanent in nature. It is a fluid state that needs a flexible, tailored response from firms. Many people in vulnerable situations would not diagnose themselves as 'vulnerable'. We can all become vulnerable, at some point in our lives.

One way for firms to identify potential vulnerability and prioritise their efforts is to use a **risk factor approach**. Multi-layered vulnerability, and sudden changes in circumstances, are particular indicators of high risk.

The following list of vulnerabilities is not exhaustive, but are recognised to be 'proxies' associated with a range of circumstances contributing to financial detriment that may apply to consumers in a range of vulnerable circumstances.

- **Long-term / significant illness.** Individuals with a long-term or significant illness, covering a broad range of physical and mental health conditions.

- **Diagnosis of a critical illness.** Individuals, or their families, where diagnosis of a life-threatening condition may impact income and cause financial difficulty.

- **Carers.** Individuals acting as carers – either formally or informally – for people with a range of conditions, including old age, physical disabilities and learning disabilities.

- **Older people.** Individuals over the age of 65.

- **Low basic skills.** Individuals who struggle with literacy and / or numeracy, with or without the presence of a formally diagnosed learning difficulty.

- **Job loss / unemployment.** Individuals who are out of work, for a wide variety of reasons and lengths of time.

- **Bereavement.** Individuals who have recently lost a partner / spouse or a parent.

8.10.3 Causes and effects of vulnerability and difficulty

Vulnerability is not just to do with the situation of the consumer.

- It can be caused or exacerbated by the actions or processes of firms.
- The impact of vulnerability is strong and many people are trying to cope with difficult situations and limited resources, energy and time.

Stress can affect state of mind and the ability to manage effectively. In such conditions, being confronted by a complex telephone menu system that gives no option of talking to a person; a 'computer says no' response; a call handler without time or inclination to listen, or a system that fails to record what may be distressing circumstances and forces the customer to repeat themselves at every point of contact, can all create a spiral of stress and difficulty, resulting in detriment.

8.10.4 The incidence of vulnerability

The following facts can help to understand the extent of vulnerability in the customer base of a typical financial institution.

- **Literacy and numeracy**. One in seven adults has literacy skills that are expected of a child aged 11 or below. Just under half of UK adults have a numeracy attainment age of 11 or below (Department for Business, Innovation and Skills, 2012).
- **Internet**. Of the 7.1m adults in the UK that had never used the internet in May 2013, over half were disabled (3.7m) and nearly half were over 75 years of age (3.1m) (Department for Business, Innovation and Skills, 2013).
- **Savings**. Almost half of adults do not have enough savings to cover an unexpected bill of £300 (Money Advice Service).
- **Cancer**. Every two minutes, someone in the UK is diagnosed with cancer (Cancer Research UK, 2014). By 2020, half of the UK population can expect to be diagnosed with cancer at some point in their lives (Macmillan 2014).
- **Caring responsibilities**. 6.5m people in the UK have significant caring responsibilities. Carers UK projects that this will reach 9m by 2037. 1 in 8 adults care, unpaid, for family and friends (Carers UK, 2014).
- **Living with dementia**. There are 800,000 people in the UK living with varying degrees of dementia, and this is expected to double over the next 40 years. Dementia affects 1 person in 6 over 80 (Age UK, 2013).
- **Disability**. 16% of working age adults have a disability (Family Resources Survey, 2011/12).
- **Mental illness**. In any given year, one in four adults experiences at least one mental disorder (NHS, 2007).
- **Old age**. Over 1.4m people in the UK are aged 85 or over. The number of people over 85 in the UK is predicted to double in the next 20 years and nearly treble in the next 30 years (Age UK, 2013).

8.10.5 Understanding vulnerable consumers' interactions with banks and other firms

Research commissioned by the FCA (reported in *Vulnerability Exposed*, December 2014) included the following findings.

- **Financial services, products and systems often 'streamline' consumers** and are not designed to meet non-standard needs of those who do not fit into a set mould.
- The response of **frontline staff** – whether it is in a branch or on the phone – is crucial to the customer's experience. The firm may have great specialist teams or policies, but if frontline staff do not deal with the situation appropriately, access to a good outcome may be missed.
- Staff on the frontline do not need to be experts, but they need **sufficient training** to facilitate a proper conversation, to know where internal expertise lies, and know how and when to refer on.
- Most problems relate to **poor interactions, or systems that do not flex** to meet needs, therefore making people's situations more difficult.

- Some **consumers are overwhelmed by complex information** and can find it hard to distinguish between promotional material and important messages about their products.

- In some areas, an inaccurate interpretation or **over-zealous implementation of rules** (such as those around data protection or affordability) is preventing firms from meeting the needs of vulnerable customers.

- **Many vulnerable consumers may be valuable customers** if firms respond to their needs and treat them flexibly. However, these consumers may withdraw from the mainstream market and their problems may spiral if their needs are not met.

CASE STUDIES

The FCA has presented the following case studies on vulnerable consumers. What are your views on what happened or what should have happened in each case?

A **registered blind person** was asked to go into his branch with photographic identification to withdraw funds from his account as his card had been blocked following fraud on his account. He did not possess a driving licence or passport, and was told by the bank that his blind person's bus pass with a photo on it was not adequate. He was unable to obtain money from his account while awaiting new cards.

A **mortgage customer who was diagnosed with terminal lung cancer** made a claim on a critical illness policy. The customer decided to repay the outstanding mortgage with the proceeds. The customer subsequently received a letter from the lender to say that an early repayment charge was payable. Despite contact being made by the family to explain the situation, it was only with the intervention of a third party that the lender waived the charge.

A **customer awaiting surgery for cancer** was expected to make a full recovery, but would miss work for three months because of the surgery. Holding a current account, overdraft and unsecured loan with the same bank and anticipating a problem meeting repayments during this period, the customer contacted the bank to discuss options to manage the temporary loss of income. The bank refused to consider any options as no payments had yet been missed and told her to call back when in arrears.

When **Adnan's mother died**, he travelled home to Turkey for a month to **organise her funeral**. As he would need time off work, he was worried about his mortgage payments. He called his bank to explain the situation and asked if it would be possible to have a four-month 'holiday' from his payments. After valuing the house, Adnan and his wife were told they were short of £1,000 in equity in the house to be granted a holiday. Instead, they were offered two months on a reduced payment schedule. Since this time, Adnan and his wife have seen their debt levels rise from £1,000 on credit cards to £13,000 to make bill and mortgage payments, and cover expenses related to the death.

8.10.6 Helping vulnerable consumers and adapting services

Bank staff can work to achieve fair treatment of customers who are **vulnerable or experiencing difficulties** by taking the following steps.

- Identify signs of vulnerability or difficulty in customers or potential customers.
- Seek an understanding of vulnerable situations and the difficulties that customers may be having.
- Ask what support the customer may need, referring cases to specialist teams as appropriate.
- Make reasonable adjustments to the support provided to the customer.
- Be ready to provide a customer with any facilities they may reasonably be provided with.
- Ensure that vulnerable customers receive fair outcomes.

Adapting services to the needs of vulnerable customers effectively requires action throughout the bank or other firm. The FCA found that there are problems at every stage, from high-level policy, through system design, to the products that are available and ways that staff implement policies and sell products.

Policy

- Many firms lack an over-arching strategy or policy on consumer vulnerability. It is important to have in place a high-level policy on consumer vulnerability, and all relevant staff should be aware of it.

- Policies designed to prevent financial abuse and fraud can inhibit staff empowerment to use discretion, particularly regarding legitimate access by third parties.

Systems

- There can be failure of internal systems, where firms fail to communicate and connect information internally. For example, this can lead to customers having to tell firms multiple times about bereavement, resulting in numerous duplicate letters from different areas of the business being sent.

- Interfaces or channels of communication are a problem if they are not inclusive.

- Increasing automation and use of call centres may create challenges in spotting potential vulnerability and ensuring customers are referred on to specialist teams where necessary.

Products

- There may be inflexible products and services that are designed for a standardised perfect customer and do not factor real-life events into their design. Some customers who face a change in circumstances are therefore not able to receive a flexible, tailored response.

- Product and information complexity and confusing communications can present problems. Clear, simple information and explanation throughout the product life cycle is important to all consumers.

- There may be a lack of suitable affordable products for people in some non-standard situations.

- There may be a lack of solutions for temporary delegation (enabling a family member or carer to manage your affairs for a short time) which retain privacy and safety.

Implementation

- A policy/practice gap at firms may result in frontline staff not being aware of or not implementing head office policies. Frontline staff may not refer people on to specialist teams.

- Consumer time may not be valued highly and many people will give up if the process is too time-consuming, especially if they are in a stressful situation with other demands on their time.

- Arrangements around temporary delegation (enabling a family member or carer to manage the person's affairs for a short time) and accompaniment (sitting in or helping with a phone call or interview) may not be sufficiently developed and flexible to enable family and carers to help.

- Inappropriate selling and sales practices may exploit behavioural biases.

- There can be issues around disclosure of a vulnerability and data protection (inaccurate or over-zealous application can create unnecessary problems).

8.10.7 What does 'good' look like to consumers?

The regulator has sought to answer the question: **What does 'good' look like to consumers, including vulnerable consumers?** The FCA has identified the following **outcomes that vulnerable consumers need to trust that they will experience** when they approach banks and other financial services providers. As the regulator comments, many of these would equally be beneficial to all consumers.

- Having **financial products that are clear and easy to understand**.

- A **choice of ways of communicating** to be available whenever you need to make contact and for these to be **designed in an inclusive way** so that they are clear, easy to understand and meet your needs. This could relate to the **method** of communication (e.g. audio/braille/face-to-face) or the **service delivery** (e.g. agreement to talk at a particular time of day depending on carers and medication).

- Feeling that firms will **treat you as an individual** and you will not face the 'computer says no' response just because your personal circumstances do not fit the standard mould.

- Knowing that, should you experience a sudden change in circumstances, you will be offered a **flexible and tailored response** from your financial services provider.

- Being able to **talk to someone who will take the time to listen**, who is flexible enough to let the conversation take its natural course, and who is sufficiently trained to spot signs of vulnerability and refer on to specialists where necessary.

- Being referred on to someone who has the authority and discretion to take a tailored approach to your situation and **offer flexible solutions, including use of specialist sources of help and advice** if necessary.

- Feeling confident that **your firm encourages disclosure**, that they will work with you in your best interests.

- Knowing that if you do disclose information about your needs, that **information will be recorded properly** so that you do not have to repeat it every time you make contact with all departments of a particular firm.

- Knowing firms will **pro-actively contact you** if they suspect you may be having financial difficulties.

- Knowing appropriate **action will be taken if a firm spots suspicious activity** that may signal abuse or fraud.

- If you are trying to speak to a firm in a **caring capacity**, finding that **the firm listens and makes a note of your concerns** even though it may not be able to divulge any information to you.

- If you are recently bereaved, have a power of attorney or a third party mandate, receiving **consistent advice and treatment**.

9 Complaints

9.1 Recognising a complaint

Regardless of how good the service is that you and your bank provide, there will be times when things go wrong.

QUICK QUESTION

What is a complaint?

How do you know when a customer is making a complaint?

What could be good about the fact that a customer makes a complaint?

Write your answer here before reading on.

A customer complaint is an oral or written expression of dissatisfaction about a service the bank has provided, or failed to provide.

We know when a customer is making a complaint when they express their dissatisfaction or annoyance to us.

This can be good because if the customer did not complain we might never know that something had gone wrong so we wouldn't have a chance to put it right. Further, the customer may tell lots of other people about why they are annoyed with us and therefore damage the bank's reputation in some way.

Therefore, when a customer complains, this gives us an opportunity to:

- Make improvements and provide better service generally
- Turn an unhappy customer into a happy one
- Strengthen customer loyalty

When a customer complains:

- Welcome the opportunity to provide a better service
- Take the complaint seriously
- Learn and get better from the complaint

Pause for thought ...

Think about a time when you made a complaint.

How were you feeling?

What did you want from the person you were complaining to?

How did the person handle your complaint?

Were you happy with the way your complaint was handled?

If so, what did the person do that resulted in you feeling happy about the way your complaint was handled?

If not, what did the person do that resulted in you feeling unhappy about the way your complaint was handled?

9.2 Handling complaints

When handling a complaint:

- Listen with empathy and understanding
- Respond along the lines of 'I'm sorry that this has happened'
- Clarify your understanding about what happened
- Be willing to help
- Take responsibility for fixing the problem
- Find out what the customer wants
- Propose a solution and get the customer's support
- Do what you can to resolve it as quickly as possible

Empathy can be described as the **ability to understand and share the feelings of another**.

QUICK QUESTION

Imagine you are recruiting a world-class complaint handler for your team. What qualities would you be looking for in this person?

Write your answer here before reading on.

An effective complaints handler will be:

- Understanding
- Calm
- Empathetic
- Patient
- Polite
- Positive
- Assertive
- Willing to help

Some customers may be angry or upset when they are complaining. If so, it's essential that you deal with their feelings before you seek a solution to the problem.

QUICK QUESTION

How might you deal with a customer who expresses anger?

Write your answer here before reading on.

When dealing with a customer who expresses anger:

- Remember that the complaint is about something that's gone wrong, it's not about you personally

- Keep in mind that there could be many reasons why the customer is feeling angry at that moment

- Match the customer's energy (so that the customer can see that you are taking their complaint seriously) but do not match their anger

- Stay calm

- Invite the customer to an interview room if you are in a branch

- Avoid small talk

- Look them in the eye and show that you are concerned there is a problem

- Put yourself in their shoes – appreciate how they might be feeling

- Let the customer have their say

- Listen for information that will help you solve the problem

- Look for areas of agreement and agree wherever you can, eg 'I agree that this must have been really inconvenient for you, I can see why you're angry about this. If that had happened to me, I would have been angry too'

- Ask questions to clarify what happened, eg 'What happened? When did you return the application? What were you told?'

- Take notes so that you have a record of the conversation to refer to later

- Nod your head in agreement to encourage the customer to keep talking

- Paraphrase key points and check understanding, e.g. 'So …, and then … Do I have that right?'

- Apologise on behalf of the bank that this happened

- Take action to solve the problem

- Say what you can do, not what you cannot

- Thank the customer for telling you what happened

Always remember that when a customer is making a complaint, they are complaining about something that they are not happy about – they are not complaining about you. Therefore, do not take the complaint personally.

On the other hand, do not blame colleagues or other teams in the bank – you should still take responsibility for the complaint. In the customer's eyes, you represent the bank and, as far as they are concerned, the bank has let them down.

You should take ownership of the situation. If you make an apology to the customer, you are apologising on behalf of the bank that this happened.

9.3 A structure for dealing with complaints

9.3.1 Overview

Whether the customer is angry or not, there is a generic process or structure that you can follow whenever you deal with a complaint:

1 Empathise with the customer
2 Obtain all the relevant facts
3 Work to a solution
4 Verify that the customer is happy with the outcome

9.3.2 Empathising with the customer

QUICK QUESTION

What is empathy?

Write your answer here before reading on.

Empathy is an ability to be aware of, and understand and appreciate others' thoughts and feelings. It's about tuning in or being sensitive to what, how and why people think and feel the way they do. People who are empathetic care about others and show interest in and concern for them. Such people are able to voice their understanding of another person's perspective on a situation, even if they don't agree with it. Being empathetic can shift an adversarial relationship to a collaborative one.

Pause for thought ...

What could you do or say to show a customer that you empathise with them?

You could show a customer that you empathise with them by:

- Listening to them
- Making eye contact and showing concern
- Putting yourself in their shoes and seeing the situation from their perspective
- Appreciating how they might be feeling
- Putting into words what they (not you) are thinking or feeling

To express empathy, we need to pay attention to the words the other person uses to describe their thoughts and feelings, as well as their facial expressions and body language. For example, if a customer seems frustrated because they did not receive a telephone call they were promised by someone in the bank, an appropriate response might be an apology followed by an empathetic statement, such as: 'I'm sorry that you didn't receive the telephone call you were promised. You must feel frustrated that we haven't kept our promise to you.'

Other empathetic statements, depending on what the customer seems to be thinking or feeling and the words they use to express their thoughts and feelings, include:

- 'That must have been really inconvenient for you.'
- 'You must be really annoyed about that.'

9.3.3 Obtaining all the relevant facts

Pause for thought ...

Thinking about what you have learned so far from this section, and reflecting on your own experience, what might you do to ensure you obtain all the relevant facts?

You can obtain the relevant facts by:

- Letting the customer talk
- Listening for information
- Asking questions to clarify what happened
- Nodding your head in agreement to encourage the customer to keep talking

BPP
LEARNING MEDIA

- Taking notes so that you have a record of the conversation to refer to later
- Paraphrasing key points and checking understanding
- Remembering to thank the customer for telling you what happened

9.3.4 Working to a solution

Once you have empathised with the customer and gathered the facts, you can now work towards agreeing a solution. You may require to obtain more information from colleagues or another part of the bank to allow you to make further progress. Should this be the case, explain to the customer what it is that you are going to do and why. You should also make a firm commitment to the customer of when you will be able to get back in touch with them. If you are not able to get all the information that you require in this timescale, you should still go back to the customer to explain the up-to-date position and to let them know what the revised timescales are going to be.

Once you have gathered all the information you need, you are in a position to work to a solution, by:

- Asking the customer what they would like to happen
- Explaining your organisation's position
- Giving alternative solutions if you can

- **Asking the customer what they would like to happen**. If you know what the customer wants, then it is much easier for you to give them what they want. For example, they may want an apology, a refund, or some form of compensation; or they may want you to contact a third party to explain what has happened. For example, say the customer has a mortgage with another provider and the direct debit has been set up incorrectly. As a result, the mortgage provider has advised the customer that they are now in arrears. In this situation the customer may want you to contact the mortgage provider to explain there has been an error and to let them know when they are likely to receive the funds.

- **Explaining your organisation's position**. You may need to explain what your organisation's complaints procedure is. If the customer is looking for a refund of charges, you may not be authorised to make such a refund and the matter has to be referred on. Again you should explain this to the customer and give them timescales of when you will be back in touch. Remember to say what you can do, not what you cannot.

- **Giving alternative solutions if you can**. If this is an option, the customer can choose which solution they prefer.

9.3.5 Verifying that the customer is happy with the outcome

Once a solution has been proposed, make sure that the customer is happy with this and that they are clear about what is going to happen next. For example, you are going to make a refund to their account, or they will get a letter of apology, or you are referring the matter to a colleague who will then contact them. If they are not happy, it may be that the complaint requires to be escalated further. Where you do promise to arrange for something to be done, follow this up to make sure it is actually done.

Pause for thought ...

What, in outline, are your bank's procedures for dealing with complaints?

9.4 FCA rules on handling complaints

9.4.1 Introduction

Banks and other regulated financial services firms may receive complaints from their clients about the way the firm has provided financial services or in respect of failure to provide a financial service. This could include allegations of financial loss whether or not such losses have actually yet occurred: for example, in the case of a mis-sold pension contract, future losses may be involved.

A complaint is defined as: 'any oral or written expression of dissatisfaction, whether justified or not, from, or on behalf of, a person about the provision of, or failure to provide, a financial service, which alleges that the complainant has suffered (or may suffer) financial loss, material distress or material inconvenience'.

9.4.2 Complaints handling by firms

A firm is required to have **written procedures** to ensure complaints from eligible complainants are properly handled. To aid consumer awareness, firms must: publish a summary of their internal processes for handling complaints; refer customers to this summary at or immediately after the point of sale; and provide the summary when acknowledging a complaint, or on request.

A firm's **complaints handling procedures** must:

- Be effective and transparent

- Allow complaints to be made by any reasonable means (which might include email messages, or telephone calls, for example)

- Recognise complaints as requiring resolution

Those handling complaints should be persons other than those who provided the service being companied about.

Firms are permitted to **outsource** complaints handling, or to arrange a 'one-stop shop' for handling complaints with other firms.

Having regard to the regulators' **Principle for Businesses 6** *(Customers' Interests),* which requires that firms treat customers fairly, firms should consider acting on their own initiative in respect of customers who may have been disadvantaged but have not complained. This is an example of how, in line with its emphasis on 'principles-based regulation', the regulator expects firms to adopt an ethical stance and to consider themselves how to apply the Principles for Businesses.

Complaints time limit and reporting rules (covered later in this Section) do not apply to complaints which are resolved by the **next business day** after the complaint is made.

9.4.3 Eligible complainants

The rules on how firms must handle complaints apply to **complainants who are eligible** to have a complaint considered under the **Financial Ombudsman Service (FOS)**.

An **eligible complainant** must be:

- A consumer

- A smaller business – that is, with fewer than 10 employees and turnover or annual balance sheet not exceeding €2 million (called a **'micro-enterprise'**)

- A charity with annual income of less than £1 million, or

- A trust with net asset value of less than £1 million

9.4.4 Time limit rules

On receiving a complaint, the firm must:

- Send to the complainant a prompt written acknowledgement (no specific time limit is stated) providing 'early reassurance' that it has received the complaint and is dealing with it, and

- Ensure the complainant in kept informed of progress on the complaint's resolution thereafter

By the end of **eight weeks** after receiving a complaint which remains unresolved, the firm must send:

- A final response, or

- A holding response, which explains why a final response cannot be made and gives the expected time it will be provided, informs the complainant of his right to complain directly to the FOS if he is not satisfied with the delay, and encloses a copy of the FOS explanatory leaflet

The regulator expects that, **within eight weeks of their receipt**, almost all complaints will have been **substantively addressed**.

9.4.5 Complaints reporting

Banks and other regulated firms must provide a complete **report to the FCA** on complaints received, **twice a year**. There is a standard format for the report, which must show, for the reporting period:

- Complaints broken down into categories and generic product types

- Numbers of complaints closed by the firm: within four weeks of receipt; within four to eight weeks; and more than eight weeks from receipt

- Numbers of complaints: upheld; known to have been referred to and accepted by the FOS; outstanding at the beginning of reporting period; outstanding at the end of the reporting period

- The total amount of redress paid in respect of complaints

9.5 Financial Ombudsman Service (FOS)

The FOS is the official independent expert in settling complaints between consumers and businesses providing financial services. It deals with complaints from consumers against regulated firms, at no charge to the consumer. The FOS can require firms to pay compensation.

The FOS can look at complaints about most financial problems, for example involving:

- Banking
- Insurance
- Mortgages
- Credit cards and store cards
- Loans and credit
- Pensions
- Savings and investments
- Hire purchase and pawnbroking
- Money transfer
- Financial advice
- Stocks, shares, unit trusts and bonds

A complainant should first go to the authorised firm being complained against. If the authorised firm does not resolve the complaint to his satisfaction, the complainant may refer it to the Ombudsman.

Under a rule introduced in 2015, the FOS may also agree to consider a complaint if both the complainant and the firm agree that it should be referred to the Ombudsman.

The FOS offers an informal method of independent adjudication of disputes between a firm and its customer. It is a body set up by statute and, while its Board is appointed by the FCA, it is entirely independent from the regulator and authorised firms. The FOS is, however, accountable to the FCA and is required to make an annual report to the regulator on its activities.

The FOS has set the following **time limits** beyond which it will not normally consider complaints.

- When six months have passed since the firm sent the consumer a final response
- When more than six years have passed since the event complained about, or
- More than three years since the person became aware of or could reasonably be expected to have become aware of the problem

After these time limits have expired, the firm against which the complaint is made may object to the Ombudsman looking at the complaint on the grounds that it is 'time-barred'.

If a firm misses a time limit, the FOS may move to the next stage of the complaint and may make provision for inconvenience or distress caused, in its award. If a complainant misses a time limit, the FOS may move to the next stage, or dismiss the complaint.

Where a complaint is determined in favour of the complainant, the Ombudsman's determination may include one or more of the following.

- A **money award** against the respondent (i.e. the firm complained against)
- An **interest award** against the respondent
- A **costs award** against the respondent
- A **direction** to the respondent

The Ombudsman may investigate the merits of the case and may also convene a hearing if necessary. Where the Ombudsman finds in favour of the complainant, it can force the firm to take appropriate steps to remedy the position including the payment of up to **£150,000 plus reasonable costs** (although awards of costs are not common). This figure will normally represent the financial loss the eligible complainant has suffered but can also cover any pain and suffering, damage to their reputation and any distress or inconvenience caused. If the Ombudsman considers that a sum greater than £150,000 would be fair, he can recommend that the firm pays the balance (although he cannot force the firm to pay this excess). An **interest award** may provide for interest from a specified date to be added to the money award.

Once the Ombudsman has given a decision, the complainant may decide whether to accept or reject that decision.

- If the complainant accepts the Ombudsman's decision, the authorised firm is bound by it
- If the complainant rejects the decision, they can pursue the matter further through the Courts

Once the Ombudsman has given a decision, the **complainant may decide whether to accept or reject** that decision. If the complainant accepts the decision, the bank or other authorised firm is bound by the decision. If the complainant rejects the Ombudsman's decision, they can pursue the matter further through the courts.

10   Financial Services Compensation Scheme (FSCS)

The **Financial Services Compensation Scheme (FSCS)** is not concerned with customer complaints about services provided. It is a scheme that protects customers by paying compensation when a bank or other firm gets into financial difficulties. The compensation scheme is independent, but accountable to the regulators and HM Treasury for its operations. The FSCS works in partnership with the FCA in delivering the regulator's objectives, particularly that of consumer protection. The FSCS is funded by levies on authorised firms.

The FSCS will compensate eligible claimants where a bank or other authorised financial services firm is unable or likely to be unable to meet claims against it. Generally speaking, therefore, the scheme will apply where the bank or other firm is **insolvent or bankrupt**.

To seek compensation from the scheme, someone must be an **eligible claimant**, the official definition of which covers most individuals and small businesses. The time limit for a claim will normally be six years from when the claim arose.

For protected **bank deposits**, the FSCS compensation limit is **£75,000 per person per claim** (a level established as being approximately equivalent to 100,000 euros), however many accounts are held by the claimant at the failed institution.

The European Deposit Guarantee Schemes Directive (DGSD) requires payout of compensation within twenty days. The FCA expects that payout will be faster, with a target of seven days.

Consumer awareness of the FSCS is promoted by a rule which requires firms to provide information on the existence of the FSCS and level of protection it offers to depositors, as well as pro-actively informing customers of any additional trading names under which the firm operates.

KEY WORDS

Key words and phrases from this chapter are given below. Make sure you know what they mean and add any other words or phrases that you want to remember. You can use the space provided to write your own revision notes.

- Types of customer
- Deposits and savings
- Borrowing
- Customer life cycle
- Payment systems
- Customer contact centre
- Internet banking
- Quality service
- Vulnerable customer
- Handling complaints
- Financial Ombudsman Service
- Financial Services Compensation Scheme

REVIEW

To help you reflect on and review the content of this chapter, give some thought to the following questions.

- What are the different types of bank customers?

- What products and services does your bank offer?

- Which products and services are suitable for which types of customers?

- What do these products and services give the customers or allow them to do?

- What might be suitable products and services for customers at each stage of the customer life cycle? In what ways are these products and services suitable?

- What are the factors that contribute to the provision of a quality customer service?

- What will be the key aspects of your approach to identify and help customers who are in vulnerable circumstances?

- How do you know when a customer is making a complaint?

- How might you show respect to a customer?

- How might you deal with a customer who is angry or upset?

- What generic structure could you follow when dealing with a complaint?

- What is the purpose of the Financial Ombudsman Service?

- What is the purpose of the Financial Services Compensation Scheme?

chapter 4

CREDIT AND LENDING

Contents

Learning objectives

By the end of this chapter, you should be able to:

- Outline the scope and key principles of The Lending Code
- Describe the factors that influence the interest rates charged by lenders
- Identify key information required in a lending application
- Explain the key principles of credit and lending and how these can be used to make professional and ethical lending decisions
- Describe the attributes of a good security for lending
- Explain why banks use credit scoring when assessing a lending proposition

Introduction

As we learned in Chapter 1, the basic functions of banks are to accept deposits and lend money. An understanding of lending is vitally important to those working in financial institutions.

In normal economic circumstances, income from lending is the major source of revenue to a financial services provider and enables the business to pay interest to providers of capital, meet its costs in full, discharge its tax and make a profit. In turn, some of the profit creates new capital that can be used to increase the asset base. Lending is also the platform upon which banks can generate further revenues. For example, if a lender creates a mortgage, it can then attempt to generate commission income by offering buildings and contents insurance and other products.

The aim of this chapter is to increase your knowledge and understanding of the key principles (or 'canons') of credit and lending and how these can be used to make professional and ethical lending decisions.

1 The Lending Code

1.1 Scope

The **Lending Code** is a self-regulatory code which sets minimum standards of good lending practice when dealing with:

- **Consumers**
- **Micro-enterprises** – that is (as we saw in the previous chapter in relation to complaints), businesses with fewer than 10 employees and turnover or annual balance sheet not exceeding €2 million
- **Charities** with an annual **income of under £1m** (encompassed within the definition of 'microenterprise customers' as used in the Code)

The Code covers:

- Loans (but see below regarding mortgage loans)
- Credit cards
- Charge cards
- Current account overdrafts

The Code does not apply to merchant services, non-business borrowing secured on land (that is, mortgage loans), nor to sales finance. Compliance with the Code is monitored independently and it is enforced by the **Lending Code Standards Board**.

Compliance with the Lending Code is independently monitored and enforced by the Lending Standards Board to ensure that subscribers are compliant with the following legislation.

- Consumer Credit Acts of 1974 and 2006

- Consumer Credit (EU Directive) Regulations 2010

- Equality Act 2010

- Other relevant legislation, such as the Consumer Rights Act 2015

The current (March 2011) version of the Code was last revised on 28 September 2015.

1.2 Key Commitments

Subscribers to the Lending Code will act fairly and reasonably in all their dealings with customers by, as a minimum, meeting all the commitments and standards in the Code. The **key commitments** of the Code are shown below.

- Subscribers will make sure that **advertising and promotional literature** is fair, clear and not misleading and that customers are given clear information about products and services.

- Customers will be given **clear information about accounts and services** before, during and after the point of sale, including how they work, their terms and conditions and the interest rates that apply to them.

- **Regular statements** will be made available to customers (if appropriate). Customers will also be informed about **changes** to the interest rates, charges or terms and conditions.

- Subscribers will **lend money responsibly**.

- Subscribers will **deal quickly and sympathetically with things that go wrong** and act sympathetically and positively when considering a customer's financial difficulties.

- **Personal information** will be treated as **private and confidential**, and subscribers will provide **secure and reliable banking and payment systems**.

- Subscribers will make sure their **staff are trained** to put this Code into practice.

Areas covered by the Lending Code:

- Communications and financial promotions
- Credit reference agencies
- Credit assessment
- Current account overdrafts
- Credit cards
- Loans
- Terms and conditions
- Financial difficulties
- Complaints
- Monitoring

2 Lending rates

The general level of **interest rates** at which banks lend is determined mainly by the base rate declared by the Monetary Policy Committee (MPC) of the Bank of England each month. This rate sets a standard for interest rates throughout the industry. In turn, the MPC's decision will be influenced by a wide range of factors, the most important of these being to ensure that the level of price inflation in the economy is contained within the government's target range. The MPC will also consider matters such as general economic trends, including unemployment, and the actual and forecast economic growth rate.

Generally, if the MPC announces an increase in the rate, banks will follow suit, though not necessarily in a uniform manner. Likewise, when the MPC decides to reduce interest rates, the rates offered by lenders (and deposit takers) will also fall. The interest rates charged (and paid) by banks vary widely according to the product. Most lenders have a Reference Interest Rate, which serves as a platform for determining rates charged on each product. The Reference Interest Rate means the Bank of England Bank Rate (also known as the base rate), or other such externally set rate as the bank may decide. The major determinant of the interest rate for each product is risk. If the product exposes the bank to high risk, a higher rate is charged and *vice versa*. Therefore interest rates on unsecured loans tend to be higher than interest rates on secured loans, as the lender is able to fall back on the value of the collateral for the latter. The lender has to rely on the personal covenant to repay in respect of unsecured loans. Likewise, products with historically low default rates, such as residential mortgages, have lower interest rates than products where there is a high risk of default, such as consumer finance and credit cards.

Interest rates charged by lenders are also affected by other factors, including:

- The term of the lending facility
- The income generated by cross-selling related products, such as protection insurance
- The income from fees, charges and commissions
- Administration costs, including default and recovery management
- The level of business targeted, relative to other lending products offered
- The interest rates charged by competitors for comparable products
- Other factors, including the ability to tie in the customer for a given period of time

3 Lending documentation

Each bank uses its own standard lending application documents. Although these may vary from bank to bank, the main areas will be very similar. Below is a sample lending application. Take a few minutes to familiarise yourself with its content and layout.

Lending Application

Date: / / /

Customer Details

Account Number	Identification Number	Branch/Office
Sort Code		

Name 1	Occupation
Name 2	Occupation
DOB 1	Employer 1
DOB 2	Employer 2

Date Bank Connection Established:

Proposed Facility:

Facility Requested for:

A/C Type and No	Limit Requested	Present Balance	Discounted Security Value	Interest Margin	Fee	Previous Limit	Previous Margin

Other Bank exposure – e.g. guarantees, contingent liabilities

Total Exposure

Statement of Assets and Liabilities as at / /			
Assets		**Liabilities**	
Property (Main Residence)		This Bank Total Facilities (as above)	
Other Property		All Other Borrowing (detail)	
Life Policies (SV)			
Investments			
Cash Balances			
Other(s) – Please detail			
Total Assets			
Less total Liabilities			
Net Means			

Available Funds as at   /   /

Annual Expenditure		Annual Net Income	
Mortgage/Rent		Self	
Council Tax		Partner/spouse	
Finance Companies/Loans		Other income (detail)	
Store/Credit Cards			
School Fees			
Other fixed outgoings		Total Income	
		Less: Total Expenditure	
Total Expenditure		Annual Net Free Funds	

Security:

Type	Details	Gross Value	Discount (%)	Net Value
Held				
Offered				

Introduction

One paragraph summary of submission, covering the 4 points below.

- One sentence summary of submission
- Introductory source
- Relationship history, if any
- Compliance with existing credit policy/guidelines, with any exceptions highlighted

Borrowers Analysis

Gives a high level picture of the customer and sets the scene before considering the proposition

Personal Borrower

- Personal circumstances, if appropriate, e.g. married with 2 children, inherited capital from deceased father
- Occupation, including comment on future stability and history of employment (e.g. works for struggling investment bank, having recently moved from another, and earns £100k basic and average £300k pa performance bonus) and perceived ability
- Financial position, e.g. owns unencumbered domestic property £2m jointly with wife and has investments worth £1.5m in sole name with net means of £x

Facility Analysis

Assesses the proposition structure and the customer's ability to pay

- Amount, purpose, term
- Repayment profile and sources, including assessment of customer's ability to make repayment
- Security, including nature, ranking, acceptability, value realisability (= 'safety')
- Covenants, if any
- Conditions precedent

Risk Analysis and Mitigants

- What risks are identified?
- How can there risks be mitigated?

Pricing

- Margin
- Fees

Additional Services

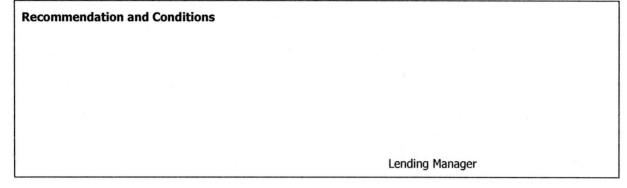

Recommendation and Conditions

Lending Manager

QUICK QUESTION

For what reasons do you think banks use lending forms like the sample provided?

Write your answer here before reading on.

There are several reasons why banks use lending applications forms like this, such as the following.

- It ensures that no important information is missed out of the lending assessment.

- It ensures that all of the relevant information is set out in a standard format, so that retrieval of this information at a later date is easier.

- As all of the relevant information is recorded, the lender can show, if required, that they have taken all of the relevant information into account when sanctioning the borrowing.

- As a number of people could be dealing with the customer over a period of time, using a standard format means that it is easy for others to identify the information that they need.

- Having all of the information summarised in one place makes the job of a lender easier.

- The idea that the lender must record all of this information means that all of the key factors in the decision are being taken into account.

4 The principles of lending

4.1 Overview

Although the range of bank lending products has increased considerably over the years, the principles of lending have remained unchanged and can be applied to any lending situation. So, whether a friend asks you to lend them £25 to tide them over until pay day, or you are dealing with a commercial lending application for £25m, the principles that you will apply to assess the proposition should be the same.

Following the general principles of lending will enable you to take a consistent and structured approach to the assessment of each case, thus leading to a balanced decision. A challenge could come from a customer whose application you have decided not to support and the customer could argue that, under the **'Treating Customers Fairly'** principle, they have been treated unfairly. By following this structured approach, you would be able to demonstrate that you had indeed treated this customer fairly as it would have been unfair to put them in a situation where they would have been unable to repay the loan.

When coming to a decision about lending, we need to look at:

- The person
- Amount, purpose and term
- Repayment

QUICK QUESTION

Having fully appraised these factors, you have decided to lend to the customer. What other factors should you now think about?

Write your answer here before reading on.

Having made the decision to lend, you should then consider:

- Security
- Reward (to your bank, by way of interest and fees)
- Other services that you could offer the customer to meet other financial needs

4.2 The person

Whenever we are approached with a lending proposition, the first area that we consider is the person and in particular the different aspects of:

- Character
- Capacity
- Commitment/capital

These are often referred to as the 'three Cs'.

QUICK QUESTION

What particular characteristics would you look for in the person?

Write your answer here before reading on.

- **Character**

The integrity of the borrower is paramount, otherwise interviews and discussions would be futile. Many questions will be raised by the lender throughout the course of discussions; honest and reliable answers are expected from the customer. If the customer promises certain action, we must be assured that this action will actually be carried out. References may be obtained in respect of new customers as integrity is very difficult to assess in a single interview.

If you are dealing with a customer who is not known to your bank, you must follow the laid down procedures for recording and verifying the customer's identity in order to comply with current anti-money laundering (AML) procedures. Each bank will also have regulations regarding the validation of the identity of existing customers who are opening new accounts, or obtaining loans.

You would look for the following characteristics to be demonstrated by a customer who has asked you to lend them money:

- Respectable and trustworthy
- Honest
- Dependable
- Of high integrity

- **Capacity**

The will to take action is not necessarily the same as an ability to see the action through, so we must also be assured as to the customer's good health, drive and energy. Equally, you should not let enthusiasm mask any potential weaknesses in capability. Often, customers who retire early or are made redundant seek to tackle new ventures of which they have had no previous experience, such as ex-footballers wishing to run a pub or a customer with no experience of house building, and, having undertaken little research, want to borrow money from the bank to finance a self build project.

For a personal lending application, you would look at the following factors:

- **Age of the customer** and therefore the **timescale** of the borrowing – for example, will they be able to repay the borrowing before their planned retirement age?

- **Experience** – does the customer have experience in the field in which they are intending to get involved?

- **Reputation** – have we lent funds to this customer before? If so, what was their repayment record like? Did they adhere to the commitments and promises that they made to us at the outset?

- **Commitment/Capital**

The amount of capital or finance provided by the customer can indicate the customer's commitment to the purpose of the advance. For a personal lending proposition, if the customer is intending to use the advance to purchase an asset, then how big a contribution are they making towards the overall cost? Also, if the customer has approached you for a mortgage, what percentage of the total cost of the house are they looking for you to provide?

With car finance, it is common to find that the customer's contribution comes from the trade-in of their previous car, therefore, rather than making a physical cash deposit to the total cost, they are still contributing financially by deducting the value of their trade-in from the total cost of the new car.

Generally, the more of their own resources the customer has committed to the project, the greater their commitment to its success is thought to be.

Other personal information

We will now look at some of the other information about the customer that we'll need to analyse to help us come to a decision. We need to determine the customer's personal circumstances, as these are going to affect the decision about the lending application.

Some of these factors we have already discussed, such as the customer's age. Other factors that should be considered include the following.

- **Marital/civil partnership status**. The customer's marital/civil partnership status can affect their ability to repay the borrowing; for example, with a couple, they have the potential to both be earning and so increase the amount of spare funds that they have available to repay the loan.

- **Dependants**. This could affect repayment. A couple may have a joint income, but by having a family, their monthly outgoings will be far greater than if there were no dependants. Does the customer have elderly parents dependant on them?

- **Employment**. The customer's employment has a great bearing on repayment as employment directly affects the customer's income. You will also know how their salary is broken down between an annual salary and bonuses.

  Normally only regular salary is taken into account for repayment, as overtime and bonuses cannot always be relied on. Employment details will also give you an insight into their future earning potential – are they employed with an established employer in a sector of the economy that is growing, or are they working for an unknown organisation in an economic sector that you know is in decline?

- **Previous connections with your organisation**. For example, other accounts/products that this customer uses. Have previous loans been repaid on time and within the terms and conditions of the borrowing?

QUICK QUESTION

You now have lots of information about the customer. How else could you use this information?

Write your answer here before reading on.

You will be starting to build up a picture of what the customer's circumstances are and so you will be able to start identifying their likely financial needs. Bear in mind that what you are seeing here are *likely* needs and that you still need to verify and agree these needs with the customer before you start talking about specific products – otherwise you may come across as trying to push products for which they cannot see a real need.

Customer's assets and liabilities

In the final section of the 'person' section, we shall examine the information we need to record about the customer's assets and liabilities. While the specific documentation used to record this information will vary from bank to bank, you will find that the type of information is very similar and is normally recorded on a standard document.

The need to consider this information is to help build as full a picture as possible of the customer and so this must include what assets the customer owns as well as looking at what financial obligations they have.

An added advantage to looking at the customer's means is that, later in our credit assessment, we may decide that it will be necessary to ask the customer for security before authorising the advance. There are some types of security that are of more value to the lender than others. However, if we know what assets the customer has, we can make an informed decision about the type(s) of security we wish to ask for.

QUICK QUESTION

What are typical types of assets and liabilities that a customer may have?

Write your answer here before reading on.

Typically, a customer may have some or all of the following assets:

- Property – as well as their main property, the customer may also own a holiday house, property that they let out to tenants, or even property that other members of their family use

- Stocks and shares

- Government securities, such as Treasury Stock

- Life assurance policies

- Bank/building society accounts

- Others, such as antiques, paintings, classic cars, or boats

The most current value for each of these assets should be recorded. For example, a current surrender value for a life assurance policy would give the most accurate description of the value to the bank.

Typically, a customer could have the following liabilities:

- An outstanding mortgage or mortgages on their property
- Loans/credit card debts
- Guarantees

Again, the most up-to-date figures should be recorded against these items.

Having looked at a high level at the customer's assets and liabilities, it is a straightforward task to sum up their asset value and deduct from this the total of their liabilities. The resulting figure is usually referred to as the customer's **net means**.

We now have an overall picture of the customer's assets and liabilities, and therefore their net means. However, as the purpose of credit assessment is to make an informed decision on the request that the customer is making, we need to look in more detail at the customer's assets and liabilities.

QUICK QUESTION

Refer back to the list of the customer's assets. What other information would you like to have about these assets to inform your lending decision?

Write your answer here before reading on.

Property	Where the property is, type of property, valuation, date of the valuation.
Stocks and shares	In what companies are the shares held and for what amounts, type of shares (such as ordinary, preference) current stock exchange valuation.
Government securities	Types of stock, coupon rate, redemption date, current stock exchange valuation.
Life policies	Name of assurance company, current surrender value, maturity date of policy.
Bank/building society accounts	Name(s) of bank/building society, type of account (for example, instant access, notice), term of notice (if any), balances.
Others	Depends on type of asset held; generally you are looking for a description of each asset, a note of the most recent valuation, the basis of the valuation and the date of the valuation.

You should always exercise care with the reliance you place on any of the assets listed – For what reason do you think this might be?

It is easy to place a value on a building society account because it is easy to value and realise. The same cannot be said for an original painting, for example, because it can be difficult to place a value on it, as the value may fluctuate widely based on the demand for a particular type of art at any time. If the customer wishes to sell the painting, it may take some time to find a suitable buyer with both the desire and the means to buy it. As a result, you should be cautious when dealing with this type of asset and it is wise not to place too much reliance on them.

QUICK QUESTION

Look at the liabilities listed earlier. Again, make a note of the additional information you would like to have on these to enable you to make an informed decision.

Write your answer here before reading on.

Mortgage loans	The amount outstanding, the property that the mortgage refers to, the type of mortgage (capital and interest or interest only), the date of the final payment.
Loans/credit cards	The amount outstanding, the name of the lender, the type of debt (e.g. loan, card), the date of the final payment.
Guarantees	Details of the guarantee – the amount, the name of the debtor, the name of the lender, the date of anticipated repayment of the loan.

4.3 Amount and purpose

What we are looking at under this heading is: how much does the customer want to borrow and for what reason do they want to borrow the money? You need to be sure that the customer is asking for the right amount of money. If they ask for too much, they are going to pay more in interest than is necessary. You will also need to be happy that the customer can afford the proposed repayments.

QUICK QUESTION

How could you establish that the customer is looking for the correct amount?

Write your answer here before reading on.

The specific steps that you take to establish that the customer is looking for the correct amount will vary with each lending proposition. For example, if a personal customer wants to take out an advance to help with home improvements, you would ask to see estimates for the proposed work.

There are several advantages to both you and the customer in taking this approach:

- You will be able to ascertain quickly that the customer is looking for the right amount

- Bearing in mind that you will probably have been faced with this type of request before, you will be able to determine if the estimates are reasonable for the work being proposed

- If you have asked the customer to obtain more than one estimate, you will be able to compare these

QUICK QUESTION

How could you establish that the customer is looking for the correct amount?

Write your answer here before reading on.

Another aspect to consider under the heading of 'amount' is loan to value. **Loan to value** (or **LTV**) is the ratio of the size of the borrowing compared to the value of the asset being purchased. For example, if a customer is looking for an advance to purchase property valued at £250,000 and the mortgage is for £200,000, the LTV is 80%. You should note that when calculating LTV, the figure taken for the asset should be the lower of the cost or the realisable (or current resale) value of the asset.

LTV is one of the measures of risk for a lender. Higher LTV advances are viewed as having a higher risk and to compensate for this, a lender will charge a higher rate of interest on the borrowing. You may also have come across LTV when dealing with mortgages where the mortgage is expressed as a percentage of the value of the property.

When looking at the amount and purpose, you should also give consideration to the term of the borrowing. This is significant because a number of factors can be influenced by the term of the borrowing, including:

- We will know whether we are dealing with short term, medium-term or long-term borrowing

- The repayment amount – the longer the period over which the advance is being repaid, the lower the monthly repayments will be

The other figure affected by the term of the borrowing is the total amount of interest paid over the life of the advance. Assuming all other things are equal, the longer the term of the borrowing, the higher the total amount of interest that the customer will have paid.

You will also want to compare the term of the borrowing with the anticipated **useful life** of the asset that the advance is financing. For example, if a customer approaches you looking to borrow money to part finance the purchase of a car, you would look for the borrowing to be repaid during the lifetime of the car, which is why you will not see a car loan with a term of 10 years.

QUICK QUESTION

Some people might argue that repayment is the most important aspect of lending. What do you think might be the reason for this?

Write your answer here before reading on.

4.4 Repayment

Those who argue that repayment is the most important aspect will state that there is no point in lending money to someone if you are not going to get it back. At times, you may come across a customer who states that, provided you have enough good quality security in place, repayment is guaranteed, so why are you so concerned with repayment? As you will see later, we should lend against the viability of the proposal – not the quality of the security.

The conditions of the advance concerning repayment and interest need to be established clearly at an early stage. These conditions vary, depending on the nature of the advance; for example, bridging loans are typically for large amounts but are repaid very quickly.

Flexibility is necessary and repayment arrangements should be based on fair reflections of profit/surplus income and/or liquid flows that the customer will have.

It is important that the customer is happy that they can meet the proposed repayment schedule. It is often necessary to emphasise to the customer the commitment that they are undertaking.

When a customer approaches a lender, their focus of attention is usually on whether or not you are going to lend them the money. It is not until they have the money and are then faced with meeting the repayment schedule that their minds turn to this in a more realistic way.

As lenders we look to future income or earnings to provide the source of repayment, not the realisation of security. This point cannot be emphasised too much.

QUICK QUESTION

There could be a situation where the customer can make the scheduled repayments at the time the advance is agreed. What other factors could come into play that would affect their ability to maintain these repayments in the future?

Write your answer here before reading on.

Factors to consider here are:

- For borrowing with a variable interest rate, what would happen if interest rates were to increase: could the customer still make the required repayments?

- How stable is the customer's employment/income source? What would happen if they were to lose their job? There are protection products that the customer could take out to mitigate the risk.

QUICK QUESTION

When dealing with a personal customer, how might you ascertain whether or not they will be able to meet the proposed repayments?

Write your answer here before reading on.

Most banks use some form of **income and expenditure statement** that they will ask a prospective borrower to complete in order to assess whether or not they will be able to service the borrowing. While the detail of the customer's income and expenditure may be recorded on a separate document, it is usual for this information to be summarised on the main credit approval form used by the bank.

The information recorded for income is fairly straightforward. You would expect to see the salary details of the borrower(s). These figures are normally recorded as net of tax, therefore this is the amount of income that the customer receives.

Other types of income that could be shown include the following.

- Child benefit

- Rental income – the customer could be letting either part of their property or an entire property on a commercial basis

- Dividends/interest income – in this case, you would want to find out information about the investments that are yielding this income; you may be able to verify this by looking at the record of the customer's assets and liabilities

- Bonus – remember the points we looked at earlier regarding any bonus that a customer may earn; a bonus will not be guaranteed and should not be regarded as a primary source of repayment for the loan

- Income from a second job – perhaps the customer does part time work in the evenings or weekends to supplement their income, in which case you should find out how regular this income is and for how long it is reasonable to expect it to continue

If you are dealing with an existing customer, you will be able to verify much of this information by looking at the run of their account. It is also useful to look at the customer's pay slips/salary advices. The advantage to be gained from looking at these documents is that not only will you be able to verify that the salary information is correct, but you will also see what the breakdown of the salary is. For example, how much of the salary comprises bonus or overtime payments? If overtime has come into the equation, again you need to find out how often the customer works overtime and how guaranteed this overtime is.

Like a bonus, it is unlikely that you would want to rely on overtime payments as a primary source of repayment for the loan.

To get a clear picture of the customer's salary it is usual practice to ask to see salary slips for the past three months. This will allow you to check if the customer has a regular level of income, or whether there are fluctuations in their income levels.

If the person does not maintain their account with you, it is also possible to verify the applicant's wage/salary by scrutinising pay slips/salary advices. Again, you would be looking for at least the last three months slips.

Looking at regular monthly financial outgoings, typical items would include:

- Mortgage/rent
- Council tax
- Insurance/assurance
- Telephone/mobile phone/e-mail
- Electricity/gas
- Travel expenses
- Car loan repayments
- Car running costs
- Food
- Clothing
- Hobbies/interests
- Holidays
- Loan repayments (other than those covered earlier in the list)
- Credit card/store card repayments

Again, if the customer keeps their account with you, you will be able to verify much of the information supplied by looking at their standing order and direct debit records.

It is important that you do not just accept everything that the customer states about their income and expenditure – if a figure seems to be out of line, you should ask the customer about this. This assessment is vital when looking at the customer's ability to repay the borrowing and you want to be assured that you are making an assessment based on realistic and well thought out figures.

When considering how realistic the information is, you should compare the customer's figures with:

- Your personal experience – do these figures seem realistic compared to your outgoings?
- The information held on record from other customers in similar circumstances

It is also normal practice to look at other borrowing that the customer has outstanding, either with your organisation or with others. One reason for doing this is to ensure that the customer is not becoming financially overcommitted.

The information you gather here should be cross-referenced to the information that you already hold regarding the customer's expenditure. You must be happy that the monthly loan/credit card repayments detailed under monthly expenditure relate to the loans and credit cards that are listed as liabilities outstanding.

While you are gaining information on the customer's income and expenditure primarily to verify if they can make the scheduled repayments, at the same time you are gaining information about other likely financial needs that the customer may have. For example, if a loan they currently have to finance the purchase of a car is about to expire, the customer may be thinking about changing their car at the loan expiry date, in which case your organisation could help them finance this purchase, as well as providing other ancillary services such as car insurance.

Remember that this information is helping you to identify likely financial needs that the customer may have – it is only by talking to the customer that you will be able to ascertain if your suppositions are correct.

The specific information about a customer's outstanding obligations can be organised under the following headings:

- Source of loan – Is the customer borrowing from another organisation, a finance company, a credit union, credit cards or store cards?

- Lending institutions – Under the headings in the bullet points on the previous page, list what organisations the customer may have been dealing with; the customer may have already approached one of these companies for the loan and their application may have been rejected, in which case you would want to know the reason(s) behind this.

It is also useful to have information on the original amount of each loan, how much is currently outstanding, what the monthly commitment for each loan is and when each loan will be repaid.

Having identified and interpreted all of the information in the repayment category, you will now be in a position to make an informed decision about whether or not the customer can afford the loan that they are requesting.

Remember that it is important to record all of this information in accordance with your bank's policies and procedures. By doing this, you will be showing that you have made the best decision based on the information that was available to you at the time.

Pause for thought ...

In what ways can following the key principles of credit and lending result in the making of a professional and ethical lending decision?

Overall viability

In our examination of the principles of lending, so far we have been considering the viability of the proposal. Now we will examine other factors –security, remuneration and other services that we might be able to offer the customer, provided these services would be of value to them.

If by this stage in the lending assessment we find that the proposal is not viable, then we can stop at this point and convey this decision to the customer. After all, if the proposal is not viable, and we have decided not to grant the loan, there is no point in looking at security, or thinking about the level of fees that we might charge.

4.5 Security

4.5.1 Introduction

In the first instance, the proposition must be basically solid and repayment should come from the usual sources such as income or sale of an asset. However, all lending bears some element of risk, quite simply because lending involves the future and the future is uncertain. Therefore, no matter how attractive and realistic the proposition might be, there is always a risk that what was anticipated does not materialise.

The ultimate risk which the lender must guard against is the borrower's bankruptcy and, should you consider that the advance is more than the unsupported credit justifies, then security should be taken. The taking of security covers the situation where the lender asks the borrower to provide an asset, as a protection against the borrowing not being repaid. The lender obtains the right to realise that asset in order to repay the borrowing.

QUICK QUESTION

What would you look for in an asset to make it good security?

Write your answer here before reading on.

4.5.2 Attributes of good security

If you know the attributes of good security and you have some appreciation of what each type of security is, then it is much easier to make an assessment of what the advantages and disadvantages are in taking security over each of these assets.

There are three things that a lender looks for in a security:

- Simplicity of title
- Stability of value
- Realisability

Each form of security does not always fall entirely on the plus side of each attribute – most also have negative aspects.

- **Simplicity of title**

  It is important for both the lender and the borrower that the formalities of arranging the security can be completed easily, quickly and cheaply. This is equally important later with regard to the discharge, realisation or release of the security.

  This attribute can be found in most types of security taken by banks with the notable exception of security over property which can be time consuming and costly for investigation of title and for the formalities of completion of the security.

  Ideally, a lender must look for the title to the subject of the security to be free of all liabilities or encumbrances of any nature which might prevent any future action that they may want to take with the security.

  An example of this is if the customer offered security over their property, but they already had an outstanding mortgage against the property. In this situation, if the customer defaulted on the loan and after following all of the recovery procedures the lender felt that they had no option but to realise the security, they may find this difficult as they would need to obtain the agreement of the first security holder.

QUICK QUESTION

Why is stability of value important to a lender when looking at security?

Write your answer here before reading on.

- **Stability of value**

It is also important that you can rely on the value placed on a security. You know what you want the security to be worth when you take it but you also wish to be as sure as you can be that it will be worth the amount you need when you need it.

The overriding rule here is that you ensure that the margin, or the difference between the borrowing you grant and the value of the security, is sufficient to allow for depreciation in value. As a lender you will want to ensure that the value of the asset does not fall below the amount of the borrowing. Be particularly aware of security which may be subject to sudden and wide fluctuations in value, such as speculative kinds of share. Furthermore, when considering the matter of value, you must also take into account whether or not the value is easy to assess at any time during the lifetime of the security.

The easiest types of security to value are:

- Cash lodgements
- Assignations of life policies
- Quoted stocks, shares and gilts

It is more difficult to value:

- Specialised or commercial property
- Unquoted shares

- **Realisability**

Repayment of borrowing may not always follow the agreed course and you may have to seek to 'cash in' – in other words, realise the security held. To do so, the security must be capable of quick realisation without undue formality. Any delay in the procedures for realisation can increase the possible loss of the principal debt and interest.

If you have taken a security which has a value that cannot readily be realised, such as a house subject to a tenant's rights or shares in a private company, this may result in the debt not being cleared at short notice.

It is worth re-emphasising that you should always look to the viability of the proposal for repayment – not for security. As the name suggests, security is there as a backup to guard against any unforeseen events that may occur during the life of the loan that will prevent the customer from making the promised repayments. As such, you should never look to security as the principal means of repaying an advance.

It is better to think of security in the same way that a trapeze artist looks at their safety net. The trapeze artist will have prepared for their act with the intention of completing it as planned – not by plunging into the net. However, the fact that the net is there will give the trapeze artist peace of mind. So it is with security – you will expect the borrowing to be repaid as agreed at the outset; but if there are any mishaps along the way, the security will give you peace of mind.

Finally, always keep in mind that no amount of security will turn an unviable proposition into a viable one.

4.6   Reward

A financial services organisation is no different to any other business – it needs to make a profit and the income comes from a number of sources, such as:

- The difference in the interest rates charged to customers who borrow and the interest rates paid to customers who deposit funds

- Arrangement fees in respect of lending facilities

- Charges for services provided directly, such as safe custody services, or night safe facilities

- The commission and payments received from other institutions for business passed to them, such as insurance commission

QUICK QUESTION

How does your bank make a profit from lending to customers?

Write your answer here before reading on.

The two main ways in which profits are generated from loans are:

- The arrangement fees charged to set up the loans
- The interest rates charged on loans

It is important that the correct amount is charged for services provided to customers. If this is not right, the profitability of the business will be undermined.

Arrangement fees

When a customer gets a loan, there are costs that the lender will incur. These include the cost of:

- Staff time spent preparing for and carrying out any interviews with the customer

- Assessing the application, either by manually underwriting the proposal or putting it through a credit scoring procedure

- Processing the borrowing on the computer system – setting up the account and the direct debit for the repayments, and arranging the drawdown for the customer

- Preparing the loan documentation, e.g. the offer letter and other supporting documentation

- Reviewing the borrowing at any review dates

In order to cover these costs, a lender may charge an arrangement fee to a customer to be paid at the time the borrowing is agreed. The fee may either be added to the borrowing or paid separately by the customer. Normally an arrangement fee will be lower for the renewal of an existing loan facility as opposed to the setting up of a completely new one. This is because it is less time consuming to review an existing facility than to set up a completely new facility.

The amount of the arrangement fee will be negotiated between the lender and the customer at the time the borrowing is agreed. While there will be some discussion as to the level of the arrangement fee, there are some parameters around which the lender will need to operate. This information should be published within your bank.

Interest rates

While some customers may express surprise from time to time regarding the need to pay an arrangement fee, they will all expect to pay interest on the borrowing. How do we decide on what level of interest rate to apply?

For some products the rate of interest will be fixed at the start and will remain fixed for the duration of the loan. The simplest example is the personal loan. Here the bank decides on the pricing of the loan based on interest rates and market conditions at the time the loan is taken out, along with the amount and term of the loan.

EXAMPLE

A customer is planning to borrow £7,500 to finance the purchase of a car over three years, with an interest rate of 7%. The interest calculation is:

$$£7,500 \times 7\% \times 3 \text{ years} = £1,575$$

Therefore the total repayment (excluding the arrangement fee) is:

$$£7,500 + £1,575 = £9,075$$

This is a simple situation – the bank decides on the interest rate and then applies it.

For other types of borrowing, we must negotiate with the customer what the rate of interest will be. As you will remember from the start of this chapter, the rate of interest is usually related to the Bank of England Bank Rate (or base rate) and will fluctuate in line with this rate.

EXAMPLE

The interest rate could be quoted as 6/BR which means that the interest charged is at 6% over the current Base Rate. Therefore, if at the time the advance is agreed, Base Rate is 4.5%, then the interest rate at the start of the loan will be 10.5%. Say two months after the borrowing is agreed, Base Rate is increased to 5%, then the interest on the borrowing will be increased to 11%.

On what do we base our decision of what rate to charge?

The fundamental way in which banks decide on rates of interest for lending is by comparing risk to reward. Basically, this means that the more risk is involved for the lender, the higher the rate of interest that will be charged. The idea behind this is that the higher the likelihood that the bank may lose its money, then the more interest it will charge the customer to compensate for this.

BPP
LEARNING MEDIA

QUICK QUESTION

What factors within a lending transaction could constitute risk?

Write your answer here before reading on.

Several factors are relevant here. For example, the purpose of the lending or the customer's previous borrowing record may present risk. As we have seen, one way in which the risk to the lender can be mitigated is by the customer providing security. Therefore, all other things being equal, if a customer offers suitable and adequate security, the rate of interest charged by the lender should be lower.

It is important that, when agreeing a rate of interest with the customer, thought is given as to what the risk is and the rate of interest should be charged accordingly. This will help to ensure that you are consistent in your approach to customers. You must always be able to justify why you are charging a particular rate of interest, rather than it appearing to be an arbitrary decision.

If there is not this consistency and the customer subsequently becomes aware that you are charging different interest rates for very similar types of borrowing, this will have an adverse effect on the image and professionalism of both you and your bank.

It is normal practice for banks to set guidelines for staff regarding the rates of interest that they should be charging.

4.7 Other services for the customer

In the past, a bank would respond to the request that a customer made but would not necessarily look beyond that request. For example, if the customer were seeking a personal loan to finance the purchase of a car, the lender might not have thought of other services that might benefit the customer, such as car insurance. This was unfortunate from both the customer's and the bank's point of view as, although the customer had a real need for car insurance, they may have had to go to another provider to have this need met.

However, this approach has changed since the mid-1980s. Banks have faced increased competition from one another and from other players who have entered the market in recent years. While firms are always keen to attract new customers, they are also very aware that it costs less for them to obtain new business from existing customers than to go out to the market to win business from new customers.

An ideal opportunity to identify additional products that the customer may need is by scrutinising a lending application. By showing the customer that you are considering all their financial needs, you are being professional. However, at this stage you are only identifying the customer's potential needs; it is only possible to ascertain if these needs are real and unfulfilled by discussing them with the customer.

QUICK QUESTION

What is your understanding of the term 'credit scoring'?

Write your answer here before reading on.

5 Credit scoring

5.1 Overview

Credit scoring is an automated technique used to assist lenders in the analysis and assessment of loan applications. It enables large volumes of applications to be processed, acting as a filtering mechanism for loans that will be automatically declined, as well as estimating the risk profile presented by each case. When implemented efficiently, credit scoring enables loan applications either to be sanctioned subject to the verification of information submitted, declined, or flagged for an 'override' decision by a lender.

Credit scoring is especially useful in managing large volumes of applications for relatively **small credit facilities**. However, some institutions have developed sophisticated models that can be used to evaluate complex applications, such as business loans.

At its simplest, credit scoring can take the form of a credit scorecard – a set of rules that create a numeric score for the various elements in a credit application. Examples include how long the customer has lived at their current address, or whether or not they have a land telephone line. Each score is added up to produce an overall figure that represents the risk for the application and so determines whether or not the loan should be approved. The minimum score that an application must obtain is the cut-off score.

The scores attributed to each variable can be positive or negative. For example, empirical evidence suggests that couples who are legally married are less likely to default than those who are not legally married. Although this is a generalisation, this should lead to a more positive score for married couples than for unmarried couples. It is also known that those in regular, permanent employment present a lower risk than the self employed, so the lender may award a negative score (or lower positive score) for those in self employment. Negative scores are often given for those who have been subject to Sheriff Court or County Court judgements for debt in the recent past, and to those who have been declared bankrupt in the past, even if the bankrupt has been discharged.

The premise behind credit scoring is that by looking at past performance, we can predict the future repayment patterns of customers who share similar characteristics. The technique therefore relies on statistical probabilities being applied to historical information, with the assumption that this will be a guide to future outcomes. Thus by looking at similar customers to the one making the application and how they have repaid in the past, we have a good indication of what their repayment record will be in the future. Credit scoring is therefore a measure of risk – the risk in this case being the non-repayment or default of the customer.

Advantages of credit scoring

- Speed in processing large volumes of applications

- Reduction in operating costs

BPP
LEARNING MEDIA

- Decisions can often be made by more junior managers or staff

- Ability to process large volumes of information in a consistent manner

- Reduction in administration in dealing with cases that will be automatically declined

- The ability to change the system as economic, social and other conditions change over time

- The ability to highlight cases that require human intervention, enabling lenders to focus the energies of lending staff on matters that require personal attention

Disadvantages of credit scoring

- It is heavily reliant on historical information, and so may be unsuitable when conditions are changing rapidly

- Dehumanisation of the lending process

- Reliance on probabilities and inability to identify certain unique features of certain cases

- Like any automated system, it will create some 'nonsense' outcomes where attractive applications may be declined and unattractive applications are sanctioned

- It is unsuitable for assessing certain types of application, such as where the applicant has no credit history whatsoever

- Some of the raw data may be subject to error (such as incorrect or out-of-date information supplied by a credit reference agency)

If a customer passes the set cut-off score, the bank is saying that this person represents an acceptable risk. On the other hand, if the person does not pass the cut-off score, the bank is taking the view that they do not represent a reasonable risk.

Credit scoring can use either a bottom-up or a top-down approach. With a bottom up approach, a high score is good and a low score is bad. With a top down approach, the opposite holds true, in that a high score is bad and a low score is good.

When we refer to a scorecard in the context of credit scoring, we are looking at the points based on the characteristics of the applicant which have been drawn from their loan application. This score is then compared to a number of previous applicants who either:

- Repaid fully on time
- Were slow to repay
- Did not repay the loan in full

Points are allocated to a range of characteristics in the application to determine this end score.

Fraud detection techniques can also be built into the credit scoring process to highlight potentially fraudulent applications. Typically this will be internal to the bank and is where verification checks are carried out for specific products or credit applications. This can produce significant savings for banks as they help to prevent advances being made where the loan would eventually be written off due to fraud.

Originally, credit scoring was used in generating credit card limits or approving fixed rate personal loans. Its use has now been extended to include current accounts of personal customers in setting overdraft limits and determining whether or not items presented to the account should be paid or if their payment would result in an irregular position on the account.

Credit and behavioural scoring has been further extended to small business customers when considering borrowing of anything from a maximum of £100,000 to £2,000,000.

5.2 Behavioural scoring

Credit scoring has been further developed into **behavioural scoring**, a method of determining the credit risk associated with an existing account.

Factors that could be considered include turnover through the account, regularity of credit payments, and any unpaid items. Information on previous and current credit facilities may also be taken into account.

Behavioural scoring is being further enhanced by live feeds of information from credit reference agencies which can verify the behaviour of the account.

KEY WORDS

Key words and phrases from this chapter are given below. Make sure you know what they mean and add any other words or phrases that you want to remember. You can use the space provided to write your own revision notes.

- Lending Code
- Lending rates
- Principles of lending
- Person
- The three Cs
- Assets and liabilities
- Amount and purpose
- Repayment
- Security
- Simplicity of title
- Stability of value
- Realisability
- Reward
- Credit scoring

REVIEW

To help you reflect on and review the content of this chapter, give some thought to the following questions.

- What is the scope of the Lending Code?

- What are the key principles of the Lending Code?

- What factors influence the interest rates charged by lenders?

- What key information is typically required in a lending application?

- What are the key principles of credit and lending?

- In what ways can the key principles of credit and lending be used to make professional and ethical lending decisions?

- What are the attributes of good security for lending?

chapter 5

RISK MANAGEMENT IN BANKING

Contents

Learning objectives

By the end of this chapter, you should be able to:

- Explain what is meant by 'risk' and 'risk management'
- Explain how risks can be identified, assessed, mitigated and monitored
- Identify the characteristics of key risk types
- Understand the role of the regulator in risk management

Introduction

The business of banking is primarily concerned with risk. For example, when a bank agrees to lend money to a customer and repayment is scheduled for some point in the future, and as the future can never be predicted with absolute certainty, there is obviously some degree of risk.

The aim of this chapter is to increase your knowledge and understanding of approaches to risk management in banking. We will consider what is meant by 'risk' and 'risk management' and discover how risks can be identified, assessed, mitigated and monitored. Risk cannot be totally eliminated, for either individuals or businesses. Indeed, regulators see it as both impossible and undesirable to remove all risk and failure from the financial system.

Risk occurs in many different areas and we will explore the elements of credit risk, regulatory risk, operational risk and reputational risk, and how these can be quantified, managed, and prevented from recurring. Risk management is not the sole preserve of senior management. Risks affect all businesses at all levels, and quite often it is an awareness of risks and taking responsibility to communicate concerns about risks that is the first step in mitigating risks and minimising the harm to the organisation. Everyone in the organisation must be aware of the risks confronting it.

In the aftermath of the late 2000s financial crisis, risk management is at the top of the agenda of regulators as well as banks and other firms across the global financial industry to an extent not experienced before.

QUICK QUESTION

What is 'risk'?

Write your answer here before reading on.

1 Risk and risk management

1.1 The nature of risk

Risk – 'the possibility of incurring misfortune or loss'. There are many definitions of risk but, using this one, the following key issues emerge.

- **Possibility**. This is the chance or likelihood of an event happening in the future. The event has not yet happened: it exists as one of a number of possible outcomes that may occur in the future, some quite likely and others not so probable. This is an important type of observation because it suggests that people can put in place a plan or take an action today that may reduce the chance of the event occurring in the future.

- **Misfortune or loss**. The potential outcome is regarded as negative. It is a potential occurrence that people are trying to avoid. This is also called the 'downside' of risk. Of course, some outcomes may be extremely serious and others of relatively minor significance.

In the context of banking, risks are faced by different persons or entities, at different levels. Here are some examples.

- For the banking **customer**, for example, taking out a variable rate loan presents the risk that interest rates will rise, making repayments more expensive in the future. At any current time, the future course of interest rates is unknown. This is **interest rate risk**.

- A **shareholder** of a bank is a part-owner of the bank. The shareholder faces the risk that the value of her shares may fall. There could be an economic downturn, adversely affecting the share prices of many banks and other companies. The shares held could suffer a fall in their value even when share markets generally are on the rise, perhaps because analysts' expectations of the bank's future profits have been lowered. In general terms, the uncertainty in the market value of shares and other assets in an investor's portfolio can be called **market risk**.

- A **bank**, like other **firms**, has the general objective of maximising shareholder value, through making profits and paying dividends. This objective aligns with that of the shareholder, although an ordinary shareholder is not totally committed to the particular bank, since she can easily sell her shares and buy the share of another company, within seconds. There are various risks that a bank faces and should seek to manage. For example, in lending money to a customer, the bank faces the risk that the customer may fail to repay the debt – that is, there is **credit risk** (also referred to as 'default risk' for the bank).

- **Regulators and central authorities**, such as the Bank of England and its subsidiary the Prudential Regulation Authority (in the UK), seek to ensure the stability of the financial system in the wider economy – the 'macro'-economy. There has been much commentary since the financial crisis of the late 2000s about certain banks and other financial institutions being 'too big to fail', and regulators categorise some larger financial firms as **'systemically important financial institutions' (SIFIs)**. Prudential measures are primarily concerned with sound banking practice and the protection of depositors at the level of the individual bank. These matters as they bear on the individual bank have been called 'micro-prudential' risks. To the extent that unsoundness of a bank could affect the market and the economy as a whole, there is a **macro-prudential risk**. Regulators may seek to monitor and manage this risk by checking on the financial health and soundness of banks and other financial firms.

Phrases such as 'run the risk' and 'taking a risk' are commonplace in our normal conversation, and we all should know that life is risky. We learn from an early age and throughout our professional lives that mistakes, errors of strategy, and foolhardy behaviour can lead to calamity. Risk is all around us in our daily lives and, as businesses begin to emerge from the economic turmoil of the credit crunch of the late 2000s, which delivered an unprecedented impact upon global finance and economics, we should now all be more attuned to the risks businesses face, particularly in the financial sector.

The phenomenon of risk is not new but is so much more demonstrably powerful today. As a result, the managers of financial institutions, indeed anyone in a senior position, must contribute to the overall duty of a firm to manage its risks. Executive managers must have a firm grasp of the businesses for which they are responsible. They should set in place a structure of control processes which looks critically at risk sources and addresses them effectively.

Risk manifests itself in various ways and one of the basic steps for firms to take is to understand the nature of different types of risks, their sources, the events which can occur, and the resultant impacts.

1.2 Managing risks

Knowing what risk is will not in itself prevent either an individual or an organisation from suffering loss or injury as a result of the risk. What we must do is to devise ways to manage risk. Whenever a bank lends money to a customer, there is a risk that that customer will not repay it. The fact that this risk exists does not prevent banks from lending money. They do however look for ways in which risk can be managed to an acceptable level so that enough loans can be made to make a profit.

QUICK QUESTION

What is meant by 'risk management'?

Write your answer here before reading on.

Risk management is the sum of all the actions taken by an individual or organisation to manage risks that could occur.

Having a car with airbags does not guarantee motoring immortality, but having airbags reduces the level of risk in an accident to a level that most people accept. Also, by taking out breakdown cover, a driver does not guarantee that their car will never break down. What they are doing is putting something in place to deal with a potential breakdown and to minimise its consequences, possibly at lower cost than the alternatives. Similarly, organisational risk management does not remove risk completely; it seeks to identify potential risks, then puts procedures in place to minimise these risks and instigates measures to deal with any potential loss, injury, disadvantage, or destruction arising.

Managing risk is thus an essential skill and responsibility of those who run financial institutions. Those who do manage risk well will benefit from significant rewards and those who do not may well see their businesses fail completely.

QUICK QUESTION

Think about the risks that you have encountered in the last month. What actions did you take to manage these risks?

Write your answer here before reading on.

If you were to ask ten people this question, you would probably get ten different answers.

Here are some of the steps that you might take to minimise risk:

- Buy a car with safety features, such as airbags
- Buy breakdown cover for your car
- Purchase an extended warranty when buying a major and expensive item
- Take out life assurance
- Warm up before working out at the gym
- Fit a strong lock to your bicycle
- Apply sun block
- Fit a computer keypad with wrist rests
- Look both ways before crossing the road

If individuals take steps to manage risk, it follows that it is sensible for organisations to do the same.

QUICK QUESTION

What items or services have you purchased recently that included a feature to minimise risk?

Write your answer here before reading on.

1.3 Types of risk

1.3.1 Introduction

You are expected to be able to differentiate between different types of risk, in particular the following types of risk affecting banks: **credit risk, regulatory risk, operational risk** and **reputational risk**.

1.3.2 Credit risk

The fundamental business of banking is that banks take deposits from some customers and lend money to other customers. When anyone lends money to another party, there is a risk that the loan will not be repaid – either in full or in part. This is what is meant by credit risk, although the risk can be wider than this simple explanation may suggest. For example, if we take shares as security (collateral) from a customer and they default on their repayments, there can still be a credit risk if the value of the shares falls and the bank does not obtain full repayment of the loan.

Much of what we looked at in the previous chapter of this Study Text on *Credit and Lending* is about identifying credit risk and, where possible, mitigating it.

1.3.3 Regulatory risk

Regulatory risk is the risk of material loss, reputational damage or liability arising from the failure to comply properly with the requirements of regulators or with codes of practice that oversee the way in which banks and other financial organisations conduct their regulated business.

EXAMPLE

The following are examples of regulatory risk.

- A laptop was lost by a manager working in a bank, with the possibility that confidential data relating to personal customers would fall into the wrong hands. The company admitted the loss of the computer and took action to ensure that the data would quickly become worthless. However, as the organisation had breached the provisions of the Data Protection Act 1998, it was ordered to pay a substantial fine.

- In 2009, a company launched an initiative that claimed that it could work on behalf of credit card holders to get their balances outstanding cancelled. The advertising campaign was aimed at individuals with large balances owing on credit cards and little prospect of reducing these balances in the short term. The argument put forward by the company to potential customers was that there was strong evidence to suggest that credit card providers were often not fully compliant with the procedures set out in the Consumer Credit Acts, and by going through the credit agreements in detail, significant errors and omissions could render the whole agreement unenforceable. This would enable the debtor to force the lender to write off the debt.

1.3.4 Operational risk

The Basel Committee, set up by the Bank of International Settlements to discuss the handling of supervisory issues and to improve the quality of banking supervision globally, has produced a definition of **operational risk**:

> '... the risk of direct or indirect loss resulting from inadequate or failed internal processes, people and systems or from external events.'

Thus, **operational risk** takes a number of forms.

- **Process risk** is the risk that comes from the processes carried out within the bank or other business. As you will be aware from your day-to-day work, there is a myriad of these processes – from the automated payments systems to the manual processes used to open and lock up a bank branch securely at the start and end of the working day.

  Risk is evident when these processes are inefficient or ineffective. A balance needs to be struck between efficiency and effectiveness. The cost of providing a watertight process may be prohibitive and so a bank may accept that there are some inherent risks. However, risks need to be at an acceptable level for the bank and the regulator. Sometimes a bank, or any other organisation, may be thrown into chaos by process or systems failure.

EXAMPLE

While 'chip and PIN' cards had been adopted by banks in Europe several years previously, up to 2014 major banks in the US had not yet adopted this system for payments within the US: they apparently estimated the costs of introducing chip and PIN cards to be greater than the fraud losses that would be saved. This was to change in 2015, with the introduction of 'chip and PIN' in US banking.

- **People risk**: it is often said that one way in which an organisation can differentiate itself from the competition is through its people. However, with people comes risk. Errors can occur due, for example, to a lack of knowledge or skills, having too few people in the right place at the right time, or from poor management.

  Another element of people risk is fidelity risk, which arises from dishonesty. In its simplest form, this may involve theft of cash and equipment. More elaborate criminals may pay accomplices to join the staff of a bank to help circumvent anti-money laundering procedures. Criminals also infiltrate contact centres by securing the services of individuals who are prepared to work there for, say, 3 to 4 months and then gather confidential customer data from computer screens by simply writing it down. If a fraud is then committed against those on whom the data is held and sufficient time has elapsed since the capture of the data, this crime can be almost undetectable.

There is no such thing as a perfect system or a perfect control system. Perhaps one of the most unpredictable issues that has to be managed is the participation of people in processes. Sometimes, actions may be routine in nature but may be overlooked in error or the panic of a situation.

EXAMPLE

A major airline reported that, in the evacuation of an aeroplane that crash landed (without casualties), the experienced pilot had to be reminded of how to unfasten his seat belt. He had successfully completed the dangerous tasks of ditching the aircraft but the situation caused him to forget the most basic of routines.

- **Systems risk** is mainly about the technology employed by banks to assist in their operations. With technology come the risks of systems failure, poor data quality, and a lack in security of the data held. This last area has received more attention from high profile publicity of the failure of some organisations to keep confidential information out of the public domain. The banker's duty of confidentiality makes this area even more important for a bank.

- **External risk**. No organisation operates in a vacuum, therefore risks from external events will always be an area for consideration. These are the risks that come from the external environment in which the organisation operates. Unfortunately the bank will have little or no control over these events, but the effects of external risk can be mitigated by the bank having contingency plans.

    There are various external risks to consider, such as a change in the tax regime, a change of government, financial fraud perpetrated by persons external to the bank, or the raids that can be carried out on bank branches.

QUICK QUESTION 8

In what way is the risk of loss of reputation dangerous for a bank?

Write your answer here before reading on.

1.3.5 Reputational risk

This is the risk of a bank suffering damage to its standing in the market, in the media, or with clients, due to some action on its own part such that the bank receives adverse publicity. The problem of reputational risk is especially sensitive for the retail banking sector, which has been regarded in the past as steady, conservative, and secure – whether rightly or not.

Reputational risk can result in a fall in the bank's share price and, consequently, shareholder value. A bank will always want to protect its brand image and value: these factors are intangible, but any adverse impact upon them will have a tangible effect by way of loss of business and/or revenue.

Reputational risk has been spectacularly demonstrated during the credit crisis. It has been triggered by general failures of institutions to deal with exceptional economic and financial circumstances, and also by the adverse press coverage of so-called 'fat cat' bonuses, executive remuneration packages and exit payments. Reputations were also damaged when some banks were required to seek government funding and, as a result, their standing within the community was tarnished.

EXAMPLE

A financial institution lost a disk on which confidential payroll information was stored. Although the institution escaped punishment on this occasion, the affair severely damaged the reputation of the business through the ensuing negative publicity.

Pause for thought ...

Thinking about the different types of risk, which ones do you come across most frequently in your role in the bank?

1.4   Stages in the management of risk

1.4.1   The risk management life cycle

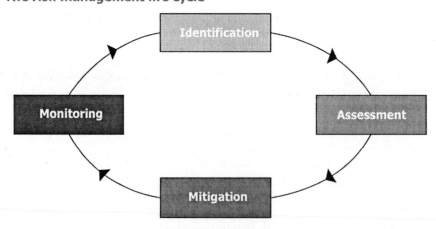

The process of risk management is a **continuous** cycle: it is not time-limited. It starts with the **identification** of risk, then moves on to risk **assessment**, then risk **mitigation**, to the **monitoring** of risk. Monitoring risk is in itself a continuous process as new risks will be identified and so the cycle continues.

1.4.2 Risk identification

It is vital that the process of risk management is pro-active because, rather than waiting for the risk event to occur and then deciding how to deal with it, we must be constantly identifying any risks before they happen. The process of risk identification must therefore produce a clear understanding of what the potential risks are. As a bank operates in a dynamic environment, the identification of risk must be an ongoing process in order to keep track of any potential risks arising. In a credit scenario, for example, risk identification needs to be carried out at both the credit assessment stage and during the life of the loan, as the customer's circumstances may change and that could present new risks or alter some of the risks already identified.

There are several ways of carrying out risk identification and we now consider some specific techniques.

Workshops. This technique is often used when an organisation is about to start a project or implement some form of major change. Representatives of the project will come along to present a brief outline of the proposal, while the other attendees assist in the identification of any potential risk through their expertise from their own specialist areas. You will probably find that, if your bank has a dedicated **operational risk team**, they will facilitate the workshop.

It is vital that everyone present participates fully in the workshop and it is useful if there are people who can think creatively and thus initiate the creativity of the other participants. The workshop should continue until all of the likely risks have been identified.

When the workshop has concluded, the outputs should then be assessed using the risk assessment techniques adopted by the bank. (We'll look at risk assessment in the next section).

Questionnaires. These can be used to identify high level risks that can then be assessed in more detail. Careful wording for the questionnaire is required to ensure that all risks are identified and that the questions are not worded in such a way that could lead to a particular outcome.

Loss data capture and analysis. If a risk has not been identified by the bank, it can become apparent when it causes a loss to the business. While this is an unsatisfactory state of affairs, steps can now be taken to ensure that there is no repetition of the situation. The bank must identify what the cause of the loss was; in effect risk identification is being carried out retrospectively, but this should help avoid a repetition of the event and thus the loss.

Near miss analysis and experience. Under the last heading, risk identification occurs retrospectively after a loss had occurred. There is also the potential for retrospective risk identification when the business has not suffered a loss, but there has been a near miss.

You could relate this to driving a car – you may alter your style of driving as a result of an accident (this would fall into the loss data capture and analysis category) but you may also alter your driving technique as a result of a near miss – perhaps a potential collision that was only narrowly avoided.

PESTEL analysis. This form of analysis can be used to help identify various sources of risk for a bank or other business, as the sources may be of the types indicated by the **PESTEL** mnemonic: **P**olitical, **E**conomic, **S**ocial, **T**echnological, **E**nvironmental, or **L**egal.

- **Political factors**. The profitability of a bank may be affected by uncertain future political outcomes in the countries in which it operates, such as an election, the removal of a government by a revolutionary coup, or a change in government policy. This could have a transforming effect upon the ability of the business to produce or continue to produce viable results.

- **Economic factors**

    - **The trade cycle** – will the state of the economy affect the likely success of the bank? For example, if base rate is increased to reduce demand in the housing market, how much will this affect the risk associated with home loan products?

    - **Interest rates** – what is the current trend of interest rates, and what is the outlook for interest rate stability? How is this likely to affect risk around, say, savings products?

- **Unemployment** – what is the current level of unemployment in the bank's target markets, and how likely is this to fluctuate? In what ways might this affect the business?

- **Structure of the economy** – has there been a move away from manufacturing to service industries? We can consider what the impact of this trend will be for risks that the bank is facing.

- **Social factors**

  - **Population demographics** – how are these likely to affect the business? For example, can we tell from demographics that demand for some of the traditional products will decline, and so does this present a risk? Could demographic changes affect the numbers of school or college leavers, so affecting the pool of talent for recruitment?

  - **Lifestyle changes** – will these influence consumers' buying decisions, and in turn the business?

  - **Levels of education** – if our customers are becoming more financially aware and so making the market much more competitive, how will this trend affect current initiatives? Can this trend be quantified?

- **Technological factors**. New developments in technology affecting the bank. While developments in technology provide opportunities for businesses, there are also associated risks, some of which may be identified only after the new technology has been implemented. The other side of the technology coin is that as technology brings us new advances, it also renders traditional technology obsolete. For example, as more people use internet banking, what impact does this have on customers' use of contact centres? As a particular working practice or delivery channel moves towards obsolescence, what risks might this bring? The possibility of IT systems being hacked brings significant risks, including of fraud losses, and loss of customer goodwill.

- **Environmental factors**. Increasing focus on the environment has had an impact on business generally. This has affected the ways in which organisations operate – and with any change there will come risks. For example, natural disasters can halt the operations of a business, and contingency plans may be put in place to address such issues.

- **Legal factors**. Legislation and changes in the law can affect business enterprises in various ways. An example is health and safety legislation. There is a requirement on employers to carry out a risk assessment. Employers with five or more employees need to record the significant findings of the risk assessment. Risk assessment should be straightforward in a simple workplace such as a typical office. It should only be complicated if it deals with serious hazards such as those in a laboratory or on an oil rig. These duties are qualified by the principle of 'so far as is reasonably practicable'. In other words, an employer does not have to take measures to avoid or reduce the risk if they are technically impossible or if the time, trouble or cost of the measures would be grossly disproportionate to the risk. The law requires what good management and common sense would lead employers to do anyway: that is, to look at what the risks are and take sensible measures to tackle them.

1.4.3 Risk assessment

Once we are clear about the risks we face, we then have to decide how likely it is that these risks will actually occur and if they do occur, what the likely effects on the business are going to be. The risk assessment process therefore needs to start as soon as possible after the risk has been identified, as one potential outcome is a change of direction for the business.

In a situation potentially initiating change, the risks need to be assessed immediately as, depending on the likelihood and impact of each risk occurring, the best decision might be not to proceed with the change. The sooner this decision is made, the better for the business, as less time and fewer resources will have been invested.

Steps involved in assessing risks

1   Identify the risks
2   Categorise and group the risks
3   Carry out an initial assessment of all of the risks
4   Plot the risks on an **impact and probability grid**
5   Prioritise the risks and allocate them to 'risk owners'
6   Further assess the risks that merit further analysis
7   Update the risk register
8   Develop mitigation actions
9   Review risks regularly

An **impact and probability grid** is shown below.

PROBABILITY	**LOW IMPACT/ HIGH PROBABILITY**	**HIGH IMPACT/ HIGH PROBABILITY**
	LOW IMPACT/ LOW PROBABILITY	**HIGH IMPACT/ LOW PROBABILITY**

IMPACT

- **High impact/High probability**. These risks should be understood and addressed first. These are the risks to avoid as they are the most likely to happen and, if they do happen, they are going to have a significant effect.

- **Low impact/High probability**. Although these risks may not represent a high cost to the bank, the likelihood of occurrence means that they should not be ignored. These risks could represent a significant cost once all the small impacts are summed – therefore they should be controlled.

- **High impact/Low probability**. Although these are risks that will typically occur only infrequently, when they do, the impact will be serious. It is likely that this type of risk would be managed by risk transfer.

- **Low impact/Low probability**. It is still worth considering these risks as circumstances can alter and they may become more significant. Often, this type of risk is accepted by organisations.

Before looking at options for mitigating risks, keep in mind that risks cannot always be fully mitigated. Mitigation can reduce a risk to an acceptable level, but an element of risk may remain – this is **residual risk**.

Having assessed the probability and impact of the risks, we can move on to decide how best to mitigate the risks. An impact and probability grid indicates how the risks could be dealt with.

1.4.4   Risk mitigation

There are the following options for mitigating risk.

Risk avoidance. This is where the risk is such a threat to the business that it must simply be avoided. In other words, the risk event is beyond the organisation's current risk appetite. An example of personal risk avoidance would be a decision not to kayak due to a fear of water.

An organisation can employ proactive avoidance or abandonment:

- Pro-active avoidance is where the bank deems that a risk is so great it will avoid it. For example, it may be planning to launch a new product, but changes in the market lead it to abandon its plans as the risks associated with the product launch are now too great.

- Risk abandonment occurs when the bank is already pursuing a particular strategy and it decides to abandon this due to an unacceptable risk. In the example above, the business may have launched its new product before the market changes occur; however, as a result of these changes in the market, the business then decides to withdraw its product.

While the avoidance of the risk can be viewed positively in that the bank will no longer suffer from the risk event occurring, there is also a negative element – any potential benefits that could have come from the course of action will no longer be available.

QUICK QUESTION

What is your understanding of a joint venture?

Write your answer here before reading on.

Risk sharing. This is where the overall risk is reduced to an acceptable level by the organisation sharing the risk with another party, such as through a joint venture, which is when two or more organisations collaborate to deliver a product or service. By doing so they are sharing the risks associated with the venture.

Another example of risk sharing is outsourcing, where the risk associated with the outsourced activity is shared with the company to whom the business has been outsourced. The extent to which the risk is shared will depend on what is contractually agreed between the two companies. As with risk avoidance, there is also a disadvantage to risk sharing – if the risk is shared, the benefits that come from the activity will need to be shared with the other party.

Risk transfer. Risks might be transferred to another party who accepts the risk. Risk transference can apply to the risk itself or the financial consequences of the risk. An example of risk transference in banks is when security companies are hired to transfer cash around the organisation and it is the security company that accepts the risks associated with this activity. Another common example is where an insurance policy is taken out to mitigate risk, such as motor insurance.

Risk acceptance. There are times when the bank will feel that, although risks are present, they are worth accepting, possibly due to the potential resultant benefits. The consequences of the risk may be low, or the likelihood of the risk event occurring is low.

Risk acceptance also occurs if the risk is larger initially, but is mitigated to a certain level and the bank thinks that the level of residual risk is acceptable. Taking out an insurance policy with an excess attached is a similar situation.

Risk reduction. The aim of risk reduction is to reduce the chance of the risk event actually occurring, or to reduce the impact of the risk if it does occur. For example, air traffic control measures are designed to reduce the likelihood of an air collision occurring. An example closer to home could be that when your bank developed a disaster recovery plan, this may have highlighted particular risk possibilities that the bank has taken steps to reduce. For example, if all the back office processing is done in one location, there is a risk of business disruption if this building becomes inaccessible, perhaps due to flooding. One risk reduction technique could be to have this work backed up and carried out in various locations, so that if one place becomes inaccessible, then operations can continue as normal from the other locations using the backed-up information.

Risk retention. This can be planned or unplanned. For example, a risk manager may have identified a risk using the concepts previously outlined. She may have determined that, rather than transfer the risk, the most effective approach is to retain the risk within the bank but to adopt other mitigation actions to reduce the retained risk to an acceptable level. This is sometimes referred to as '**buying the risk**'. The bank has decided to accept the level of risk, but has plans in place to mitigate the impact of the risk event should it occur. If a risk has not been identified, the bank will not have any mitigating strategies in place, should the event occur. This is **unintentionally retained risk**.

1.4.5 Risk monitoring

The management of risk should be an ongoing process; thus risk should be **monitored on an ongoing basis** so that any new or amended risks can be identified quickly and dealt with through the other processes in the risk management cycle.

1.4.6 Management process

An approach to addressing risks and the risk assessment procedure which identifies, analyses and evaluates risks is summarised in the diagram below.

(Note the **continuing processes of monitoring and review** accompanied by active open communication and consultation.)

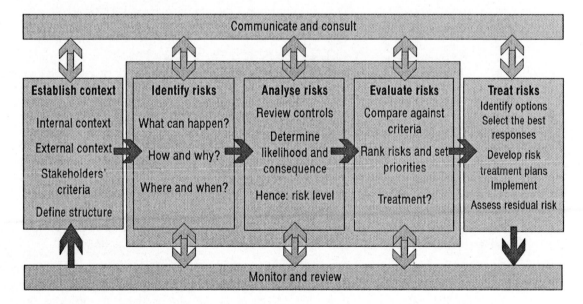

Pause for thought ...

Think about your role in the bank.

What are the key risks?

How are the key risks identified?

How are they assessed?

How are they mitigated?

How are they measured, monitored, and reported?

What could you do in your role to help minimise risk to the bank?

1.5 Key risk indicators (KRIs)

Managers have always looked at information to tell them how well their business is doing. An obvious source of indicators of performance is financial information, such as the profit and loss account or the sales figures. **Performance Indicators (PIs)** are essential management information. What they do not generally indicate, however, is how much risk is being run to achieve that performance.

By identifying and assessing the severity of risks and properly understanding the cause of the chain of events, objective measurement criteria can be chosen to measure ongoing risk status. These measures are called **risk indicators**. They are a 'health check' on the performance of the business and are used by all functions to ensure that risk is satisfactorily controlled. They usually measure the effects (rather than the cause) of risk at set control points in the business and act as early warning signals or forward-looking measures to alert management to problem areas.

Risk indicators facilitate the monitoring and control of risk. Indicators are metrics used to monitor identified risk exposures over time (*Institute of Operational Risk*, 2010). The indicator becomes 'key' when it tracks a particularly important risk exposure (a key risk), or it does so particularly well (a key indicator). Ideally the indicator does both, that is, it tracks a particularly important risk exposure particularly well.

BPP
LEARNING MEDIA

A metric is considered a key risk indicator (KRI) when it can be used to measure:

- The amount of exposure to a risk or risks

- The effectiveness of any controls that have been implemented to reduce or mitigate a risk exposure

- How well the risk exposures are being managed

QUICK QUESTION

What is a key risk indicator (KRI)?

Write your answer here before reading on.

An operational KRI provides information about the level of exposure to a given risk at a certain time. It should therefore be related to the specific risk whose exposure it represents. An example is the relationship between the number of customer complaints and the risk of process errors. As the number of complaints increases, there is an increased probability of the occurrence of process errors.

Risk indicators are early warning devices about whether or not exposure to risk is changing.

Thresholds or limits are typically tied to risk indicators (threshold levels (or changes) which, when exceeded, alert management to areas of potential problems. Some of the key risk indicators will be that a specific limit has been exceeded and that action will be required. Of course if the limit is exceeded by a comparatively small amount then one action may be required, whereas another action may result from a greater level of excess.

KRIs tell the most about the risks that are important to a particular business. It is therefore possible that a risk indicator may be a KRI in some businesses but only an RI in another.

QUICK QUESTION

What other examples of KRIs can you think of?

Write your answer here before reading on.

Other examples of KRIs

- Staff turnover (linked to, for example, staff shortages)
- Number of data capture errors (linked to, for example, process errors)

■   Number of computer virus attacks (linked to, for example, IT systems failure).

An effective monitoring and reporting process is essential for adequately managing operational risk. Regular monitoring and reporting activities can offer the advantage of quickly detecting and correcting deficiencies in the policies, processes and procedures for managing operational risk which can substantially reduce the potential frequency and/or severity of a loss event. Therefore, in order for risk to be managed, KRIs are monitored and reported.

2   Use of a risk register

A **risk register** (or 'risk log') is a risk management tool that can be used in the monitoring and reporting of risk. The register is used to log key risks associated with a project, or that could arise within an operational business area. It also contains details of the control measures that have been identified to mitigate the risks.

The example of a risk register shown **on the next page** logs the following information.

■   Name of project/operation

■   Date reviewed and modified, and by whom

■   Reference numbers assigned to each identified risk

■   Identified risks

■   Possible consequence if the risk is not mitigated

■   The probability, or likelihood, of the risk occurring, for example:

      5 – Definite
      4 – Very likely
      3 – Likely
      2 – Occasional
      1 – Rare

■   A rating based on the extent of damage the risk could cause, for example:

      5 – Disastrous
      4 – Serious damage
      3 – Moderate damage
      2 – Minor damage
      1 – Insignificant

■   A risk score that indicates the importance or urgency of mitigating the risk; the score is obtained by multiplying the risk rating by the risk probability

■   The control measures identified for handling the risk

■   A control score that indicates whether the proposed control measures are sufficient to completely mitigate the risk, for example:

      3 – Sufficient
      2 – Reasonable
      1 – Insufficient

For risks that have a control score of 1 or 2, the four columns on the right hand side of the risk register can be used to record the:

1   Consequences that would still remain, even after adopting all the control measures
2   Probability of any unaddressed parts of the risk cropping up
3   Risk rating for those parts of the risks that are not addressed by the control measures
4   Risk score after the control measures have been implemented

BPP
LEARNING MEDIA

Risk Register

Name of Project:

Modification Date:

Review Date:

Created by:

Reviewed by:

Ref No.	Risks	Consequence	Probability	Risk Rating	Risk Score	Control Measures	Control Score	Consequence (after improvement)	Probability (after improvement)	Risk Rating (after improvement)	Risk Score (after improvement)

Source: Adopted from http://www.brighthub.com/office/project-management/articles/100274.aspx

A risk register can take an individual event and state what the loss value might be should the risk occur, and then will apply an impact assessment to it. Consider, for example, a case of potential fraud where the risk impact might be assessed at £5m, with a 15% chance of its occurrence in any one individual year. Multiplying these together, £5m x 15% would give a severity of £0.75m in any one individual year. Of course, this would not mean that the company would expect a loss of £5 million or even £0.75 million. The actual cost would be based upon the distribution of losses. So, the loss could be at least £0.25 million with a 75% likelihood, or up to £2 million with a 25% likelihood.

Any assessments are based upon actual knowledge from real loss events that have occurred, together with additional assessment made by management and risk specialists regarding the quality of the control environment and control and risk self-assessment key performance indicators.

The severity could be calculated by assessors who might be asked to choose from, say, a number in the range of 1 to 10 for each of the risk issues that they are addressing. These expectation (or likelihood) levels would then be multiplied to come up with a severity. Hence, expectation multiplied by impact would deliver the severity figure.

The risk manager, or the person administrating the risk register and the assessment, would be the person who would then take the different expectations and convert them into something more meaningful in terms of real values rather than levels of severity. An expectation of 6 could equate to say 30% and an impact of 5 could equate to £10m. This then would give the severity of £3m, i.e. 30% of £10m. The point of this exercise would be to translate the general severity analysis from the managers who initially assessed the issue into real numbers to apply to the business.

At the next level however, one is faced with the change of other events, for example business volumes. Should business volumes go up by 1%, would the expectation increase by 1%? Would the impact increase by 1%? It could be that the expectation changes but not the impact, or *vice versa*. It could also be that both of these might occur, but that one is more than a 1% increase, rather than the other. (This is the beginning of the concept of 'stress testing'.)

3 Risk management and the regulators

3.1 PRA – assessing and acting on prudential risks

As we have seen, the **Prudential Regulation Authority (PRA)** has responsibility for the **prudential regulation** of banks and other prudentially significant firms. This regulator oversees banks from the point of view of their safety and soundness: the main risks here are that unsound banking practices could result in a bank being unable to repay customers' deposits, and could affect the wider market if the bank were to fail.

In order to deliver its objective of stability of the financial system, the PRA will uses a framework to assess risks to financial stability arising in the firms it oversees.

The PRA identifies risks by making use of:

- Baseline monitoring
- Investigation and assurance
- The macroeconomic and business context

The PRA take a forward-looking and judgment-based approach to supervision. **Baseline monitoring** will be undertaken for all firms, including those that can be resolved with minimal disruption to the financial system (e.g. credit unions and small deposit-takers). This monitoring will include a review of a firm's resolvability (i.e. its prospective ability to manage failure in a controlled manner) at least once a year, analysis of a firm's financial position, discussions with senior management and ensuring compliance with minimum prudential standards for capital, liquidity and large exposures, as well as early interventions (where necessary) driven by what the PRA calls its **Proactive Intervention Framework (PIF)**.

The PRA classifies the firms it supervises into five categories, from high impact (1) to low impact (5), based on their potential impact on the stability of the UK's financial system.

- Firms that are most significant, given their size, complexity, interconnectedness and business type, have the capacity to cause 'very significant disruption' to the UK financial system, and so are categorised as **high impact firms**.

- **Low impact firms** have no significant capacity on their own to cause disruption, even though there is the potential that they could contribute to disruption that is occurring across a sector of the financial system.

The PRA will take into account how close a bank is to failing when considering the intervention actions it would take. The regulator's PIF will characterise, in the form of five clearly demarcated PIF stages, its judgement about a bank's proximity to failure.

3.2 FCA – assessing and acting on conduct risks

3.2.1 Introduction

We saw earlier that the **Financial Conduct Authority (FCA)** is the **conduct regulator** for banks and other financial services firms. While the PRA's focus is on the safety and soundness of financial services firms, the FCA's focus is on how regulated firms interact with their customers.

It is perhaps not surprising that **conduct risk** was a term adopted early in the life of the FCA as the UK's 'conduct regulator'. So, what is conduct risk? The concept has been related to 'a range of inherent factors [that] interact to produce poor choices and outcomes in financial markets.' *(FCA Risk Outlook 2013)*

The FCA has referred to conduct risk as the risk of '**consumer detriment** arising from the wrong products ending up in the wrong hands, and the **detriment to society** of people not being able to get access to the right products.'

Note that this definition recognises the need for a balance between these two sources of potential detriment. On one hand, regulatory action may seek to stop the wrong products being made available to consumers, while on the other hand regulation should not stifle or inhibit the financial services industry from making suitable products available.

As we saw in Chapter 2, the regulator identified a number of more specific categories of risk with which it was concerned, within the financial services industry:

- **Prudential risk** – the risk that the company could collapse as a result of poor or ineffectual management

- **Bad faith risk** – may be caused by mis-selling, fraud, misinterpretation, or failure to disclose important information

- **Complexity or unsuitability risk** – resulting from a lack of understanding on the part of the consumer, leading to the wrong choice of product

3.2.2 The regulator's assessment of risks

The regulator considers risk to be the combination of impact (the potential harm that could be caused) and probability (the likelihood of the particular issue or event occurring).

These impact and probability factors are combined to provide a measure of the overall risk posed to the regulator's statutory objectives. This measure is then used to prioritise risks and make decisions on what, if anything, its regulatory response should be. The regulator also uses this information to set its strategic aims and outcomes and to allocate resources based on its regulatory priorities.

RISK	=	IMPACT OF THE PROBLEM IF IT OCCURS	×	PROBABILITY OF THE PROBLEM OCCURRING

This approach is designed to:

- Identify the main risks to objectives as they arise
- Measure the importance of the risk
- Mitigate risks, and
- Monitor the progress of the risk

This helps the regulator to plan how to address those risks and allocate resources.

In the FCA's approach to risk management, some firms in some sectors may experience a highly intensive level of contact with supervisors over months or even years. Other, low-risk firms may only be contacted by one of the FCA's supervisors once every four years. The FCA will focus their attention on firms and sectors of the industry that could cause, or are causing, consumers harm or threaten market integrity.

3.2.3 The FCA's supervision model

The **FCA's supervision model** is based on three pillars.

1   **Firm Systematic Framework (FSF)** – preventative work through structured assessment of the conduct of firms.

2   **Event-driven work** – dealing faster and more decisively with problems that are emerging or have happened, and securing customer redress or other remedial work where necessary. This will cover issues that occur outside the firm assessment cycle, and will use better data monitoring and intelligence.

3   **Issues and products** – fast, intensive campaigns on sectors of the market or products within a sector that are putting or may put consumers at risk. This approach is driven by what the FCA calls **sector risk assessment**, which looks at what is currently and prospectively causing poor outcomes for consumers and market participants. It will use data analysis, market intelligence and input from the firm assessment process, as well as working closely with the FCA's Policy, Risk and Research area.

3.2.4 The Firm Systematic Framework (FSF)

The FSF is designed to assess a firm's conduct risk, and aims to answer the question:

'Are the interests of customers and market integrity at the heart of how the firm is run?'

It does this by using a common framework across all sectors, which is targeted to the type of firm. The common features involve:

- **Business model and strategy analysis (BMSA)**: to give a view on how sustainable the business would be in respect of conduct, and of where future risks might lie.

- Assessment of how the firm embeds fair treatment of customers and ensures market integrity in the way it conducts its business, and the assessment has the following four modules.

  - **Governance and culture** – to assess how effectively a bank or other firm identifies, manages and reduces conduct risks

  - **Product design** – to determine whether the firm's products or services meet customer needs and are targeted accordingly

  - **Sales or transaction processes** – to assess firms' systems and controls

- **Post-sales/services and transaction handling** – to assess how effectively a bank or other firm ensures its customers are treated fairly after the point of sale, service or transaction, including complaints handling.

■ Deciding what actions are required by the firm to address issues that the FCA has identified.

■ Communication to the firm, setting out the assessment and actions required.

The assessments will help the regulator to come to a view about the extent to which the firm embeds fair treatment of customers and integrity in the way it is run. This, at the most intensive end of assessment, covers the product lifespan from design through to sales and after-sales handling. The assessment of governance and culture will be crucial, as these are key factors that drive whether a firm treats its customers fairly (TCF) and can achieve the consumer outcomes set out through the TCF initiative, which we considered in Chapter 2 of this Study Text.

3.2.5 Event-driven work

Having fewer supervisors allocated to specific firms means that the FCA will have more flexibility to devote resources to situations in firms where there is heightened risk to consumers; or where consumers have experienced some loss and prompt action is required to stop the situation from worsening. The regulator's response could be prompted, for example by a whistle blower alleging misconduct in a firm, or a spike in reported complaints at a firm. The regulator will have a consistent and efficient process to ensure that 'event-driven' cases are dealt with quickly and that they get the right outcomes for consumers.

3.2.6 Issues and products

Being more flexible in how they deploy supervisors means that the FCA can react promptly to emerging issues, and carry out more reviews on products and issues across a sector or market. They will use a **sector risk assessment (SRA)** to drive this '**issues and products**' work. As the name suggests, this will provide an assessment of the conduct risks across a sector (such as the investment intermediary sector, or the retail banking sector).

This will complement the FCA's firm-specific work, so that together they identify risks, whether there are cross-firm issues, firm-specific issues or product issues. Working with colleagues from across the organisation, the FCA will use a range of data, information and intelligence from firms, consumers and trade bodies for example, to help identify the biggest risks and to prioritise work.

Here are key questions that the SRA will seek to answer:

■ What are the cross-firm and product issues that are behind poor outcomes for consumers or endanger market integrity?

■ What is the degree of potential harm?

■ What is the discovery or mitigation work proposed?

Specialist sector teams will work together to deliver these assessments, making appropriate use of external data and market intelligence. The FCA will consider the full range of mitigation options before deciding what to do, including policy, competition, enforcement and other interventions, in addition to or instead of a wholly supervision-based response. If they identify sector risks, they will carry out cross-firm issue and product work. This is where firms will experience a more intrusive approach, with specialist supervisors spending more time on a single issue and delving deeper into information, including files, recordings of calls from customers, and mystery shopping in firms' high street branches and offices. The FCA will look for the root causes of issues that they find, rather than just focusing on the effect they have.

KEY WORDS

Key words and phrases from this chapter are given below. Make sure you know what they mean and add any other words or phrases that you want to remember. You can use the space provided to write your own revision notes.

- Risk management life cycle
- Risk identification
- PESTEL
- Risk assessment
- Risk mitigation
- Risk avoidance
- Risk sharing
- Risk transfer
- Risk acceptance
- Risk reduction
- Risk retention
- Risk monitoring
- Key risk indicators
- Risk register
- Credit risk
- Regulatory risk
- Operational risk
- External risk
- Reputational risk
- Firm Systematic Framework (of FCA)

REVIEW

To help you reflect on and review the content of this chapter, give some thought to the following questions.

- What is meant by 'risk' and 'risk management'?
- What is a suitable approach to managing risk in banking?
- How can risks be identified?
- What risks might be identified by using the PESTEL framework?
- How can risks be assessed?
- How can risks be mitigated?
- How can risks be monitored?
- What is meant by risk avoidance?
- What is meant by risk sharing?
- What is meant by risk transfer?
- What is meant by risk acceptance?
- What is meant by risk reduction?
- What is meant by risk retention?
- How might a risk with high probability and high impact be managed?
- How might a risk with high probability and low impact be managed?
- How might a risk with low probability and high impact be managed?
- How might a risk with low probability and low impact be managed?
- What is a key risk indicator?
- How can a bank use key risk indicators to manage risks?
- What is a risk register?
- How can a bank use a risk register to manage risks?
- What different types of risk are there in banking?
- What is meant by operational risk?
- What is the role of the regulator in risk management?
- What is the FCA's Firm Systematic Framework (FSF) designed to do?

chapter 6

CONDUCT AND PROFESSIONALISM IN BANKING

Contents

Learning objectives

By the end of this chapter, you should be able to:

- Understand what is meant by ethics and differentiate between a range of ethical theories and approaches
- Explain what is meant by professionalism and differentiate between rules-based and principles-based codes of practice
- Explain the purpose and describe the content of the Chartered Banker Code of Professional Conduct and describe the potential impact of unethical and unprofessional behaviours
- Explain mechanisms for identifying, reporting and resolving ethical dilemmas and conflicts of interest
- Explain the social responsibilities of a bank

Introduction

A sustainable and successful banking industry is built on foundations of high ethical and professional standards. Banks deal with money that belongs in the main to their customers, and they take risks to generate income and create wealth. Trust is therefore a vital element of the relationship between a bank and its customers. The extent to which the public trusts its banks will be influenced by what banks do and how they do it, and the values and principles that guide their actions.

The aim of this chapter is to increase your knowledge and understanding of ethics and professionalism and to provoke your thoughts about what this means for you as a *Professional Banker*.

1 Ethics

1.1 Introduction

Ethics: derived from the Greek word *ethos* meaning custom, habit, character or disposition.

Ethics can be described as 'a system of moral principles and a branch of philosophy which defines what is good for individuals and society'. Ethics affect how we make decisions and lead our lives.

Ethics encourages us to think about:

- How to live a good life
- Our rights and responsibilities
- Moral decisions – what is right and wrong, or good and bad

Ideas about ethics have come from different religions, philosophies and cultures.

1.2 What is ethics used for?

We can use ethics as a framework to:

- Think about moral issues and dilemmas
- Decide what is the right thing to do
- Take responsibility for our own choices and actions

Core to the concept of ethics is a concern about others. When we think ethically, we are thinking about someone or something beyond ourselves.

1.3 Stages of ethical decision making

Ethical decision-making can be characterised as a four-stage process, and is influenced by individual and situational factors.

BPP
LEARNING MEDIA

Four stages of ethical decision-making – with examples:

1   **Recognise the moral issue** – for example, 'lying to customers about products can increase sales'

2   **Make a moral judgement** – e.g. 'lying to customers is wrong'

3   **Establish moral intent** – e.g. 'decide to be honest'

4   **Engage in moral behaviour** – e.g. 'tell the truth'

These stages distinguish between knowing what is the correct thing to do and the action taken. Therefore, the employee could still lie to customers about products even though they have recognised that this is immoral behaviour.

The moral decision taken will depend on:

- **Individual factors:** the unique characteristics, qualities and experience of the individual making the decision

- **Situational factors:** the context of the circumstances that cause an individual to make an ethical or unethical decision

Individual factors become more important in higher-level decisions in that the decision maker is making ethical decisions because they themselves believe that is the correct course of action.

Situational factors appear to be more important at lower-level decisions in that the decision maker may make decisions based on what is expected of them in that situation, rather than on their own values and beliefs.

1.4   Ethical theories: overview

Ethical theories can be categorised into three areas.

1   **Meta-ethics** considers the nature of moral judgement, and the origins and meaning of ethical principles.

2   **Normative ethics** is about the content of moral judgements and considers the criteria for what is right or wrong.

3   **Applied ethics** is concerned with controversial topics such as war, animal rights and capital punishment.

We will consider normative ethical theories in more detail later.

1.5   Moral rules: Absolutism v Relativism

One of the big questions in moral philosophy is whether or not there are moral rules that apply in all cultures and at all times. Religious views of ethics tend to be absolutist.

Some people think that there are universal rules that apply to everyone. This way of thinking is called **moral absolutism**.

Moral absolutism argues that:

- There are some moral rules that are always true and apply to everyone

- Acts that break these moral rules (immoral acts) are wrong, regardless of the circumstances or consequences

- As there is one set of rules for everyone, universal rules such as the Declaration of Human Rights can be drafted

QUICK QUESTION

Why might people disagree with moral absolutism?

Write your answer here before reading on.

Some people disagree with moral absolutism because they may:

- Feel that the consequences of an act, or the circumstances surrounding it, are relevant to whether that act is good or bad

- Think that absolutism does not take account of respect for diversity and tradition

Moral relativists dispute the idea that there are some 'super-rules' that all cultures ought to obey. Moral relativism argues that:

- Different cultures or different periods in history have different moral rules

- What is 'good' depends on what a particular group of people approve of

- Relativism respects the diversity of human societies and responds to the different circumstances surrounding human acts

QUICK QUESTION

Why might people disagree with moral relativism?

Write your answer here before reading on.

Some people disagree with moral relativism because they may:

- Feel that there is more to moral rules than the general agreement of a group of people

- Think that moral relativism does not provide a way to deal with moral differences between societies

Another view is that both absolutism and relativism have some good points and that:

- There are a few absolute ethical rules, and
- Many ethical rules depend on the culture

BPP
LEARNING MEDIA

Pause for thought ...

Consider the example of an absolute moral rule that it is good to keep promises. If we believe that it is good to keep promises, is it always good to keep promises? When might it be OK not to keep a promise?

Complete the following, according to what you believe.

It is right or good to:

1

2

3

Is it always right or good to do the things you have written? When might it not be right or good?

It is wrong or bad to:

1

2

3

Is it always wrong or bad to do the things you have written? When might it not be wrong or bad?

There is no right or wrong answer. What you have written will reflect your own moral rules that you feel a duty to live by.

QUICK QUESTION

According to the Concise Oxford English Dictionary, ethics are 'the moral principles governing or influencing conduct'. What moral principles do you think influence your conduct at work?

Write your answer here before reading on.

Perhaps you thought about your moral principles in relation to certain qualities, characteristics or certain virtues that you value; or perhaps you thought about certain duties you feel obliged to fulfil; or did you think about your moral principles in light of the potential consequences of your behaviour?

Ethics considers what is right and wrong and whether conduct by individuals and organisations is either good or bad. Yet what we consider to be right or wrong, good or bad, will depend on our values and beliefs. It will depend on what we think and the judgements we make about what people or organisations do in a given set of circumstances.

If we accept the subjective nature of ethics, we can rarely conclude that a behaviour or outcome is *absolutely* right or wrong. What we can do is consider various theories and approaches to ethics to help inform our thinking and reach our own conclusions.

1.6 Ethical theories

1.6.1 Introduction

As stated earlier, normative ethics is about the content of moral judgements and considers the criteria for what is right or wrong. Normative ethics can therefore help us arrive at moral standards that regulate right and wrong conduct.

Normative ethics can be viewed from several perspectives. The theories that we shall consider here are:

- Virtue theory
- Duty theory
- Consequentialist theory

1.6.2 Virtue theory

Ethics based on virtue is one of the oldest approaches and is rooted in the work of ancient Chinese and Greek philosophers, such as Plato and Aristotle. Virtue ethics is concerned with the moral character, or virtue, of a person carrying out an action. As such, it is based on the person, rather than ethical duties or the consequences of their actions. Although virtue ethics provides guidance on the personal qualities, or characteristics, a good or virtuous person would seek to embrace, it does not provide clear guidance on how to deal with an ethical or moral dilemma.

Key concepts:

- A virtue is a moral characteristic that a person needs to live well – what Aristotle called 'a good life'.

- A virtuous person is one who acts virtuously (as the result of rational thought).

- A person acts virtuously if they possess and live the virtues.

- An action is right only if it is one that a virtuous person would carry out in the same circumstances.

Virtue ethics addresses questions such as:

- What sort of person should I be?
- How should I live my life?
- What personal characteristics should I demonstrate?

Virtue theorists say that there is a common set of virtues that all human beings would benefit from, and that these are natural to mature human beings, even if they are hard to acquire. Yet, as different societies have different views about what these virtues should be, there is no general agreement about what these virtues are. Therefore it could be that what these virtues are will depend on the culture and society to which they relate.

Examples of virtues are:

- Objectivity
- Altruism
- Loyalty
- Wisdom
- Courage

QUICK QUESTION

What other virtues can you think of?

Write your answer here before reading on.

Other examples of virtues are:

- Honesty
- Kindness
- Fairness
- Prudence
- Justice

Pause for thought ...

Imagine you are creating characters for a blockbuster film about the banking world. There are two opposing characters. One is the most virtuous banker the world has ever seen. The other is the least virtuous. Complete the Table below.

What qualities does the most virtuous banker possess and live by?

What qualities does the least virtuous banker possess and live by?

In what ways does having and living by these qualities affect their respective behaviours?

	Character	Qualities	Behaviours
Most virtuous			
Least virtuous			

1.6.3 Duty-based ethics

Duty-based ethics are concerned with what we do, not with the consequences of our actions. It is about doing the right thing. According to this approach, we cannot justify an action by showing that it resulted in a good outcome or consequence. Therefore, some actions are right or wrong in themselves, regardless of the consequences.

Duty theories are sometimes called **deontological theories**, from the Greek word *deon*, or duty.

Key concepts:

- Do the right thing for the right reason, because it is the right thing to do.

- There are universal, absolute moral rules or principles, such as that it is wrong to steal, or it is good to keep promises.

- People have a duty to do the right thing, even if it produces a bad result.

- The right thing to do is established by clear rules or criteria established in advance.

- If we do something because we know it's our duty to do it, then we have done the right thing.

 Q U I C K   Q U E S T I O N

Ethics based on duty suggests that actions should be judged according to criteria established in advance. In your role at work, what criteria established in advance do you have a duty to act in accordance with?

Write your answer here before reading on.

You may have included in your answer examples of some of the following:

- Laws
- Rules and regulations
- Codes of conduct
- Industry guidelines
- Bank policies and procedures

One of the most influential writers on **duty-based ethics** was the German philosopher Immanuel Kant (1724-1804). Kant taught that there were some moral rules or laws that all human beings should obey and that every rational human being could work out what was right or wrong for themselves. Kant believed that his ideas would help people deal with moral dilemmas and provide us with a guide to acting in the right way.

Kant's views can be summarised as follows.

- Facts are neutral; they do not indicate what we should do or what we should be.

- The criteria we use to make moral judgements about facts are separate from the facts themselves.

- The criteria we use to make moral judgements and the actions we take are based on our own interpretation of what is right and wrong and what we think is 'good'.

- There are absolute, universal, moral rules that are true in all circumstances. Kant calls these rules categorical imperatives.

- Moral rules must respect human beings. We should value others and treat them properly. We should view others as an end in themselves rather than as a means to an end just to get something we want.

- An action taken out of 'a good will' is a right action, regardless of the consequences.

- We should always act in such a way that we would be willing for it to become a general law that would apply to everyone else in the same situation.

- If the ethical rule we claim to be following cannot logically be made a universal rule, then it is not a valid moral rule.

QUICK QUESTION

Consider the saying: 'The end never justifies the means'. What would be an example of treating someone as a means and not an end?

Write your answer here before reading on.

Examples of treating someone as a means to an end include coercing, bullying, or deceiving them to get what you want.

1.6.4 Consequentialist ethics

Consequence-based or consequentialist ethics are concerned with the consequences of our actions. According to this approach, correct moral conduct is determined solely by a cost-benefit analysis of the consequences of an action. If the good consequences (benefits) are greater, then the action is morally proper. If the bad consequences (costs) are greater, then the action is morally improper. Consequentialist theories are sometimes called **teleological** theories, from the Greek word *telos*, or end, since the end result of the action is the sole determining factor of its morality.

Key concepts:

- Ethics based on consequences judges actions by looking at outcomes. It considers the question: Will my actions do good or harm to others?

- Whether an act is right or wrong depends only on the results, or consequences, of that act.

- The more good consequences an act produces, the better or more right that act.

- When faced with a moral dilemma, we should choose the action that maximises good consequences.

- People should live so as to maximise good consequences.

Consequentialist theories became popular in the 18th century by philosophers who wanted a quick way to morally assess an action by appealing to experience, rather than by appealing to gut instinct or long lists of questionable duties.

There are the following three main forms of consequentialism that have different views about what good thing should be maximised.

- **Ethical egoism**: an action is morally right if the consequences of that action are more favourable than unfavourable specifically to the person performing the action. 'Egoism' is about what is best for the individual. This approach is based on the idea that pursuit of personal interests will promote desirable outcomes for society more widely.

  Key question: *What decision would be best for me?*

- **Ethical altruism**: an action is morally right if the consequences of that action are more favourable than unfavourable to everyone except the agent.

  Key question: *What decision would be best for everyone else?*

- **Utilitarianism**: an action is morally right if the consequences of that action are more favourable than unfavourable to everyone.

  Utilitarianism is about maximising human well-being and that the ethically right choice in a given situation is the one that produces the most happiness and the least unhappiness for the largest number of people. Jeremy Bentham (1748-1832) was a utilitarian writer who maintained that decisions should reflect what would result in the greatest good for the greatest number of people.

  Key question: *What decision would result in the greatest good for the maximum number of people?*

Pause for thought ...

In your opinion, what are the main advantages and pitfalls of ethics based on virtue, duty and consequence?

Approach to ethics	Advantages	Disadvantages
Virtue		
Duty		
Consequence		

Suggested answer

Approach to ethics	Advantages	Pitfalls
Virtue	Provides guidance on the personal qualities, or characteristics, a good or virtuous person would seek to embrace and develop.	Some 'virtues' might be hard to acquire. It does not provide clear guidance on how to deal with an ethical or moral dilemma.
Duty	Values and respects every human being. Having rules to follow can make it easier to decide what action to take. Deals with intentions and motives.	It can be hard to reconcile conflicting duties. Sets absolute rules with too little regard for consequences of actions.
Consequences	Encourages us to think about the consequences of our actions and the effect on others. Focuses on the greatest good for the greatest number of people.	It can be difficult to predict and evaluate the consequences of our actions. Should the rightness or wrongness of our acts be judged on what we thought was going to happen or what actually happened? There may be different short and long term consequences. There may be different consequences for different groups of people, eg good outcomes for the majority and not so good for the minority.

QUICK QUESTION

What is your understanding of the terms 'profession', 'professional' and 'professionalism'?

Write your answer here before reading on.

2 Professionalism

According to the Concise Oxford English Dictionary:

- A profession is a paid occupation, especially one involving training and a formal qualification

- 'Professional' means worthy of a professional person; skilful or competent; or a person having impressive competence in a particular activity

- 'Professionalism' is the competence or skill expected of a professional

Distinguishing features of a profession:

- There is some degree of specialism.

- The specialism is relied on by the public, or sections of the public.

- The public expects high levels of integrity to be maintained.

- Integrity can extend to a person's private life, which means that certain events could result in expulsion from the profession, for example, being found guilty of a crime.

- There are barriers to entry in that jobs with a profession usually require the successful completion of professional exams and/or robust assessments.

- Professional activities are overseen and possibly governed by a professional body or association that is membership-based.

- The professional body sets minimum accepted standards of behaviour, usually in the form of a code of conduct or ethics.

- There are disciplinary and reputational consequences of failing to comply with these standards of behaviour. This could result in the refusal of a licence to practise, either for a specific period of time or indefinitely. For many professions, if a member is expelled, they will not be able to obtain employment in the same field.

- The professional body may stipulate requirements for Continuing Professional Development (CPD) and different levels of membership.

Central to the concept of professionalism is that a professional:

- Has a specialist knowledge base that underpins their professional judgement and decisions
- Exercises a high degree of autonomy
- Provides a service based on the needs of their clients (Eraut, 1994)

Generic features include:

- The understanding and application of knowledge

- Competence in relevant skills

- Reflective practice, using critical thought and informed, ethical judgement to make decisions in a range of contexts

- Responsibility and accountability to others

- Engaging in lifelong learning to develop as a professional, and develop the profession itself

[Source: Katz, T. (2000) *University Education for Developing Professional Practice* in *New Directions in Professional Higher Education* edited by Bourner, T., Katz, T., and Watson, D. UK: SRHE and Open University Press, pp. 19-32.]

Pause for thought ...

To what extent do you think banking is a profession?

What different types of professionals does your bank employ?

What are the CPD requirements of these different types of professionals?

3 Codes of conduct

3.1 Introduction

Professional activities are overseen and possibly governed by a professional body or association that is membership-based.

Members of a professional body are usually expected to commit to a set of standards in the form of a code of practice, conduct or ethics. If they breach this code, they could be subject to disciplinary action and may even be prevented from working in that profession in future.

3.2 Rules-based and principles-based codes

Codes can be described as either rules-based or principles-based.

- **Rules-based approach**. The rules-based approach is prescriptive in that it sets out details of what members can and cannot do. It therefore focuses on compliance, leaving little room for misunderstanding.

- **Principles-based approach**. The principles-based approach sets out broad 'high-level' principles with which members should comply; how members go about complying with these principles is up to them. High-level principles may, for example, involve treating customers fairly, and acting with professional integrity. It is up to the professionals, and the firms they form a part of, to develop rules and procedures that are consistent with the high-level principles of the code. As this approach is more about providing guidance that can be applied to various circumstances, it is more flexible than a rules-based approach and encourages the taking of responsibility and the exercising of professional judgement which, as we have seen, are key aspects of professionalism.

The aim of the principles-based approach is thus to prevent unprofessional conduct, within a focus on high-level principles such as fairness, rather than compliance with detailed rules. There will therefore be some degree of subjectivity when interpreting the code.

Principles-based codes usually refer to:

- Acting in the public interest

- Adopting ethical or 'high-level' principles

- A framework setting out the safeguards that apply to address the threats posed by non-compliance

In practice, many codes are a mixture of both rules and principles.

 QUICK QUESTION

What does it mean to 'act in the public interest'?

Write your answer here before reading on.

Acting in the **'public interest** is usually about the professional's duties and responsibilities to make decisions and act in a way that promotes the collective well-being of the community served by the profession. The community may therefore include key **stakeholders**, such as customers, employers, employees, investors, the business and financial community, who rely on the work of the profession.

Pause for thought ...

Which professional bodies are you a member of?

Which of these bodies has a code of practice, conduct or ethics?

What standards do these codes include?

3.3   Aspects covered in professional codes

Typically, standards set out in professional codes will refer to:

- Integrity
- Objectivity
- Professional competence and due care
- Confidentiality
- Professional behaviour

Integrity. The professional should be straightforward and honest in all their professional and business relationships.

Objectivity. Members of the profession should avoid bias, conflicts of interest and the undue influence of others when making a professional or business judgement.

Professional competence and due care. There is an ongoing duty to maintain professional knowledge and skill to ensure that a client or employer receives competent professional services in line with current technical and professional standards of practice and legislation.

Confidentiality. The professional should respect the confidentiality of information they acquire as a result of their professional and business relationships and not disclose this information to third parties unless there is a legal or professional duty to disclose it; nor should the professional use this information for personal benefit.

Professional behaviour. Members should comply with relevant laws and regulations and avoid any action that discredits the profession.

Pause for thought ...

The issues contemplated by the ancient Greeks 2,500 years ago are still relevant and worthy of thought today. For example, traders in the markets would ask Socrates how their need to sell could be compatible with being ethical. This was important because if they didn't sell their goods to make a living, their families could starve and there was a danger of being sold into slavery. Socrates observed that the more ethical traders were the most successful. They were trusted by their customers and therefore did more business.

In what way is a bank's need to sell its products and services compatible with being ethical and professional?

3.4 Chartered Banker Institute

The **Chartered Banker Institute** is the trading name of the **Chartered Institute of Bankers in Scotland (CIOBS)**, the oldest banking institute in the world and the only remaining banking institute in the UK. The Institute develops and promotes professional standards for bankers and provides professional qualifications for the financial services industry in the UK and overseas. As the professional body for bankers in the UK, the Institute is unique in being entitled to award the 'Chartered Banker' designation to qualified members.

All individuals working in the banking and financial services industry are required to act in a fair and honest manner. This is to protect the interests of customers, colleagues and counterparties; and the wider interests of society as a whole. As a minimum, compliance with legislation, regulation and industry/employer codes and standards is expected.

Membership of the Chartered Banker Institute brings with it additional responsibilities. All members are expected to display the highest **standards of professionalism** and a commitment to **ethical conduct**, giving at all times due care and consideration to others and **putting the public interest first**.

To help members maintain these high standards, the Institute's Code of Professional Conduct identifies key attitudes and behaviours expected of members and provides guidance to help members recognise and develop appropriate behaviours. Failure to meet the high standards expected may result in suspension or expulsion from the Institute.

Chartered Banker Institute Code of Professional Conduct

The Institute's Code of Professional Conduct requires members to:

1   At all times act in a professional and ethical way and uphold the highest standards of honesty, trust, fairness, integrity and diligence.

2   Consider the risks and implications of their actions, be accountable for them, and for the impact their actions may have on others.

3   Comply with all current regulatory and legal requirements, and endeavour to follow best industry practice.

4   Treat information with appropriate confidentiality and sensitivity.

5   Be alert to and manage potential conflicts of interest which may arise whilst performing their role, and not act for personal gain or advantage.

6   Treat all customers, colleagues and counterparties with respect and take responsibility for the advice and services provided to them.

7   Lead by example and act as a positive role model to others.

8   Continuously develop and maintain their technical and professional knowledge and competence.

9   Uphold the name and reputation of CIOBS and the banking profession.

3.5   Chartered Banker Professional Standards Board (CB:PSB)

3.5.1   Overview

The **Chartered Banker Professional Standards Board (CB:PSB)**, set up in 2011, is a voluntary joint initiative by eight UK banks and the Chartered Banker Institute.

The CB:PSB was set up to:

■   Develop a series of professional standards to support the ethical awareness, customer focus and competence of those working in the banking industry

■   Facilitate industry and public awareness and recognition of the standards

■   Establish mechanisms for the implementation, monitoring and enforcement of the standards

■   Help build, over time, greater public confidence and trust in individuals, institutions and the banking industry overall, and enhance pride in the banking profession.

The CB:PSB is not a regulatory body, and the professional standards have no statutory force.

The Board's overall aim is to restore public confidence and trust in the industry, and promote a culture of professionalism amongst individual bankers by creating industry-wide standards for professional knowledge, skills and competence.

Members of the CB:PSB are senior executive or non-executive directors from banks with significant UK-based operations, committed to funding the CB:PSB's activities and embedding its ethical and professional standards within their organisations. Collectively the CB:PSB member banks serve more than 70 million UK customers, and employ more than 350,000 individuals working in banking in the UK.

The CB:PSB serves as a public demonstration of banks' collective commitment to restoring trust in the banking profession and emphasising their responsibilities to customers, colleagues and wider society.

The CB:PSB developed and published its Chartered Banker Code of Professional Conduct (see below), which sets out the ethical and professional values and behaviours expected of bankers by the CB:PSB. Banks supporting the CB:PSB have agreed to subscribe to the Code. CB:PSB member banks will determine how the Code's broad principles may best be implemented and embedded in their organisations.

Note that the **CB:PSB Chartered Banker Code of Professional Conduct (supported by CB:PSB member banks),** set out below, is a different document from the **Chartered Banker Institute Code of Professional Conduct (for CIOBS members)**, which was set out earlier in this Section.

3.5.2 CB:PSB Chartered Banker Code of Professional Conduct

This Code states the following.

'I will demonstrate my personal commitment to professionalism in banking by:

1 Treating all customers, colleagues and counterparties with respect and **integrity**

2 Developing and maintaining my professional knowledge and acting with **due skill**, **care** and **diligence**, considering the risks and implications of my actions and advice, and holding myself accountable for them and for the impact

3 Being **open** and **cooperative** with the **regulators**, complying with all current regulatory and legal requirements

4 Paying **due regard to the interests of customers and treating them fairly**

5 **Observing** and demonstrating **proper standards of market conduct** at all times

6 Acting, at all times, in an honest and trustworthy manner, being alert to and managing potential conflicts of interest; and

7 Treating information with appropriate confidentiality and sensitivity

Pause for thought ...

Consider the key principles of the CB:PSB's Chartered Banker Code of Professional Conduct, supported by member banks, and the Chartered Banker Institute's Code of Professional Conduct, for its members.

How might you act in accordance with these key principles and industry best practice when:

Identifying, communicating, and meeting customer needs?

Responding to and dealing with complaints?

Applying legal and regulatory requirements?

Dealing with confidential and sensitive information?

Articulating decisions and the decision-making process?

Faced with an ethical dilemma or conflict of interest?

3.5.3 CB:PSB Professional Standards

Without the appropriate technical knowledge and skill, individuals cannot be expected to apply the Code consistently. The CB:PSB, therefore, has begun to develop a series of professional standards for bankers. These will define key components of banking professionalism, provide a framework for the development of professional judgement, and actively promote the improvement of banking skills, competence, and appropriate behaviours. Over time, the standards will sustain a strong culture of ethical and professional development across the banking industry.

The CB:PSB's standards will:

- Define key components of banking professionalism

- Provide a framework for the development of ethical and professional judgement

- Promote the improvement of banking skills and competence

- Enable benchmarking of individuals' competence and organisations' learning and development activities against industry standards

The standards will support bankers at all stages of their careers, and help banks and others design and deliver learning and development programmes that will aid the development of the requisite knowledge, skills and competence.

The CB:PSB is developing professional standards at three levels:

- **Foundation** – basic standards of professional and technical competence required by all those working in the banking industry (first published in 2012)

- **Intermediate** – comprising standards covering specialist roles

- **Leadership** (previously known as 'Advanced') – standards for experienced and senior bankers committed to demonstrating ethical and professional leadership (published on 30 September 2014)

3.6 Corporate codes

Corporate codes are produced either by groups of organisations or individual organisations. Sometimes these corporate codes will have been produced in response to some negative publicity that the organisation has received.

Typically, a corporate code of ethics contains:

- A general commitment from the company and its employees to ethical standards
- An allusion to a number of desirable values, such as honesty, integrity and trust
- A commitment to the interests of customers and stakeholders
- A commitment to comply with the law, regulation and universally accepted best practice
- A commitment to fair competition and the avoidance of restrictive practices or anti-trust policies
- An expression of respect for the environment
- A commitment to community and social responsibility

Typically, a corporate code wil be signed off at the highest level in the organisation, with the organisation's compliance function monitoring adherence to it.

QUICK QUESTION

Does your bank have any corporate codes of conduct or ethics? If so, provide examples of standards included in these codes.

Write your answer here before reading on.

CASE STUDY

Kwik Fit is probably the best-known car tyre and exhaust fitting company in the UK. It has been in business since the 1970s and has a large chain of outlets throughout the country. One way in which the company sought to differentiate itself was to introduce a nine point code simply called the 'Kwik Fit Code'. Ethical standards in the motor repair business can be perceived negatively by the public. Customers often know little about cars and, as a result, they can be overcharged or sold work that is either not necessary or not actually done. Kwik Fit identified this issue and incorporated principles in its code that sought to reassure customers that they would not be exploited in this way. The company's code explicitly states that a customer will not be sold something that is not required.

QUICK QUESTION

How effective do you think codes of conduct are?

Write your answer here before reading on.

Pause for thought ...

Imagine a bank that is perceived by customers to be the most trustworthy bank in the world. What does it do? How does it do it?

Think about what the bank does, for example, to:

- Identify, communicate and meet customer needs

- Respond to and deal with complaints

- Comply with legal and regulatory requirements

- Deal with confidential and sensitive information

- Invest customers' money

- Lend customers money

- Take and manage risks

- Contribute to society

- Make decisions

How does the world's most trustworthy bank treat its:

- Employees?

- Customers?

- Shareholders?

- Competitors?

3.7 Effectiveness of codes of conduct

Although codes of conduct promote greater awareness of professional standards and ethics, codes alone will not guarantee that all bankers or others will act ethically at all times. This is because:

- No matter how much a person reads and hears about ethics, that in itself is no guarantee that they will always act ethically; the same holds true for other forms of education – a person may attend a number of leadership seminars, yet this will not necessarily make them a better leader

- Not all people employed in the banking industry are members of a professional body

- Not all professional bodies recognise that they have a role to play in setting or promoting ethical standards

- Some businesses may act unethically in the pursuit of their aims

- The banking industry is a global industry and there could be cultural differences as to what ethical standards should be.

4 Threats to professionalism

4.1 The impact of unethical and unprofessional behaviour

In the current banking environment, a number of scandals have engulfed the global financial system, and international banks are under investigation by regulators in several countries. They are alleged to have committed offences ranging from fixing inter-bank lending rates to failing to stop their banks being used for money laundering.

Ethics and professionalism are therefore high on the agenda. Much of the debate over the professionalisation of banking has been stimulated as result of these high profile scandals where the actions of individuals and corporate decision-makers have been called into question. Whether these actions were illegal, unethical, or simply an error of judgement, they have undermined public trust and confidence in the banking profession.

Pause for thought ...

Think about the banking scandals that have hit the press in recent years.

In the Table below, write down examples of unethical or unprofessional behaviours associated with these scandals and either the actual or potential impact of these behaviours. For example, think about the impact on the individuals concerned, their colleagues, customers, other members of the public, the bank itself, other banks, the banking industry, and society as a whole.

Unethical or unprofessional behaviour	Impact

Although most of us will not have directly witnessed such severe instances of unethical or unprofessional behaviour, many of us will probably have encountered what we consider to be unethical and unprofessional behaviour at work, even what some may consider relatively minor examples such as inappropriate use of the bank's resources, or time taken for personal interests. While some instances of unethical or unprofessional behaviour may *seem* trivial, if we combine the effects of such occurrences over the organisation or indeed the sector as a whole, then the effects can be much more wide-reaching.

Unethical and unprofessional behaviour could have an impact on the individual, the bank, the industry and even society as a whole. We now look at some examples.

The individual. Time spent worrying about what to do is time not spent doing what we are paid to do. Further, if the individual who discovers this unacceptable behaviour thinks about it outside of work, this can result in domestic friction, lost sleep, reduced feelings of well-being and increased anxiety. All of this may well have an impact on how they perform at work. For the person who is acting inappropriately, once they have crossed the line into this area of behaviour, it may be hard to stop and may well set off a spiral of further, perhaps more serious unethical and unprofessional behaviour.

The bank. There could be financial loss to the bank, either in time, money or other resources. There is also the threat of reputational risk. Once the behaviour is in the public domain, the bank's reputation can be damaged in the eyes of both present and potential customers. Once the bank has a damaged reputation, it can be very difficult to regain. Remember that the essence of banking is trust.

The industry. The banking industry has had its fair share of troubles in recent years. While much of this emanated from the financial crisis which started in 2007, the reputation of banks in the eyes of the public has been adversely affected, with customers looking for more ethical ways to transact their business, for example through the use of credit unions and mutual societies.

Society. If a society has sanctioned, either explicitly or implicitly, unethical and unprofessional behaviour, this could open the door to the inappropriate use of power, with corruption soon becoming rife, and ultimately affecting key stakeholders as well as the economy.

4.2   Types of threat

There may be circumstances where the professional's compliance with fundamental principles is threatened. **Threats** may be created by a broad range of relationships and circumstances and may be categorised as shown in the following diagram.

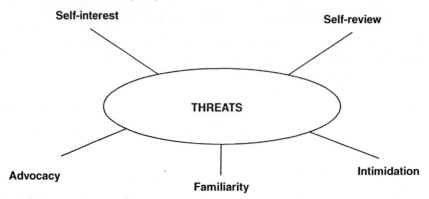

4.3   Self-interest threat

The **self-interest-threat** arises where a financial or other interest inappropriately influences the professional's judgement or behaviour. For example, the individual may have a financial interest in the transaction proceeding. A common example of this is where the professional will receive either a commission or bonus if the transaction goes through.

It is also possible that the individual has a close business or personal relationship with the client, and this can have a big effect on business operations. For example, if the business manager and the client have a close personal relationship, it may be less straightforward for the banker to return cheques unpaid, or to refuse a request for additional funding. This is more likely to occur where the amount involved is small as there are likely to be procedures in place to review credit decisions.

4.4   Self-review threat

A professional might not appropriately evaluate the results of a previous judgement they have made or a judgement made by a colleague on which the professional has relied when forming their own opinion.

The **self-review threat** can often arise where a person is involved in auditing or evaluating the work of others. For example, say at some stage in your career you work in the bank's internal audit department and are required to audit the effectiveness of a procedure that you, in a previous role, were responsible for developing and implementing. In such a situation it would be expected that the internal auditor has a preconceived notion about the system and so is not in a position to make an objective assessment of it.

When we obtain valuation reports on property for security purposes, it is vital that the valuation comes from an independent valuer, rather than someone who was involved in the design of the particular property.

Conflicts of interest may also arise in situations where a banker finds that a client is also an ex-employer.

C A S E   S T U D Y

Alexei joined his bank in the IT department but is now a member of an inspection team in the compliance department. He moved to the department having developed an interest in law and regulation when studying for his professional examinations.

Alexei and his colleagues have been asked to prepare a special report on the effectiveness of substantive testing programmes. He has welcomed this new task, as he was instrumental in designing the software used by the bank.

Should Alexei participate in the project?

Alexei should make his manager aware of his involvement in the development of the programme. It is then up to the manager to decide whether Alexei can be sufficiently independent when considering the effectiveness of the software. He may have a valuable role to play, but it is unlikely that he will be totally objective.

4.5 Advocacy threat

The **advocacy threat** is the threat that a professional will promote a client's or employer's position to the point that the professional's objectivity is compromised.

It could arise where a professional firm is called upon to support a client. For example, a bank may provide credit facilities to a business customer with whom it enjoys a good relationship, based on the fact that the account is conducted in the agreed manner. A problem could arise if the customer has granted a second security over its premises to another lender and the second lender asks for the bank's support in realising its security. A bank can reduce the threat of advocacy by taking a neutral stance when considering the client's business plan.

4.6 Familiarity threat

Due to a long or close relationship with a client or employer, a professional will be over-sympathetic to their interests or too accepting of their work, leading to a **familiarity threat**, for example:

- Where the bank has a long-established relationship with a client, and there is the danger that the senior management teams of the business and the bank become too familiar with one another

- Where there is a personal or family relationship between the banker and customer

The bank could mitigate this risk by:

- Rotating people's roles on a regular basis
- Involving others who do not have a personal relationship with the client
- Obtaining independent reports or reviews

4.7 Intimidation threat

There is an **intimidation threat** where a professional is deterred from acting objectively because of actual or perceived pressures, including attempts by another to exercise undue influence over them. An example is the threat of litigation by a customer against the bank. This threat may be real or perceived.

As a result, the outcome could be:

- Loss of the client's business
- Damage to the reputation of the bank – even if the bank is without blame
- Financial consequences such as compensation and costs

CASE STUDY

Yvonne has a mortgage with JKL Building Society. She is angry because the society is advertising 20% discounts for new applicants for household insurance. She has insured her property with the society for many years. She was not offered any discounts when she took out the policy and has not been offered any concessions since then. Yvonne is particularly annoyed that the society's advertising makes it clear that the deal is open to non-members only, which seems to be at odds with the society's claim that it exists for the benefit of its members. Yvonne is threatening to take her insurance elsewhere if the society does not offer her the same 20% discount.

Should the building society make any concessions to Yvonne?

The advertising campaign, pricing structure and offer to non-members seems to conflict directly with the society's stated mission of bringing benefits to members. Yet it could argue that by generating further commissions from insurance sales, the society is able to generate more profits which in turn lead to better interest rates.

The society is unlikely to be able to offer Yvonne any special deal unless it does so for all of its policyholders.

The risk posed by litigation is common as there is a perception that banks are well able to defend themselves and pay appropriate compensation, no doubt fuelled by the **compensation culture** evident today. The most likely threat is an action for professional negligence.

Although the threat of litigation may be reduced, it will never be completely removed. Consequently, any organisation that provides professional services must ensure that it has adequate professional indemnity cover in place, so that compensation and costs can be paid if action against the bank is successful. However, all such cover does is ensure that these monies can be paid – the case may also end with damage to the bank's reputation.

Many regulators and professional bodies will insist that organisations under their sphere of influence have appropriate cover in place. If litigation does ensue, it may be necessary to move some individuals or teams to other duties while the action is ongoing.

The threat of intimidation may also arise where the customer seeks a second opinion from another professional firm. The provider of the second opinion may take a different view from the first. Although two views could be taken on the particular case, where a second opinion has been sought, this could result in risks. It is quite possible that the person seeking the second opinion does not provide the second firm with exactly the same information as was made available to the firm that provided the original opinion, thus making the difference in opinion far more likely to occur.

Second opinions will come with their own ethical considerations; for example, should the organisation being asked for the second opinion contact the provider of the original opinion?

4.8 Safeguards

Safeguards are actions or other measures that may eliminate threats or reduce them to an acceptable level. They fall into two broad categories:

- Safeguards created by the profession, legislation or regulation
- Safeguards in the work environment

Safeguards created by a profession, legislation or regulation include:

- Educational, training and experience requirements for entry into the profession
- Continuing professional development requirements
- Corporate governance regulations
- Professional standards
- Professional or regulatory monitoring and disciplinary procedures
- External review by a legally empowered third party, for example, a regulator

5 Ethical dilemmas and conflicts of interest

5.1 Overview

QUICK QUESTION

What is an ethical dilemma?

Write your answer here before reading on.

Encountering instances of unprofessional and unethical behaviour can compromise our own ideas of what is ethical and professional. Sometimes, we can be faced with an ethical dilemma or conflict of interest. The question is: what do we do about it? How do we **identify** them, **report** them, and **resolve** them?

An ethical dilemma can be described as a situation in which we find it difficult to decide what is the right or wrong thing to do. With a dilemma, we find it difficult to choose between alternative courses of action as a result of some mental conflict. For example, there could be a conflict between:

- Our values or moral principles
- Alternative courses of action, each of which has reasons for doing and not doing
- Two or more unsatisfactory alternatives.

The dilemma could occur when you choose what you believe is the right thing to do, even if it results in an unfavourable outcome; or you may choose to do something you feel is wrong for the sake of a favourable outcome. This brings us back to ethics based on duty, or actions, and ethics based on consequences.

When faced with an ethical dilemma, you may choose to focus on the actions you take and pay less attention to the consequences. You will therefore feel that you are doing the right thing, regardless of the consequences.

Alternatively, you may choose to focus on the consequences of your choice, where what you do to achieve the outcome is not as important as the outcome itself.

Pause for thought ...

Think of a time when you were faced with an ethical dilemma or conflict of interest.

What was the situation?

How did you know you were facing an ethical dilemma or conflict of interest?

What professional and/or ethical issues did this raise?

In what ways was your own and others' professionalism compromised?

How did you feel?

Who was/might have been affected? In what ways?

What challenges did this present:

- For you?

- For others involved?

What choices of action did you have?

In what ways did these actions either conform with or contravene professional and/or ethical standards?

What did you do?

How did you decide that this was the right thing to do?

What was the outcome?

How do you feel about it now?

What lessons have you learned from this experience?

How might you apply these lessons in future, either to your own situation or across the banking profession?

Given the very nature of a dilemma, there is often no clear-cut response to an ethical dilemma. You may have discovered something you believe to be illegal or fraudulent or something that contravenes a professional code, such as the Chartered Banker Institute Code of Professional Conduct for its members, or the CB:PSB Chartered Banker Code of Professional Conduct.

As a professional banker and member of the Chartered Banker Institute, you have a responsibility and professional duty to exercise good judgement and be accountable for your actions both to the banking profession and to the public. So how do you identify ethical dilemmas and conflicts of interest as they arise?

If you have concerns about the situation, then it is likely you are facing an ethical dilemma. The longer you leave it unresolved, the greater the likely repercussions for you, your bank and the banking profession.

CASE STUDY

A regular feature in the Chartered Banker Institute's *Chartered Banker* magazine is the consideration of ethical dilemmas and conflicts of interest. Back issues of the magazine are available in the Members and Students section of the Institute's website.

5.2 Chartered Institute of Management Accountants checklist

The Chartered Institute of Management Accountants (CIMA) has a **checklist** to help its members identify and act on ethical dilemmas and conflicts of interest. This can be used in conjunction with the key principles of integrity, objectivity, professional competence and due care, confidentiality and professional behaviour.

Below are **key elements** of the checklist, adapted for your role as a professional banker.

1   Check all your facts and, where possible, document.

Identify all relevant facts; do not rely on assumptions.

Is it really your problem? Can anybody else help?

2   Is it ethical? What ethical issues are involved?

Does it feel right?

How would you feel if you saw it in a newspaper?

How would you feel about your peers, friends, family knowing about it?

Have you referred to codes of ethics and professional conduct that you personally subscribe to?

Have you consulted your bank's internal code of ethics/conduct and other internal policies?

3   Is it legal?

- Is the issue in question regulated by law?
- Does it comply with rules, policies, standards and contracts imposed by relevant regulators/bodies and by your employer?

4   Which of the key principles are involved?

Integrity?

Objectivity?

Professional competence and due care?

Confidentiality?

Professional behaviour?

Other key principles of professional codes that you subscribe and commit to?

5   Identify who is affected:

- Who are the individuals, organisations and key stakeholders affected?
- In what way are they affected?
- Are there conflicts between different stakeholders?
- What might be the effects of non-action – to the organisation, to yourself and to society?

6   What are possible courses of action?

- In your role, consider what you are required to report, to whom and when
- Consider what you *should* report, to whom and when
- Escalate internally; consider grievance procedures
- Document every action that you take to resolve the conflict
- Escalate externally to auditor, legal advisors, professional body

7   Seek professional or legal advice:

- Public Concern at Work or similar local whistleblowing helpline

- Legal advisers

- Professional body

8   Refuse to remain associated with the conflict:

- If resolution seems unlikely, disassociate yourself from the issue, in writing as necessary.

- Legal advice may be necessary if this affects your employment status or if you are implicated in any way with the issue.

CASE STUDY

Laura and James work in the same sales and business development department in their bank. They joined the bank at the same time and their jobs have equal status in the organisation.

At a party, James admitted to Laura that he managed to increase his performance-related income by 'gently pressuring' customers to buy certain products and services. He went on to explain that he could do this by instilling fear that without certain products (such as insurance), the consequences to the customer's family could be disastrous. James boasted that he virtually intimidated customers into buying products by playing on their consciences and also stated that his expenses claims were a 'nice little earner' as he has some friendly taxi drivers who were quite prepared to give him blank receipts.

- Should Laura report James to a senior manager?

This case study concerns the subject of whistleblowing which can take two forms:

- Internal whistleblowing occurs when improper behaviour is reported upwards within the organisation

- External whistleblowing occurs when a matter is reported externally, to a regulator or to the press.

Many companies now have an explicit policy in respect of this. If an individual breaks the trust placed in him or her by the employer, the individual loses the right to the loyalty of co-workers.

Laura should report James's behaviour to an appropriate person within the bank. James's actions demonstrate low integrity and contempt for both customers and colleagues. If he is permitted to continue exploiting customers and the bank in these ways, the bank is vulnerable to future accusations of mis-selling. Even before that, customers will possibly be purchasing products that they cannot afford, do not need and will ultimately abandon. Once customers learn that they have been mis-sold products, they will be lost to the bank forever.

Laura is in a difficult position. From an early age we are encouraged not to 'tell' or to 'snitch' on our peers. She also has to work with James. However, the bank should have some line of communication through which she can report her concerns in confidence. She is protected to some extent by the provisions of the *Public Interest Disclosure Act 1998*. This is an Act designed to protect people who make certain disclosures of information in the public interest and which allows these people to bring action in respect of any victimisation they may be subject to as a result of making the disclosure.

QUICK QUESTION

What mechanisms does your bank have in place for the identification and reporting of ethical dilemmas and conflicts of interest?

Write your answer here before reading on.

Some organisations may have policies or procedures in place regarding, for example:

- Confidentiality, security and disclosure

- Segregating teams and individuals working on tasks where conflicts may arise

- Imposing Chinese walls – these are policies that forbid the sharing of information between divisions/departments

- Having proper disciplinary procedures in place when breaches occur

- Limiting access to information

- The use of confidentiality agreements

5.3 Institute of Chartered Accountants of Scotland framework

The Institute of Chartered Accountants of Scotland (ICAS) uses the following framework to analyse ethical dilemmas.

1   What are the readily identifiable ethical issues for your decision? (For you personally, and for the company/bank.)

2   Who are the key parties who can influence, or will be affected by, your decision?

3   What fundamental ethical principles for accountants are most applicable and is there an apparent conflict between them?

4   Is there any further information (including legal obligations) or discussion that might be relevant?

5   Is there a conflict between the 'guardian' and 'commercial' strands of an accountant's responsibilities?

6   Based on the information available, is there scope for an imaginative solution?

7   Are there any other comments?

5.4 American Accounting Association (AAA) model

The American Accounting Association's framework involves consideration of the following questions.

1   What are the facts of the case?

2   What are the ethical issues in the case?

3   What are the norms, principles, and values related to the case?

4   What are the alternative courses of action?

5   What is the best course of action that is consistent with the norms, principles and values identified in Step 3?

6   What are the consequences of each possible course of action?

7   What is the decision?

This model provides a framework within which an ethical decision can be made.

1   Establishing the facts of the case

This ensures that when the decision-making process starts, there is no ambiguity about the facts being considered.

2   Identify the ethical issues in the case

This involves examining the facts of the case and asking what the ethical issues are.

3   An identification of the norms, principles, and values related to the case

This involves placing the decision within the context of social, ethical and professional behaviour, for example by considering professional codes of ethics and conduct, or the social expectations of the profession. For example, if FCA rules are involved in the decision, then these will be a relevant factor to consider in this step.

4   Each alternative course of action is identified

This involves stating each alternative course of action, without consideration of the norms, principles and values identified in Step 3, in order to ensure that each outcome is considered, regardless of how appropriate or inappropriate that outcome might be.

5   Matching norms, principles and values to options

The norms, principles and values identified in Step 3 are mapped over to the options identified in Step 4. When this is done, it should be possible to see which options accord with the norms and which do not.

6   The consequences of the outcomes are considered

The purpose of the model is to make the implications of each outcome unambiguous so that the final decision is made with full knowledge and recognition of each outcome.

7   The decision is taken

5.5 Tucker's five-question model

Ethical decisions can be tested against **Tucker's 5-question model**. It can be used after the AAA framework has been applied, to ensure that the decision reached is 'correct'.

BPP
LEARNING MEDIA

The **Tucker model** asks if the option or decision is:

- Profitable?
- Legal?
- Fair?
- Right?
- Sustainable or environmentally sound?

In this model, the reference to profitability means that this model is often more useful for examining corporate rather than professional or individual situations.

Applying Tucker's model requires a little more thought than when using the AAA model. For example, when the model asks, 'Is an option profitable?', we might consider: 'compared to what?' Similarly, whether an option is 'fair' depends on whose perspective is being considered. This might involve thinking about the different stakeholders involved in the decision and the effects on them. Whether an option is 'right' depends on the ethical position adopted.

Thinking again about different ethical theories, different answers may result from different approaches. For example, looking at a situation from a duty-based (deontological) perspective may result in a different conclusion from a consequence-based (teleological) perspective.

QUICK QUESTION

What is your understanding of corporate social responsibility?

Write your answer here before reading on.

6 Corporate social responsibility

6.1 Introduction

'The business of business should not just be about money, it should be about responsibility. It should be about public good, not private greed.'

– Anita Roddick, human rights activist, founder of The Body Shop

Corporate Social Responsibility (CSR) is about how a company manages its business in order to have an overall positive impact on society. It can be described as an obligation, beyond that required by the law, for a business to pursue long term goals that are good for society.

CSR involves:

- Conducting business in an ethical way and in the interests of the wider community
- Responding positively to emerging societal priorities and expectations
- A willingness to act ahead of regulatory requirements
- Balancing shareholder interests against the interests of the wider community
- Being a good citizen in the community

CSR and sound business ethics run in parallel with each other, in that:

- Both are concerned with values, objectives and decisions based on something other than just the pursuit of profit
- Socially responsible firms must act ethically

The difference is that:

- Ethics concern actions which can be assessed as right or wrong by reference to moral principles, while
- CSR is about the organisation's obligations to all stakeholders, not just shareholders

6.2 Pyramid of CSR

Archie Carroll, University of Georgia, maintained in 1979 that the social responsibility of business encompasses the economic, legal, ethical and discretionary expectations that society has of organisations at a given point in time.

Carroll was one of the first academics to make a distinction between different kinds of organisational responsibilities. He illustrated the different types of responsibility in a 'pyramid of corporate social responsibility'.

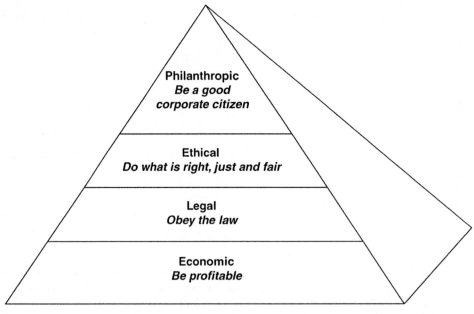

According to Carroll, a firm's economic responsibilities are the foundation on which all other responsibilities rest. A firm's economic responsibility is to produce an acceptable return on its owners' investment. An important component of pursuing economic gain within a law-based society, however, is legal responsibility – a duty to act within the legal and regulatory framework. Going one step further, a firm has an ethical responsibility to do no harm to its stakeholders and within its operating environment. Finally, firms have a discretionary responsibility, which represents more proactive, strategic behaviours that can benefit the firm and society, or both.

Economic responsibilities include:

- Earning a profit for owners
- Maintaining a strong competitive position
- Having a high level of operating efficiency

Legal responsibilities include:

- Complying with the law
- Complying with regulations
- Providing goods and services that meet legal and regulatory requirements

Ethical responsibilities include:

- Behaving in accordance with moral and ethical expectations and standards

- Not compromising ethical norms to achieve corporate goals; not just acting for profit, but doing what is right, just and fair

- Recognising that corporate integrity and ethical behaviour go beyond compliance with laws and regulations

Discretionary (or voluntary) and **philanthropic responsibilities** include:

- Behaving in a manner that is consistent with philanthropic and charitable expectations of society
- Contributing to the community, eg by participating in voluntary activities in the community
- Being a good corporate citizen, eg by promoting human welfare, goodwill and quality of life.

CSR is a form of corporate self-regulation integrated into a business model. CSR policy functions as a built-in, self-regulating mechanism whereby a business monitors and ensures its active compliance with the spirit of the law, ethical standards and international norms.

- CSR is a process that aims to embrace responsibility for the company's actions and, through its activities, encourage a positive impact on the environment, consumers, employees, communities and other stakeholders.

- CSR may guide a company's mission, what it stands for, and what it promises to provide to customers. The recognised standard for CSR is ISO 26000.

6.3 ISO 26000 – *Social responsibility*

Business and organisations do not operate in a vacuum. Their relationship to the society and environment in which they operate is a critical factor in their ability to continue to operate effectively. It is also increasingly being used as a measure of their overall performance.

ISO 26000:2010 is an International Standard that provides guidance on how businesses and organisations can operate in a socially responsible way. This means acting in an ethical and transparent way that contributes to the health and welfare of society.

ISO 26000:2010 provides guidance rather than requirements. It helps clarify what social responsibility is, helps businesses and organisations translate principles into effective actions and shares best practices relating to social responsibility. It is aimed at all types of organisations regardless of their activity, size or location.

Although it is recognised that not all parts of the Standard will be of equal use to all organisations, certain core subjects have been identified. Within each core subject are a number of issues for organisations to consider.

Core subjects are:

- Organisational governance, i.e. the way the organisation is managed

- Human rights, e.g. discrimination, resolving grievances, rights at work

- Labour practices, e.g. working conditions, health and safety, training and development

- The environment, e.g. prevention of pollution, sustainable use of resources, climate change mitigation, environmental protection

- Fair operating practices, e.g. anti-corruption, fair competition, respect for property rights

- Consumer issues, e.g. fair marketing and provision of information, customer service, complaint and dispute resolution, data protection and privacy
- Community involvement and development, e.g. education and culture, employment creation and skills development, access to technology, wealth and income creation, health, social investment

6.4 Benefits of CSR

Organisations around the world, and their stakeholders, are becoming increasingly aware of the need for and benefits of socially responsible behaviour. When approaching and practising social responsibility, the overarching goal for an organisation is to maximise its contribution to sustainable development, that is, development that meets the needs of the present without compromising the ability of future generations to meet their own needs.

An organisation's performance in relation to the society in which it operates and to its impact on the environment has become a critical part of measuring its overall performance and its ability to continue operating effectively.

This is, in part, a reflection of the growing recognition of the need to ensure healthy ecosystems, social equity and good organisational governance. In the long run, all organisations' activities depend on the health of the world's ecosystems. Organisations are subject to greater scrutiny by their various stakeholders.

The perception and reality of an organisation's performance on social responsibility can influence, among other things:

- Its competitive advantage
- Its reputation
- Its ability to attract and retain workers or members, customers, clients or users
- Employees' morale, commitment and productivity
- Views of investors, owners, donors, sponsors and the financial community
- Its relationships with companies, governments, the media, suppliers, peers, customers and the community in which it operates

Pause for thought ...

Most banks publish information about their social responsibility pledges. Visit your own bank's website. What is your bank's stance on Corporate Social Responsibility?

For example, what is your bank's mission? What does it promise to provide to customers? What does it do to encourage a positive impact on the environment, customers, employees, communities, and other stakeholders?

Now visit the websites of some other banks. In what ways are the CSR pledges similar to and different from those of your own bank?

7 The impact of technology and information systems

Information systems raise new types of ethical problems as a result of the challenges posed by the Internet and electronic commerce to the protection of people's privacy and intellectual property.

Other ethical issues include:

- Establishing accountability for the consequences of information systems
- Setting standards to safeguard system quality and protect individuals and society
- Preserving values that are considered essential to the quality of life in the information age

QUICK QUESTION

What information systems do you work with in your role?

Write your answer here before reading on.

Whichever systems you work with, they need to be protected from computer fraud and abuse. We also need to protect people's privacy and to ensure data quality.

In their book *Management Information Systems (2011)*, **Laudon and Laudon** consider the main moral dimensions of an information society and specific principles for conduct that can be used to guide ethical decisions.

Ethical, social and political issues raised by information systems

- **Information rights and obligations.** What information rights do people and organisations possess with respect to themselves? What can they protect? What obligations do they have concerning this information?

- **Property rights and obligations**. How will traditional intellectual property rights be protected in a digital society?

- **Accountability and control**. Who can and will be held accountable and liable for the harm done to individual and collective information and property rights?

- **System quality**. What standards of data and system quality should we demand to protect individual rights and the safety of society?

- **Quality of life**. What values should be preserved in an information and knowledge-based society? Which organisations should we protect from violation? Which cultural values and practices are supported by the new information technology?

Three basic concepts underpin an ethical analysis of information systems and those who manage them:

1   Information systems are products of organisational and individual behaviour and actions.

2   Organisations and individuals who choose to use certain systems are responsible for the consequences of these systems.

3   Individuals can recover damages done to them through the legal system.

Laudon and Laudon's principles for conduct in relation to information systems include the following.

1   Analyse the relationships among ethical, social, and political issues that are raised by information systems

Information can be communicated, copied, and manipulated in online environments easily and anonymously. This challenges traditional rules of right and wrong behaviour. Ethical issues are faced by people who must choose a course of action, often in a situation in which two or more ethical principles are in conflict (a dilemma). Social issues emerge from ethical issues as societies develop expectations about the correct course of action. Political issues arise from social conflict and are concerned with laws that prescribe 'correct' behaviour.

2   Identify the main moral dimensions of an information society and specific principles for conduct that can be used to guide ethical decisions

These principles should be used in conjunction with an ethical analysis to guide decision making. The ethical analysis involves identifying the facts, values, stakeholders, options, and consequences of actions. Once the analysis has been completed, you can decide what to do in accordance with a particular ethical approach.

3   Evaluate the impact of contemporary information systems and the Internet on the protection of individual privacy and intellectual property

Technology enables companies to easily gather and analyse personal data about people and create profiles about them and their behaviours. Data flowing over the Internet can be monitored at many points. The activities of website visitors can be closely tracked using cookies and other Web monitoring tools. Not all websites have strong privacy protection policies, and they do not always allow for informed consent regarding the use of personal information.

4   Assess how information systems have affected everyday life

Computer errors can cause harm to individuals and organisations. Widespread use of computers increases opportunities for computer crime. Computers can also create health problems, such as repetitive stress injury, computer vision syndrome, and technostress (stress induced by computer use).

Organisations can use these principles to develop a corporate code of ethics for information systems.

KEY WORDS

Key words and phrases from this chapter are given below. Make sure you know what they mean and add any other words or phrases that you want to remember. You can use the space provided to write your own revision notes.

- Meta-ethics
- Normative ethics
- Applied ethics
- Moral absolutism
- Moral relativism
- Virtue theory
- Duty theory
- Consequentialist theory
- Ethical egoism
- Ethical altruism
- Utilitarianism
- Professionalism
- Codes of practice
- Chartered Banker Institute Code of Professional Conduct
- Chartered Banker Professional Standards Board (CB:PSB)
- CB:PSB Code of Professional Conduct
- Ethical dilemma
- Identifying, reporting and resolving ethical dilemmas
- Threats and safeguards
- Corporate Social Responsibility

REVIEW

To help you reflect on and review the content of this chapter, give some thought to the following questions.

- What is 'ethics'?
- What is 'ethics' used for?
- What is the difference between meta-ethics, normative ethics and applied ethics?
- What is the difference between moral absolutism and moral relativism?
- What is the difference between ethics based on virtue, ethics based on duty and ethics based on consequences?
- What is meant by 'ethical egoism'?
- What is meant by 'ethical altruism'?
- What is meant by 'utilitarianism'?
- What is meant by 'professionalism'?
- What is the difference between rules-based and principles-based codes of practice?
- What five key principles are typically addressed in codes of ethics or professional conduct?
- What does the Chartered Banker Institute's Code of Professional Conduct require members to do?
- What was the Chartered Banker Professional Standards Board (CB:PSB) set up to do?
- What is the purpose of the CB:PSB's Chartered Banker Code of Professional Conduct?
- What are those who subscribe to the Chartered Banker Code of Professional Conduct expected to do to demonstrate their commitment to professionalism in banking?
- What are the different types of threats that could threaten a professional's compliance with their professional code of conduct?
- What is the potential impact of unethical and unprofessional behaviours?
- What is an ethical dilemma?
- How would you know if you were faced with an ethical dilemma or conflict of interest?
- What are the key elements of the Chartered Institute of Management Accountants' checklist that is designed to help its members identify and act on ethical dilemmas and conflicts of interest?
- What are the key questions used by members of the Institute of Chartered Accountants of Scotland to analyse ethical dilemmas?
- What are the key questions used by members of the American Accounting Association to enable an ethical decision to be made?
- What are the five questions in Tucker's ethical decision-making model?
- What are the four stages of ethical decision-making?
- What is meant by Corporate Social Responsibility?
- What aspects of social responsibility appear as core subjects in ISO 26000:2010?
- What are the social responsibilities of a bank?
- What are the five moral dimensions of an information society?

QUESTIONS

Chapter 1 – The Business of Banking and the Economic Environment

To test your knowledge retention of Chapter 1, answer the following questions and check your answers.

1   Wholesale banking is about:

A   Providing pensions and insurance

B   Borrowing from and lending to larger companies, other banks and governments

C   Managing corporate mergers and acquisitions

D   Taking deposits from and lending to individuals and companies

2   Financial intermediation is a business activity that involves pooling funds from different sources and using these to:

A   Provide loans and make investments

B   Provide loans only

C   Make investments only

D   Act as an agent for payments

3   In banking, liquidity is about:

A   Maximising profits on investments

B   Balancing risk and reward

C   Having sufficient cash and other assets that can be converted quickly into cash to meet the immediate withdrawal demands of customers

D   Expanding the supply of money through deposit and loan transactions

4   The main purpose of a building society is to:

A   Raise, primarily from its members, funds for lending to members for the purpose of buying a residential property

B   Raise, primarily from the wholesale money markets, funds for lending to members for the purpose of buying a residential property

C   Offer personal financial and money transmission services to its members

D   Maximise profits for shareholders

5   Macroeconomics examines factors such as:

A   Patterns of supply and demand for a product

B   Consumers' and producers' behaviour and decision-making processes

C   Interaction between buyers and sellers

D   Unemployment, gross domestic product and inflation

Chapter 2 – The Regulatory and Legal Environment

To test your knowledge retention of Chapter 2, answer the following questions and check your answers.

1   **The regulator responsible for requiring firms to put the well-being of their customers at the heart of how they run their business, promoting effective competition' and ensuring that markets operate with integrity is the:**

A   Financial Conduct Authority

B   Prudential Regulation Authority

C   Bank of England

D   Financial Services Authority

2   **For a loan regulated by the Consumer Credit Act 2006, the upper limit for the amount of a loan to an individual is:**

A   £15,000

B   £25,000

C   £50,000

D   None – there is no limit

3   **The Data Protection Act 1998 classifies data relating to a person's religion as:**

A   Personal data

B   Sensitive data

C   Private data

D   Restricted data

4   **A negotiable instrument is:**

A   A non-transferable, signed document that promises to pay the bearer a sum of money at a future date or on demand

B   A transferable, signed document that promises to pay the bearer a sum of money at a future date or on demand

C   A non-transferable, unsigned document that promises to pay the bearer a sum of money at a future date or on demand

D   A transferable, unsigned document that promises to pay the bearer a sum of money at a future date or on demand

5   **The minimum number of people required to set up a UK private limited company is:**

A   1

B   2

C   3

D   4

Chapter 3 – Serving Customers

To test your knowledge retention of Chapter 3, answer the following questions and check your answers.

1   The maximum amount that a customer can invest in an ISA each year is:

A   £3,000

B   £6,000

C   £9,000

D   Subject to annual review

2   An equity release loan would be most suitable for a customer who wants to:

A   Bridge the gap between selling one house and buying another

B   Raise money by freeing up some of the capital that is locked in to their property

C   Take out a mortgage for their first house purchase

D   Buy a property to rent out

3   Level term assurance can be useful for a customer who wants to:

A   Secure the payment of their mortgage if the customer dies during the term of the policy

B   Ensure that the sum assured is paid on their death, regardless of when they die

C   Provide security for dependants up to a certain age if the customer dies during the term of the policy

D   Combine life assurance protection with investment

4   One way of empathising with a customer is by:

A   Making small talk

B   Demonstrating the same emotion that the customer demonstrates

C   Saying 'That must have been really frustrating for you'

D   Saying 'I'm sorry about that'

5   If a complaint is not resolved between a bank and its customer, the customer may be entitled to refer the complaint to the:

A   Financial Ombudsman Service

B   Financial Services Compensation Scheme

C   Financial Services Authority

D   Financial Conduct Authority

Chapter 4 – Credit and Lending

To test your knowledge retention of Chapter 4, answer the following questions and check your answers.

1 **The Lending Code covers good practice in relation to:**

A   Loans, credit cards, merchant services, and current account overdrafts

B   Loans, credit cards, charge cards, and current account overdrafts

C   Loans, credit cards, charge cards, and non-business borrowing secured on land

D   Loans, credit cards, charge cards, and sales finance

2 **When assessing the 'three Cs' of the person aspect of a loan application, a lender considers the applicant's:**

A   Character, capacity, and commitment

B   Character, credit card repayments, and commitment

C   Character, competence, and capital

D   Character, credit card repayments, and capital

3 **The type of income that would be most attractive to a banker as the primary source of repayment for a loan would be the customer's:**

A   Bonus

B   Overtime

C   Dividends

D   Salary

4 **Three attributes of good security are:**

A   Simplicity of title, fluctuating value, and ability to be realised

B   Simplicity of title, ability to be realised, and ability to turn an unviable lending proposition into a viable one

C   Simplicity of title, stability of value, and ability to be realised

D   Simplicity of title, stability of value, and ability to turn an unviable lending proposition into a viable one

5 **An attraction for a bank of using an automated credit scoring is because such a system:**

A   Requires lending decisions to be made by qualified and experienced bankers

B   Enables large volumes of loan applications to be processed quickly and consistently, and profiled for risk

C   Is suitable for assessing cases where the applicant has no credit history

D   Relies on historical and therefore accurate information supplied by a credit reference agency

Chapter 5 – Risk Management in Banking

To test your knowledge retention of Chapter 5, answer the following questions and check your answers.

1   A risk with high probability and low impact would typically be:

A   Accepted

B   Controlled

C   Avoided

D   Transferred

2   A risk with low probability and high impact would typically be:

A   Accepted

B   Controlled

C   Avoided

D   Transferred

3   An effective key risk indicator:

A   Is related to non-specific risks to which a bank is exposed

B   Tracks a particularly important risk exposure very well

C   Tracks the financial performance of a bank

D   Measures only the amount of exposure to a risk

4   Operational risk is:

A   The risk of direct loss resulting from inadequate or failed internal processes, people and systems or from external events

B   The risk of direct or indirect loss resulting from inadequate or failed internal processes and systems

C   The risk of direct or indirect loss resulting from inadequate or failed internal processes, people and systems or from external events

D   The risk of direct loss resulting from inadequate or failed internal processes and systems

5   From a regulatory perspective, the FCA's Firm Systematic Framework is designed to assess, for a firm, the level of:

A   Conduct risk

B   Systems risk

C   Reputational risk

D   External risk

Chapter 6 – Conduct and Professionalism in Banking

To test your knowledge retention of Chapter 6, answer the following questions and check your answers.

1   **The branch of ethics that considers the content of moral judgements and the criteria for what is right or wrong is:**

A   Meta-ethics

B   Virtue ethics

C   Normative ethics

D   Applied ethics

2   **Moral absolutism argues that:**

A   There are some moral rules that are always true and apply to everyone

B   Different cultures have different moral rules

C   What is 'good' depends on what a particular group of people approve of

D   We should respect the diversity of human societies and respond to the different circumstances surrounding human acts

3   **The idea that people have a duty to do the right thing, even if it produces a bad result, is a key concept of:**

A   Teleological theories of ethics

B   Deontological theories of ethics

C   Virtue theories of ethics

D   Utilitarian theories of ethics

4   **A professional body's rules-based code of conduct generally:**

A   Sets out the detail what members may do and should not do

B   Seeks to provide adequate legal defences for members' conduct

C   Provides guidance that can be applied to various circumstances

D   States the high-level principles that underlie the profession

5   **The CB:PSB Chartered Banker Code of Professional Conduct sets out the ethical and professional values and behaviours expected of:**

A   Members of the Chartered Banker Institute

B   Employees of all firms regulated by the Financial Services Authority

C   Members of the British Bankers' Association

D   Bankers by the Chartered Banker Professional Standards Board

ANSWERS

Chapter 1 – The Business of Banking and the Economic Environment

1   B
2   A
3   C
4   A
5   D

Chapter 2 – The Regulatory and Legal Environment

1   A
2   D
3   B
4   B
5   A

Chapter 3 – Serving Customers

1   D
2   B
3   C
4   C
5   A

Chapter 4 – Credit and Lending

1   B
2   A
3   D
4   C
5   B

Chapter 5 – Risk Management in Banking

1   B
2   D
3   B
4   C
5   A

Chapter 6 – Conduct and Professionalism in Banking

1	**C**
2	**A**
3	**B**
4	**A**
5	**D**

BPP
LEARNING MEDIA

Review and next steps

You have now completed your study of *Professional Banker Certificate*. The aim of this module was to provide you with an overview of the banking profession and enable you to:

- Develop the values, attitudes and behaviours set out in the Chartered Banker Code of Professional Conduct

- Demonstrate a general knowledge of banking practice

- Relate your banking knowledge to a range of practical banking applications

- Use a range of banking skills to serve customers, and address routine issues at work

- Apply your banking knowledge and understanding, and practise your skills to enhance customer service, improve work performance, and develop your professional banking practice.

You have learned about six topic areas:

1   The business of banking and the economic environment

2   The regulatory and legal environment

3   Serving customers

4   Credit and lending

5   Risk management in banking

6   Conduct and professionalism in banking

Now that you have completed your study of Professional Banker, you should be able to:

1   Explain the purpose and functions of a bank and describe the business and economic environment in which banks operate

2   Describe key regulatory, cultural and legal requirements that apply to banking and explain how these requirements influence the way a bank operates

3   Describe a range of banking products and services and assess their suitability for different customer needs

4   Explain the key principles of credit and lending and how these can be used to make professional and ethical lending decisions

5   Describe the role of risk management in banking

6   Explain the importance of high standards of conduct in banking and the practicalities of applying these standards

The next stage is for you to pass your *Professional Banker Certificate* exam. You can sit the exam online at one of Chartered Banker Institute examination centres throughout the UK. The exam consists of 100 multiple choice questions and you will have up to 2 hours to complete it. The pass mark is 60% and you will receive your result as soon as you have completed it.

For further information about registering for and sitting the exam, log in to the *Members and Students* area of our website at **www.charteredbanker.com**.

When you attain your Professional Banker Certificate, you are eligible to become a Certificated member of the Chartered Banker Institute. As you know, being a member of a professional body is a good way to demonstrate commitment to the profession and further develop your professional banking practice. We will contact you with details about professional membership when you attain your qualification.

To take your professional banking qualifications to the next level, you can top up your Professional Banker Certificate to a Professional Banker Diploma. You can do this by completing two modules from the Professional Banker Diploma options. Visit **www.charteredbanker.com** to find out about available modules and how to apply.

If you would like to speak to the Institute team about your next study options, please get in touch at **info@charteredbanker.com** or on **0131 473 7777**.

GLOSSARY

Glossary

Acceptance

In the context of contract law, a communication or action taken by a person to agree to an offer that has been made to enter into a contract.

Advocacy threat

A threat to independence that arises when an individual is asked to consider an action or take a decision in relation to a person or entity he or she has previously supported.

Affordability

The ability of a customer to make payments that will become due in the life of a financial product.

Agent

A person or body that acts on behalf of another person or body (the principal).

Annual Percentage Rate (APR)

An interest rate that must be quoted in all intermediate and full advertisements for lending products. It is calculated to a standard formula set out in regulations under the Consumer Credit Act 1974. Its purpose is to enable customers to compare the costs of different lending products in the market place.

Annuity

An investment product through which a cash sum invested provides a regular income for life, irrespective of how long the annuitant lives.

Articles of Association

A constitutional document of a limited company, basically forming the contract between the shareholders and the company.

Authorisation

The right to carry out business in a defined market place. It is a criminal offence to carry out most types of business in the financial services sector without being authorised.

Bacs

The Bank Automated Clearing System – a scheme for electronic processing of financial transactions within the UK. Direct debits use the Bacs system. Bacs Direct Credit is the service that is mainly used for paying benefits, wages and salaries. Payments are cleared in three days.

Bank of England

The UK's central bank.

Bank of England Base Rate

The interest rate set each month by the Monetary Policy Committee of the Bank of England. This acts as a reference point by which other interest rates in the economy are set.

Banking Conduct of Business Sourcebook (BCOBS)

A set of FCA rules and guidelines introduced in 2009, under a principles-based approach, to regulate standards of service provided by retail banks.

Bill of exchange

An unconditional order in writing, addressed by one person to another, signed by the person giving it, requiring the person to whom it is addressed to pay on demand, or at a fixed or determinable future time, a sum certain in money to or to the order of a specified person, or to bearer. Bills of exchange are most often used to facilitate international trade transactions.

Breach

A breach occurs when the terms of a contract are broken.

British Bankers' Association

A trade association for British banks.

Building society	A mutual deposit-taking and mortgage lending organisation, owned by its savers and borrowers.
Capacity	One of the 'three Cs' (along with 'character' and 'commitment') to be considered about the person making a lending application. In the context of contracts, the ability to do participate in a contract.
Capital and interest mortgage	The main type of mortgage taken out by residential and commercial customers. Regular payments are made to the lender comprising some interest and some capital. The loan will be fully paid off at the end of the term if payments are maintained.
CHAPS	A same-day automated payment system for processing payments within the UK. CHAPS is used by banks and other corporates who make large numbers of high value payments. It can also be used by individuals, typically when buying or selling a house.
Chinese wall	An administrative or physical barrier that limits communications between persons in the same organisation, in order to help prevent a conflict of interest. Chinese walls are commonly used in large consultancy firms and banking organisations to minimise the prospect of price-sensitive information being put into the public domain.
Clearing	The process through which banks settle their net indebtedness to one another in respect of money transmission services. Clearing a cheque means processing it so that funds are deducted from the payer's account and put into the payee's account.
Clearing bank	A bank that is part of a network with other clearing banks that can clear cheques for its customers whether or not the cheque originates from the same commercial bank.
Code of Practice	A voluntary statement of best practices, usually formulated on behalf of a group of organisations and administered by their trade association.
Collateral	A generic term that refers to a form of security offered by a debtor to a creditor.
Common law	The traditional system of judge-made case law passed down over many centuries.
Companies Act 2006	The main statute regulating limited companies in the UK.
Complaint	An oral or written expression of dissatisfaction about a service that a financial services firm has provided, or failed to provide. All authorised firms must have formal complaints policies in place.
Conflict of interest	Arises when a decision taker either has a personal stake in the outcome of the decision, or where a decision may affect two or more persons in different ways.
Consequentialist ethics	A branch of ethics that considers whether behaviour is ethical or not based on the consequences of acts.

Consideration	This is the value in a contract to either party. Consideration may be positive, such as the price of a good or service, or it may be negative, such as an agreement not to do something. Consideration is necessary for most types of contract to come into force in England, Wales and Northern Ireland, but not in Scotland.
Consumer Credit Acts 1974 and 2006	Acts of Parliament that regulate most types of personal lending agreement.
	Some loans, such as residential mortgages and lifetime mortgages, are regulated under the MCOB rules and not these Acts.
Consumer Credit Directive	A directive which tightens some aspects of consumer credit legislation.
Continuing professional development (CPD)	Programmes offered by professional bodies that encourage members to continue their own personal and career development.
Contract	An agreement between two or more parties, entered into on a voluntary basis, with a view to establishing a legally binding relationship in terms of specific outcomes.
Cooling-off period	A period immediately after entering into a contract, usually expressed as a number of days, during which the customer has a right to change their mind. Cooling off periods are laid down in FCA rules, in the Consumer Credit Act 1974, and in codes of practice.
Corporate social responsibility	The ways in which a company manages its business in order to have an overall positive impact on society. CSR can be described as an obligation, beyond that required by the law, for a business to pursue long-term goals that are good for society.
Counter-offer	An offer made in response to an earlier offer. The effect of a counter-offer is to cancel the original offer.
Credit reference agency	An organisation that maintains a database on individuals and/or firms in order to make this information available to lenders to support lending decisions.
Credit scoring	A technique used to assess the quality of a loan application through use of a quantitative score.
Credit risk	The risk that an obligation might not be repaid.
Credit union	A mutual organisation, owned by its savers and borrowers, typically providing mainly regular savings plans and small consumer loans, and sometimes a wider range of services. Some of the small credit unions are run by volunteers.
Damages	The main legal remedy for breach of contract, based on common law. Damages comprise a financial award to the injured party and are compensatory in nature.
Data controller	A person or organisation that holds personal data.

Data Protection Act 1998	The statute that regulates the collection, storage, and dissemination of personal data. It lays down the eight principles of data protection and provides data subjects with civil remedies.
Data subject	A living person on whom personal data is held by a data controller.
Direct debit	An instruction by a customer to a bank permitting a third party to draw down regular payments.
Director	An officer of a company accountable to the members and bearing fiduciary, common law, and statutory responsibilities.
Duty-based ethics	A branch of ethics that considers ethical behaviour and actions based on duties owed by individuals and entities to society.
Economic growth	The change in a country's national income over a period of time – generally measured by the change in gross domestic product.
Endowment assurance	A long-term life assurance contract that combines life assurance cover with long-term saving.
Equity release	A product that enables an existing homeowner to borrow capital for any purpose. In this context, equity is the difference between the market value of the property and the total value of the mortgage. Equity release can be facilitated via mortgage/remortgage, second mortgage, lifetime mortgage, or home reversion plan.
Ethics	The study of what is right and wrong, regarding rights and responsibilities, and moral decisions.
Executive director	A director with responsibilities in running the company – both a director and an employee.
Express consent	Agency may be expressly constituted by verbal or written contract.
Familiarity threat	A threat to independence through which the objectivity of an individual's actions or decisions is compromised by some connection with another party.
Faster Payments	A service enabling individuals and businesses to make internet and phone payments from their banking account to that of the payee almost simultaneously.
Fidelity risk	The risk arising from dishonest actions, such as fraud and theft.
Fiduciary	One who is entrusted with property belonging to someone else.
Fiduciary responsibility	Arising from common law, the moral responsibility of a person or organisation to act in the best interests of those to whom they are accountable.
Financial Ombudsman Service	The ombudsman scheme for financial services providers, set up under the Financial Services and Markets Act 2000. The FOS deals with unresolved complaints from consumers against firms that are regulated by the FCA and it can require firms to pay compensation.

Financial Services and Markets Act 2000	This Act provides the framework for the regulatory regime, and enables the FCA to implement regulations in relation to most activities of regulated firms.
Financial Conduct Authority	The regulator of firms' conduct across the financial services industry.
Financial Services Compensation Scheme	A statutory scheme, established under the Financial Services and Markets Act 2000, that provides compensation for customers of authorised financial services firms that are financially unable to pay the claim, eg because of insolvency.
FinTech	An industry sector comprising enterprises that create innovation in in financial services.
General insurance	A generic term for insurance business that provides protection against risk and uncertainty, usually referring to non-life assurance business.
Gross Domestic Product (GDP)	A measure of national income; the market value of the annual production of goods and services within a country.
Guarantee	An undertaking given by one person to discharge the debts of another if the principal debtor fails to do so.
High level principles	Principles laid down by the FCA that state, in very general terms, the minimum accepted requirements in relation to the standards of behaviour adopted by authorised firms. These rules are especially relevant to advertising and promotion of products, the sales cycle, how prices and interest rates are presented, and complaints management.
Holding out	Arises if a principal has had an agent conducting business on their behalf on a regular basis in the normal course of business. In this situation, the principal cannot decide to withdraw subsequently from any transaction the agent has entered into with this third party.
Implied consent	If the appointment of an agent is by implied consent, the relationship of principal and agent is constituted, not in writing or verbally, but by inference from the conduct of the parties.
Individual Savings Account (ISA)	A tax-free savings account that can consist of cash, or stocks and shares. Maximum annual limits, reviewed by the government annually, are set for the amount that can be paid into an ISA.
Inflation	The rate of change in the general level of prices in the economy over a period of time.
Insurance Conduct of Business (ICOB) rules	Detailed rules laid down by the FCA in relation to insurance products.
Integration	One of the stages in the money laundering process, when laundered funds are typically withdrawn.
Integrity	High moral standards or values.
Interest-only mortgage	A method of repayment through which the borrower pays interest to the lender on a regular basis, but discharges the capital debt at the end of the term. Provision is usually made for capital repayment by taking out a long-term investment, such as an ISA.

Intimidation threat	The threat that a professional will be deterred from acting objectively because of actual or perceived pressures from attempts by another to exercise undue influence over them.
Investment bank	A bank that specialises in the provision of services such as acceptances, corporate finance, portfolio management and treasury management. They tend not to offer retail banking products, except to high net worth individuals in some cases.
Investment business	Advising, managing, dealing in, and arranging investments regulated under the Financial Services and Markets Act 2000 (including company shares and collective investments).
Investment trust	A public limited company formed to issue shares to its members and then invest in a range of equities, bonds, property and cash deposits.
Joint and several liability	Under joint and several liability, a claimant may pursue an obligation against any single party as if they were jointly liable. It is then the responsibility of the defendant parties to settle among themselves their respective liabilities.
Layering	One of the stages in the money laundering process, involving a series of multiple transactions that are designed to hide the original source of the 'dirty' money.
Lender of last resort	A function of a central bank (in the UK, the Bank of England) through which financial institutions can still maintain necessary liquidity levels at times of crisis. Funds made available this way are usually charged at a penal rate of interest.
Lending Code	A self-regulatory code which sets minimum standards of good lending practice when dealing with consumers, small businesses (called **'Micro-enterprises'**), and charities with an annual income of under £1m.
Life assurance	Any form of insurance contract that provides cover in the event of the death of the policyholder.
Limited liability partnership (LLP)	A type of partnership in which the partners' personal liability extends only to their investment in the business. Unlike general partnerships, LLPs have a separate legal personality in their own right. They must be registered at the Companies Registry. They combine some of the benefits of a company with the flexibility of a partnership.
Loan to value (LTV)	The ratio of the value of collateral offered by a customer to the amount of borrowing sought or obtained.
Mandate	A written instruction to a bank by its customer to carry out the operation of certain aspects of the account in a prescribed manner. The term can also apply to the limit of authority for decision-taking of an individual employee or agent.
Memorandum of Association	A forming document of a company, including (under Companies Act 2006) only two clauses: a statement that the company has been formed, and a statement that the subscribers (the founding shareholders) have taken at least one share of specified value in the new company.

Micro-enterprise	A business with fewer than 10 employees and turnover or annual balance sheet not exceeding €2 million.
Minor	A person under the age of 18 years.
Misrepresentation	A statement made prior to a contract coming into effect that causes one person to be misled in relation to the meaning or significance of the contract. Misrepresentation can be innocent, negligent or fraudulent.
Mistake	Where one or both of the parties to a contract misunderstands a feature of the contract or its consequences. Mistake is called 'error' in Scotland.
Monetary Policy Committee	A standing committee of the Bank of England that meets monthly to decide the official interest rate. The Committee has responsibility for setting a rate that will achieve government targets for controlling inflation.
Money laundering	Illegal movement of funds through the financial system in order to disguise the origins of these funds, thereby making the funds appear to be legitimate.
Mortgage Conduct of Business (MCOB) rules	The detailed rules of the FCA in relation to regulated mortgage contracts.
Muslim mortgages	Mortgages which comply with Islamic Sharia law.
National Savings and Investments (NS&I)	A government agency that accepts savings and investments, mainly from personal customers. The funds raised provide finance for the Government. NS&I products are available by post and on the internet.
Negligence	When one party fails to exercise a proper duty of care to another party, with harm suffered to that party as a direct consequence.
Negotiable instrument	A transferable, signed document that promises to pay the bearer a sum of money at a future date or on demand. Examples are bills of exchange, cheques (if not marked 'not negotiable'), and promissory notes.
Non-executive director (NED)	NEDs are not employed under a contract of service by the company but do have all the duties and responsibilities under statute, common law and equity.
Offer	An invitation by a person or entity, communicated to another person or entity, with a view to entering into a legally binding contract.
Offeree	A person or entity that receives an offer.
Offeror	A person or entity that makes an offer.
Open Ended Investment Company	A collective investment entity that sells shares to the public and organisations in order to make investments in equities, bonds, property and deposits. Investments may be in regular contributions or single cash sums. (**OEICs** and **Unit trusts** are known collectively as 'funds'.)
Operational risk	Any risk to the day-to-day activities necessary for the smooth functioning of an organisation.

Ordinary share	The main type of share offered by a company. An ordinary share offers extensive constitutional rights, including attendance and voting at general meetings. Dividends are variable, based on the decision of the board of directors.
Partnership	An unincorporated business run by two or more persons. Can also be a limited liability partnership (LLP).
Payee	A person or entity that receives a payment.
Payer (or Payor)	A person or entity that makes a payment.
Payment Services Directive	Directive aimed at ensuring payments made within the European Union are as easy, efficient and secure as domestic payments would be within an EU member State.
People risk	The risk arising from failures of individuals or groups within an organisation.
Personal customer	A customer whose business with the financial services provider is not linked to a business, trade or profession.
PESTEL analysis	An assessment of the external factors affecting a business – Political, Economic, Social, Technological, Environmental, Legal. Often used in corporate planning and risk assessment.
Placement	One of the stages in the money laundering process, where the proceeds from criminal activity first enter the financial system.
Power of attorney	A type of agency that empowers one person to act on behalf of another.
Principal	One who gives instructions to an agent.
Principles-based regulation	A system of regulation based on the development of core standards that are often voluntary but agreed by the majority of participants in an industry or sector. The signatories to these standards are expected to comply with the principles or have explicit reasons for non-compliance, which can then be communicated to principal stakeholders.
Private limited company	A limited company whose shares are privately owned and cannot be traded.
Proceeds of Crime Act 2002	The primary legislation under which the money laundering regulations are implemented.
Process risk	The risk arising from failures in the processes of an organisation.
Public limited company	A limited company whose shares can be offered to the public, and traded.
Ratification	The subsequent confirmation by a principal of an agent's actions when these have been outside the scope of the agent's authority.
Regulatory risk	The risk of loss that arises from the failure of a person or entity to comply with regulatory rules and obligations.
Reputational risk	The risk of loss arising from how an organisation is perceived by the public and/or its stakeholders.
Self-interest threat	The threat that a financial or other interest will inappropriately influence the professional's judgement or behaviour.

Self-review threat	The threat that a professional will not appropriately evaluate the results of a previous judgement they have made or a judgement made by a colleague on which the professional has relied when forming their own opinion.
Social responsibility	The responsibility of an organisation to the wider society as opposed to its narrower responsibilities to its shareholders or other stakeholders.
Sourcebooks	Collections of detailed principles and rules issued by the regulators in relation to specified activities, such as training and competence, prudential management, and conduct of business.
Stakeholder	A person, organisation, group, or community that can influence an organisation or can be affected by its actions.
Standing order	An instruction by a customer to a bank instructing the bank to make a regular payment in specified amounts to a third party, or to another account in the name of the customer.
Suitability	Firms that sell regulated financial products and services must be able to demonstrate their suitability to the client, which means that the inherent features and benefits should be consistent with the customer's needs and that any drawbacks should not outweigh the benefits. Suitability must be confirmed in writing for most regulated products.
Term assurance	A type of life assurance that will pay a cash sum in the event of death of the policyholder during a specified term of years.
Title	Legal right to ownership.
Treating Customers Fairly	An initiative introduced by the then FSA in 2008, aimed at improving the customer experience when dealing with financial services providers. TCF was set up in response to the growing concerns relating to customers being mis-sold financial products and services. It extends to all customer interactions, and so affects branches, agencies, call centres, written material, website content, and marketing materials.
UK Corporate Governance Code	A code issued by the Financial Reporting Council. Listed companies are expected to comply with its provisions, or be prepared to explain to shareholders why it is not appropriate to comply ('Comply or explain').
Undue influence	Psychological or emotional pressure (eg, to enter into a contract).
Unit trust	An open-ended collective investment entity that sells units to the public and organisations in order to make investments in equities, bonds, property and deposits. Investments may be in regular contributions or single cash sums. (**Open Ended Investment Companies** and **Unit trusts** are known collectively as 'funds'.)
Utilitarianism	In the context of ethics, utilitarians pursue decisions and actions that will bring the greatest benefit to the maximum number of people.

Virtue ethics	A branch of ethics that considers the characteristics that individuals should possess if their behaviour and acts are to comply with ethical norms.
Void contract	A contract that is deemed by the courts never to have existed.
Voidable contract	A contract that is deemed by the courts to be valid but which can be set aside by one party at their discretion.
Vulnerable consumer	A consumer who, due to their personal circumstances, is especially susceptible to detriment, particularly when a firm is not acting with appropriate levels of care.
Whole of life assurance	A life assurance contract that pays a cash sum on the death of the policyholder, whenever death occurs.

INDEX